FROM VERSAILLES TO
THE NEW DEAL

VOLUME 51
THE CHRONICLES
OF AMERICA SERIES
ALLAN NEVINS
EDITOR

FROM VERSAILLES
TO THE NEW DEAL

A CHRONICLE OF THE
HARDING–COOLIDGE–HOOVER ERA
BY HAROLD U. FAULKNER

NEW HAVEN: YALE UNIVERSITY PRESS
TORONTO: GLASGOW, BROOK & CO.
LONDON: GEOFFREY CUMBERLEGE
OXFORD UNIVERSITY PRESS
1950

PRINTED IN THE U.S.A.

12501

CONTENTS

CONTENTS

FROM VERSAILLES TO
THE NEW DEAL

. .

CHAPTER I

THE END OF THE GREAT CRUSADE

WAR-WEARY Americans scanning the headlines of
their papers on Thursday, November 7, 1918,
learned that a German delegation seeking terms of
peace was on its way to General Foch. They could
hardly be blamed when later that day they accepted with little reservation a false release from
the United Press that an armistice had been
signed. The early afternoon papers carried the announcement in screaming headlines, and for a few
hours the nation went wild to the din of shrieking
factory whistles, automobile horns, church bells,
and shouting crowds. But the joy was short-lived.
By late afternoon both the War and State Departments had announced they had no knowledge of
an armistice.

Four days later came the real armistice and an

even fiercer jubilation. What happened in the great city of New York was typical of hundreds of other towns and cities. Early morning whistles awoke the sleeping citizens while the giant searchlight on the *Times* building played on hotels and apartment houses. Within two hours the celebration was well under way. Offices, factories, schools, and even courts were closed. Impromptu parades of horn-blowing, bell-ringing celebrants were joined by trucks hung with bunting and banners. Mayor Hylan headed a parade of city employees which marched from Canal Street to Columbus Circle. Early in the morning the Salvation Army held a formal thanksgiving service on the steps of the Public Library. Toward night the warships and camouflaged merchant vessels in the North River, which had been decked with flags all day, turned their searchlights up and down Riverside Drive, thronged by great crowds. Apartment houses were brilliantly illuminated; street lamps that had been dark to save coal were turned on for the celebration, while down the bay the Statue of Liberty was once more ablaze.

One incident that morning dramatized the willingness of the nation to play her part in the war but also her determination to end the military phase without delay. Eight hundred newly drafted men on their way to camp marched amid the cheering throngs from the Bronx to Grand Central.

By the time they reached the railroad station, a representative from the regional draft supervisor arrived to inform them that in view of the armistice they could return home.

The United States had entered the World War with a sense of grim duty rather than lighthearted enthusiasm. Watching the European struggle for almost three years, Americans had gained some understanding of its terrible cost. The decision once made, however, the nation unstintedly threw into the conflict her great power of men, money, and industrial resources to end the German menace. To many doughboys the crusade to Europe was a glorious adventure. For most, however, it was a painful and bewildering interference with a normal routine. Unaccustomed to the restrictions and discipline of military life, the typical soldier endured rather than enjoyed his army experience.

Though America lost few men in comparison with the other great powers, no country welcomed the armistice more joyously. Nineteen months of high effort and emotional strain had frayed the nerves of civilians. Doughboys had experienced enough of camp and trench, and were eager to be done with war. Despite high profits, manufacturers chafed under wartime restrictions; owners of railroads, telegraphs, telephones, and other communication facilities were anxious to regain control of their property. Even organized labor, which had

attained a greater recognition and larger membership than ever before, was restless under unaccustomed Government supervision. Many other Americans, deeply imbued with democratic liberalism,
had accepted with reluctance the abrogation of
civil privileges. They distrusted the Espionage Act
sponsored by the Administration and were suspicious of the furor raised by various leaders over
spies and "hyphenated Americans." It was clear
that neither the era of social reform which preceded
the war, nor the war itself, had deeply altered the
laissez-faire psychology of the average American.

Although many citizens had been a little dubious
of the European adventure as early as November,
1918, the great disillusionment which was to sweep
over the nation during the following decade was
not then evident. Nevertheless, demobilization
could not come too quickly. The war had been exciting, but the nostalgia for what Warren G. Harding later called "normalcy" was more fundamental.
The first step toward a peace basis was the demobilization of the four and a half million men in uniform. Elaborate plans for gradually disbanding the
army had been suggested, but the War Department
had given them little attention. In any event, a
gradual demobilization would not have been tol-
erated by public sentiment. The soldiers wanted
to be released; the people at home wanted them
back; the Government had no more use for them.

Under this pressure the War Department cut its red tape. Even before the armistice the Administration knew that the war would soon end. Troop trains en route to camp were reversed and recruits sent home. After the armistice, demobilization moved forward rapidly. Before the end of 1918 the army had released 652,000 men. By the end of June, 1919, it had disbanded 2,608,000, and by the end of October, 3,226,000. Altogether, more than four million young men laid off their uniforms at an average rate of ten thousand a day for over a year and streamed back into civilian life.

To those in American camps whose health had not been seriously impaired, the Government merely granted a formal discharge, issued a full uniform, provided transportation money home, and turned over what pay was due after deductions for war-risk insurance. All factors considered, the work of the army in handling this tremendous task was highly creditable. For the 2,000,000 overseas, the problem was more complicated. They were returned to America as quickly as ships could be obtained, and discharged from the thirty-two camps earlier used for mobilization and training. The greatest care was taken to protect the country against the importation of disease. After a careful examination abroad, and, if necessary, treatment in a detention camp, troops were given another medical examination and thorough disinfection on arrival in the United States. Except for the wounded, the number held for hospitalization was relatively small. Preventive medicine had largely eliminated the older camp diseases of typhoid fever, malaria, and dysentery. "Had it not been for influenza and pneumonia," reported the Surgeon General, "the total rates for the late war would have, indeed, been very small for admissions to hospitals and more so for deaths."

While the nation was busy with demobilization, it was involved in the equally complicated job of liquidating wartime contracts and disposing of un-needed war materials. At the time of the armistice the War Department had outstanding more than 47,000 contracts, calling for payments to exceed six billion dollars. So efficiently did the Government adopt economy measures that within a few weeks more than half the contracts had been terminated and two thirds of the liabilities written off. The work had been handled by a War Department Claim Board from which appeals could be taken to a group of experienced lawyers known as the Board of Contract Adjustment. Machinery was meanwhile set up to dispose of a vast amount of equipment and stores in Europe, which it was impossible or inexpedient to return to America. Surplus medical and surgical supplies were turned over to the American Red Cross, and the rest of the material to France, Poland, Spain, Belgium, and other purchasers. Needless to say, a heavy loss was incurred. Though the original cost of this material was $1,680,000,000, it was sold for $627,150,000, or only 37.3 per cent of its book value. France, the largest purchaser, paid about $400,000,000 for military equipment which had cost the American Government $1,400,000,000. While wartime contracts were being liquidated, price controls and priorities were ended with even greater speed.

Political demobilization began before the doughboys were again seeking jobs on farms and in factories. Weeks before the armistice, it was evident that the war was almost over. Republicans, unwilling to tie the hands of the Government in wartime and hesitant to risk any charge of disloyalty, had refrained from criticism and dutifully joined in voting the legislation asked for by the Administration. President Wilson had recognized this truce when he told Congress on May 27, 1918: "Politics is adjourned. The elections will go to those who think least of it, to those who go to the constituencies without explanations or excuses, with a plain record of duty faithfully and disinterestedly performed." But these words had hardly been spoken before both parties were busy preparing for the fall elections. As early as February the Republican National Committee, completely controlled by the Old Guard, had elected Will H. Hays of Indiana as Chairman and were formulating their strategy.

On the part of the Democrats, Wilson himself had vetoed the suggestion of a nonpartisan campaign.

Republican strategy was well planned. It appealed to regional bias by emphasizing the role of the "Dixie Democrats" as chairmen of important Congressional committees in formulating national war policies, presumably to the advantage of their section. It nurtured the dislike of wartime regulations and high taxes on the part of industrialists, and intimated quick relief after the war. Not only did Republicans assume an end of the lower Democratic tariff; they promised continued protection to the "war babies"—in the words of Hays, those "great new industries building up now so marvelously under war conditions. . . ." They also fanned opposition to the whole economic policy of the Democrats as revealed in the legislation of the first Wilson Administration. Since the great majority of people appeared satisfied with Wilson's foreign policy, the Republicans, with the exception of Theodore Roosevelt and a few others, avoided this issue until the end of the campaign. They made the most of opposition to wartime controls and also of the personal dislike of Wilson.

Despite partisan efforts on both sides, the campaign was comparatively quiet until almost the end. Promotion of the Fourth Liberty Loan, excited anticipations of victory, and the battle against a nation-wide influenza epidemic kept politics in the background. Roosevelt urged the voters to repudiate Wilson before Europe as the American leader. The President might have ignored this attack, but instead on October 24 he suddenly made his famous appeal for support. "If you have approved of my leadership and wish me to continue to be your unembarrassed spokesman in affairs at home and abroad," he urged, "I earnestly beg that you will express yourself unmistakably to that effect by returning a Democratic majority to both Senate and House of Representatives." Ten days later the people marched to the polls and upset Democratic control by giving the Republicans a majority of two in the Senate and 45 in the House.

It is impossible to ascertain what motive Wilson had in issuing this dramatic appeal, beyond resentment of Roosevelt's diatribes and his natural desire for a sympathetic Congress during the making of peace and the early months of reconstruction. His intimate advisers, such as House, insist that they protested against it. It is evident, however, that he had long had it in mind and that Republican leaders had expected it. Sensible as the appeal may have been in theory, it was politically unfortunate, for it lent color to the Republican insistence that Wilson was unduly enlarging the Presidential prerogative. Naturally the Republicans made the most of his misstep. Will Hays issued a formal reply, asserting that the President wanted to settle the war according to his own will and "to reconstruct in peace times the great industrial affairs of the nation in the same way, in unimpeded conformity with whatever socialistic doctrines, with whatever unlimited government-ownership notions, whatever hazy whims may happen to possess him at the time. . . ." Theodore Roosevelt, whose hatred of Wilson had become a mania, and who considered him a "Judas" who "would double-cross creation," delivered a few days later at Carnegie Hall in New York a three-hour excoriation of the President.

Impossible as it is to measure the exact effect of this appeal on the electorate, there can be no doubt that the denunciation by Roosevelt and other Republican leaders exerted real influence. So did their general demand that Wilson's leadership be repudiated. Other elements in the result included the Republican votes cast by Negroes who had migrated to the North in large numbers during the war, and by newly enfranchised women in a number of states, resentful of the opposition of Southern Democratic politicians to the impending nineteenth amendment. Republican totals were also swelled, as they were two years later, by opposition to Wilson's foreign policy on the part of German-Americans and Irish-Americans. Whatever the causes, the result was momentous. No Congressional election in American history had a more important effect on the future of America and the world. It weakened Wilson's position at Versailles and fettered him heavily when the great fight began over American entry into the League of Nations. It also ended the progressive era that had flourished under Theodore Roosevelt and Woodrow Wilson, and marked a definite reversal toward "normalcy" and *laissez-faire*. It raised the curtain upon not only the election of 1920 but the economic and political policies of the ensuing decade.

The Republican victory accelerated the loosening of economic controls. When the Sixty-sixth Congress met in special session on May 19, 1919, the Republican floor leader, Representative F. W. Mondell, crisply expressed the spirit of both houses. "The era of reconstruction and the return of old policies," he announced, "has arrived." To describe what followed as "reconstruction" would be as much a travesty on the meaning of that term as the similar use of the word in the years after the Civil War. The nation was less prepared for peace in 1918, if possible, than in 1865. Its leaders had been too busy mobilizing men and resources for war to give any attention to the problems of domestic readjustment. The President spent the spring of 1919 in Paris, devoting his entire attention to the peace treaty. When he returned, his flagging energies were largely absorbed by his

efforts to win Congress and the nation to its acceptance. After his paralytic stroke in September his
party was without leadership. Congress, as the
Congressional Record shows, was likewise more interested in debating the treaty than in tackling the
nation's home problems.

To the leaders of both major parties in 1919,
"reconstruction" meant little more than "the return
to old policies." Neither the Administration nor its
Republican opposition had formulated any real
plans to aid veterans in their search for jobs, to
demobilize wartime industry, or to preserve part
of the gains in wartime regulation of business. Mobilization for war had been a simple task in comparison with the new problems faced by American
industry, finance, labor, and agriculture. Yet, at
the moment, Congress had nothing to offer. In its
rush to return to pre-war conditions, it repealed
during the special and regular session more than
sixty wartime laws. Swept away—along with a
host of other agencies—were the Food Administration, the American Relief Administration, the War
Industries Board, the National War Labor Board,
and the Committee on Public Information. Abolished also were most of the wartime powers of the
President, a sweet consummation to Republican
Senators.

Repeal of wartime controls, however, was by no
means complete. The Lever Food and Fuel Act,

for example, remained on the statute books long
enough to enable the Administration in the autumn
of 1919 to break a bituminous coal strike by the
use of an injunction. (Fifteen years later President
Franklin D. Roosevelt was to discover powers conferred in 1918 and still unrepealed which allowed
him to act in the banking emergency of 1933.)
Furthermore, it was impossible to turn the hands
of the clock completely back. Soaring prices of
sugar, for example, led Congress in 1919 to extend
the life of the Sugar Equalization Board for a year.
Collapse of agricultural prices late in 1920 likewise
induced Congress to revive the powers of the War
Finance Corporation. The idea of price control—
whether to keep prices down or push them up—
was, as a matter of fact, reluctantly abandoned
after the war. The nation never quite returned
to that stage of *laissez-faire* which had existed before 1917.

It was in the field of transportation that the experience of wartime control was most fruitful. In
fact, the same Sixty-sixth Congress which so rapidly repealed the regulatory wartime acts launched
the Federal Government in 1920 on its peacetime
regulation of electric power. It established a Federal Power Commission consisting of the Secretaries
of War, the Interior, and Agriculture and authorized to license citizens of the United States to develop power projects on the navigable waters of

the United States and on the public lands. The
licenses were for fifty years; methods of accounting were to be standardized; and the Commission
was permitted to regulate rates for power produced
under its license and sold across state lines or in
states which had not yet created their own utility
commissions. It was also given jurisdiction over
new security issues. Far-reaching as the Federal
Water Power Act appeared to be, it was in reality
but a first feeble gesture toward Federal control
of a rapidly growing and powerful industry. Not
until the days of the New Deal was effective control extended over the interstate transmission of
electric power.

In the light of subsequent experience, Federal
utility regulation was possibly the most important
economic legislation before the Sixty-sixth Congress. At the time, however, the most pressing
problem seemed to be the fate of the railroads.
Despite their best efforts, they had failed under
private control to meet the crisis of war transportation. President Wilson had therefore issued on
December 26, 1917, a proclamation providing for
Government operation, and in March, 1918, Congress followed with a Railroad Control Act stating
the terms under which this should take place. Each
road was to be returned within twenty-one months
after ratification of the peace treaty "in substantially as good repair and in substantially as com-

plete equipment as it was at the beginning of government control."

Ratification of the peace which Wilson had brought home from Versailles was more than doubtful, and the country was still officially at war. From the standpoint of Congress there was no great hurry about returning the railroads. The problem was difficult, and men held conflicting views as to its solution. Extended hearings took place before Congressional committees. Director-General McAdoo advised continued Government regulation for five years. Railroad owners demanded immediate return of their property with full indemnity for wear and tear. On the other hand, the Railroad Brotherhoods, with the lukewarm backing of the American Federation of Labor, strongly advocated Government ownership and worked hard to popularize the "Plumb Plan." Named after Glenn E. Plumb, the brilliant attorney for the railroad unions, this called for Government purchase of the roads and their operation by a board of fifteen directors upon which the public, operating officers, and employees would be equally represented. Earnings, after operating expenses, maintenance, and liquidation of the purchase price had been provided for, were to be shared between the Government and the workers. Extensions were to be paid for by the community, and the Interstate Commerce Commission was to retain all its rate-making powers. It was an ingenious plan, which might have gone far toward solving the complicated railroad problem. In the conservative post-war reaction, however, it had no chance.

When Wilson in his annual message of December, 1918, called attention to the railroads, he indicated three possibilities: restoration to the owners under old conditions, complete Government control or ownership, or return under new conditions extending public regulation. He unquestionably believed in the last. "The one conclusion," said he, "that I am ready to state with confidence is that it would be disservice alike to the country and to the owners of the railroads to return to the old conditions unmodified. Those are conditions of restraint without development."

Despite the conservative post-war trend, Congress followed his advice. The Transportation Act of 1920, drawn up largely by Representative John Jacob Esch of Wisconsin and Senator Albert B. Cummins of Iowa, both veterans of railroad legislation, inaugurated new principles in railroad control and gave the Interstate Commerce Commission, now increased to eleven members, fresh responsibilities and powers. The Commission was authorized to divide the country into districts, in each of which it should prescribe rates which "under honest, efficient, and economical management" would give a fair return upon the aggregate value of railroad property. The determination of the "fair return," after appraisal of the property, was left to the Commission; but the rate was set for two years at $5\frac{1}{2}$ per cent, with an additional half per cent to provide for improvements and additions deemed necessary by the Commission. These rate-making provisions represented a revolutionary change in the functions of the Commission. Up to 1920 the chief business of that body had been to protect the interests of the public. Now it must also conserve the interests of the railroads. Up to 1920 the railroads, as far as rate-making was concerned, were protected only by the due-process clause of the Fifth Amendment. Now they were largely relieved of the burden of proof as to reasonableness, and responsibility was shifted back to the Commission.

The Commission was also charged with the task of providing for an adequate transportation system. If any railroad received in any year a net income in excess of 6 per cent, it was required to turn half of the excess over to the Commission to be held as a revolving fund for loans to the weaker roads. The Commission was now given power over minimum as well as maximum rates, and under certain conditions over intrastate as well as interstate rates. It was also authorized to regulate the issuance of railway securities and to supervise the use to which the proceeds might be put—a reform which, if it had been inaugurated forty years earlier, would have been of vast benefit to both railroads and public. Other powers included authority to pass upon the advisability of new lines, the abandonment of old, and the supervision of service and traffic. Finally, Congress abandoned the idea that the welfare of roads and public was dependent upon ruthless competition, and gave the Commission a mandate to work out plans for railroad consolidation into not less than twenty, nor more than thirty-five, competing groups.

Since Congress had been deeply disturbed by the severe strikes of 1919, the Transportation Act also set up machinery for the settlement of labor disputes. This, too, was an innovation. The Act encouraged the settlement of disputes not involving wages by boards of adjustment to be formed voluntarily by railroads and employees. If this failed, the controversies, including those on wages, might be taken to a Railroad Labor Board of nine members, three representing employers, three labor, and three the public. As the Board had no power to enforce its decisions, compliance depended largely on public opinion.

Such were the major provisions of the most intelligent effort which Congress made toward "reconstruction." Most provisions of the Act, particularly those relating to the regulation of capital structure, were a distinct step forward. A few proved unworkable. The provisions regarding labor

disputes were utterly inadequate and were super-
seded in 1926 by the Railway Labor Act, which
established a Federal Board of Mediation, and
which turned out to be even more useless. This
Board was to act in disputes only when asked to
do so by one or another of the parties involved.
That part of the Act of 1920 which provided for
the return of excess profits to the Interstate Commerce Commission was opposed by the railroads;
it was largely invalidated by the O'Fallon decision
of May, 1929 (St. Louis and O'Fallon Railway
Company *v.* U. S.), and finally repealed by Congress in 1933. The mandate to consolidate the
railroads received little encouragement from railway heads, and no major consolidations were made
under the act. Failure to give the Commission
adequate control over holding companies also handicapped it in dealing with railroad financing during the boom days of the twenties.

Another problem which Congress was unable to
evade was that of ocean transportation. American
dependence upon European shipping became so
acute during the first two years of the war that
Congress established a Shipping Board to supervise
ocean transportation and advise methods for increase of the merchant marine. When the United
States entered the war the Shipping Board organized the Emergency Fleet Corporation, which by
June 30, 1920, had spent over $3,000,000,000 and

held 1,502 ships of 9,358,000 gross tons. The problem was what to do with this vast flotilla now owned, and much of it operated, by the Government. Most Americans held that the merchant marine should be preserved and strengthened. The nation had made a new start; it ought never again to find itself so weak on the seas as during the World War. Yet most Americans also asserted that continued Government operation was "socialistic" and contrary to American tradition, and must be ended as quickly as possible. There seemed only one alternative, the sale of the vessels to private owners and the support of the merchant marine by direct or indirect subsidies. Under existing competitive conditions, it was doubtful if it could be maintained without aid.

The Merchant Marine Act of 1920 met the practical needs of the situation in the spirit of the postwar conservative reaction. Congressmen who denounced Government operation proved quite willing to vote lavish "handouts" to private business, while shipowners who criticized a Government-owned merchant marine as socialism were glad to accept subsidies. Briefly, the Act continued the Shipping Board and Merchant Fleet Corporation, with instructions to sell Government ships to Americans and get out of business as quickly as possible. The Board was to establish necessary shipping routes and maintain Government ships on them until private owners could be induced by loans or otherwise to take over operation. In many different ways the Act encouraged American merchant ships, and particularly their private operation. The earnings of vessels plying in foreign trade were exempted, under certain conditions, from war and excess profits taxes. Discriminations were set up in favor of national shipping, as, for example, the repeal of the Act of 1917 which had admitted foreign ships to the coastwise trade. High indirect subsidies were provided through mail contracts and loans for ship construction. This law of 1920, with later legislation, kept an American fleet on the seas, but the cost ran into hundreds of millions. The merchant marine did not flourish and the picture until the new legislation of 1936 was as discouraging as in 1920.

While Congress struggled with the problems of transportation, 4,500,000 discharged soldiers were trying to adjust themselves to civilian life. They competed with many civilians who had been engaged in war work and whose demobilization was almost as complete as if they had been in uniform. In their search for work, veterans often found their former jobs in the hands of women, of older men, or of a new crop of youth too young to have been called by the Selective Service Act. The problem was not made easier, of course, by the speed with which the armed forces were demobilized, nor by the fact that industry also was demobilizing as the Government canceled its war orders and factory owners hastened to adjust themselves to a peace-time basis. Veterans of earlier American wars, if unable to find jobs, had always been able to seek new opportunities on the frontier, and had been encouraged to do so by their Government. But now the frontier was gone.

Another element complicating the situation was the temporary slowdown of economic activity during the early months of 1919, when demobilization was at its height. Fortunately, however, this was brief. In general, the American soldier returned to a nation prosperous from wartime business and keyed to a high level of economic production which was to last for a year and a half after the armistice. After some uncertainty early in 1919, business experienced a sharp upturn and enjoyed tremendous activity during the rest of the year. Production indices were actually higher in some industries in 1919 than in 1918. Railroads reached their peak for the year in May and industries in November. Prices mounted skyward, the stock market boomed, and prosperous Americans, first made acquainted with the security market through the purchase of Liberty Bonds, hastened to buy new industrial issues as rapidly as they could be thrown on the market. Foreign trade was particularly active, exports mounting from $5,920,000,000 in 1918 to

$7,225,000,000 in 1919 and $8,228,000,000 in 1920. These three years, in fact, marked the apex of American peacetime export trade.

This economic prosperity continued until the late spring of 1920. In part it sprang from the momentum of the tremendously active war years and in part from continued heavy Government spending and active foreign purchasing. The Government was still borrowing heavily (the Victory Loan was floated in 1919) and still loaning large amounts to foreign nations, which spent the money chiefly in this country. While the continued prosperity undoubtedly helped millions to find work, the problem of unemployment was always serious. There was never a time in 1919 when several hundred thousand men were not looking for jobs. Although Congress had curtailed the work of the United States Employment Service, other Government departments leaped into the breach to help meet the situation. The Council of National Defense, an Emergency Committee of the War Department, and many local committees and employment services did yeoman work. Certain cities developed special public works projects to meet the emergency.

It is probable that the social strain of the first fifteen months after the war was primarily due to other causes than unemployment. Above all, men complained of the high cost of living. Already sky-high in 1918, prices continued to mount during the next two years. During the war, wages had to some extent followed prices in their upward trend, and there actually were a few wage earners who satisfied their longing for luxury by wearing silk shirts. In general, however, students are agreed that the American workingman was worse off at the end of the war than at the beginning. While dollar wages had jumped ahead, real wages lagged behind. To be precise, the index figures (1913 = 100) of the Department of Labor showed that while dollar wages (per hour) advanced to 162 in 1918, and to 184 in 1919, the rise in living costs were such that real wages fell to 92.9 in 1918 and 97.7 in 1919. The index figure rose, however, in 1920 to 112.2.

If wage earners suffered, far more hardship was endured by salaried and professional groups whose incomes had remained practically stationary. What made the situation worse was the fact that prices increased most sharply in the necessities of life—clothing, food, and shelter. This spurt in the cost of living was ascribed by the Council of National Defense in October, 1919, to failure to use fully the nation's productive powers, to unavoidable war waste, increase in money and credit, and considerable profiteering, both intentional and unintentional. Herbert Hoover, testifying before the New York State Lusk Committee in May, 1920, diagnosed the situation in greater detail. Among the predominating causes he listed shortage of commodities as a result of the war; inflation, particularly expansion of credit facilities; profiteering and speculation; the unfortunate adjustment of taxation, particularly in the case of the excess profits tax, passed on to the consumer; decrease in American productivity due to relaxation in effort after the war; strikes; increase in our own consumption with accompanying waste and extravagance; deterioration of the American transport system, and an expensive and wasteful distribution system. He might also have said much about the increased taxation necessitated by the rising Federal and state expenses. The Federal budget jumped from $617,382,000 in 1913 to about $4,860,000,000 in 1920, and the Federal debt from $1,193,048,000 to $24,297,918,000. Taxation was reduced in the postwar years, but it was never to approach the low levels of 1913.

It was interesting to know the reasons for the high cost of living, but this did not help people pay the bills. The situation became so acute that both state and Federal governments had to take some notice of it. President Wilson in a proclamation of November 21, 1919, resumed Government control of the nation's food supply, and Congress shortly afterward extended the life of the Sugar Equalization Board. The Government believed that it had made a little headway toward lower prices when in November the "Big Five" in the packers' trust agreed, under pressure, to confine themselves to meat packing and dairy products. At a great mass meeting in Chicago the next month, Attorney-General Palmer outlined plans for combating the high cost of living. He urged the holding of conservation economy meetings, the organization of fair-price committees in every city and county backed by prosecuting officials, organization of women to refuse to buy anything but actual necessities, remobilization of the Four-Minute Men to deliver "work and save" addresses, and the active participation of public officers in ending disturbances in industry. Although a buyers' strike of some proportions developed by 1921, it was the business collapse and depression of that year that did most to bring prices down.

Workers engaged in a bitter competition to get and hold jobs, and the middle class, crushed under advancing prices, found no consolation in the general effect of the war upon the distribution of wealth. While wage earners and professional men were, in general, worse off in 1919 than in 1913, the war had created about 1,700 new millionaires. Like every other great conflict, it had engendered a crop of profiteers, whose easy wealth was flaunted before the eyes of those who had borne the brunt of the struggle. The millions of ex-soldiers who had fought for $30 a month were embittered to discover that workers who stayed behind had often earned twice that much a week. The disillusionment that developed from all this, rather than the influence of the Russian revolution, was mainly responsible for the left-wing developments in politics, the intellectual radicalism, and the severe labor struggles of the post-war years.

Some relief from the high cost of living came in the latter half of 1920, but only at a severe price. More than a century earlier John Adams had observed: "I am old enough to remember the war of 1745 and its end, the war of 1755 and its close, the war of 1775 and its termination, the war of 1812 and its pacification. Every one of these wars has been followed by a great distress, embarrassments of commerce, destruction of manufactures, fall of the price of produce and lands." So far as America was concerned, the World War was no exception. Following a year of inflation and rapidly mounting prices, the upward sweep of the business cycle reached its peak in May, 1920, and then started to drop rapidly.

Just as the prosperity of 1915–1919 had been artificially stimulated by the European war, so the deflation was primarily the result of foreign influences. The depression began in Japan, which had experienced an even dizzier wartime financial inflation and industrial expansion than the United States, and soon spread to most of the world. The nations of Europe, impoverished by the struggle, staggering under crushing debts, and with exchange rates against them, no longer had funds or credit to make large-scale purchases. Exports from the United States, which in 1920 rose to the incredible figure of $8,228,000,000, dropped in 1921 to $4,379,-000,000, while imports, after reaching an all-time high in 1920 of $5,278,000,000, dropped the next year to less than half that figure

The radical shrinkage of the European market naturally dealt a heavy blow to American business. The automobile industry, whose production in 1921 was almost cut in half, and the metal industry, whose production declined by one third, were the hardest hit. Textiles were perhaps least affected that year. To the curtailment of the European field was added the restriction of the consumers' market at home as prices rose beyond the ability of many to purchase. The cost of living reached its highest point for the decade in June, 1920. Above all, however, many economists attribute the depression mainly to the cessation of heavy Government buying with the end of the war.

As is usual in depressions, the chief sufferers in the recession of 1920–1922 were industrial workers and farmers. Observers agreed that unemployment in the winter of 1920–1921 was twice as great as during the previous depression of 1914–1915. Estimates made during the winter months varied between 3,000,000 and 4,000,000. As 1921 progressed, the situation grew worse; in August the Secretary of Labor submitted to the Senate an official estimate of 5,700,000 unemployed. Yet less acute distress was noted than in 1914 and 1915. Many workless men were able to get through the winter on wartime savings. The declining cost of living helped, and so did savings as a result of prohibition. Organizations for temporary relief sprang up throughout the nation; employment agencies worked overtime, and in many cities public works were started. Fortunately the post-war depression was short. Early in 1922 the nation was again on the upgrade of a new business cycle. At the same time, the price structure had been so shaken that the general position of labor was improved. Real wages, which the Department of Labor had put in 1919 at 97.7 (1913=100), advanced to 112.2 in 1920, 123 in 1921 and 124.3 in 1922.

More disastrous to agriculture than to labor, the post-war deflation hit the farmers a blow from which many never recovered. Profiting from an expanded market, prices of agricultural commodities had shot up to heights which only the Government could control. To meet an insatiable demand, farmers had increased their areas of cultivation and facilities for farming. Sudden curtailment of the European market and reduced purchases at home brought the inevitable crash. Wheat, which had sold for $2.15 a bushel in December, 1919, dropped to $1.44 in December, 1920; corn from $1.35 to $.68; oats from $.72 to $.47, and cotton from $.36 a pound to $.14. Land values collapsed. While farm revenues fell precipitously, farm costs as measured in mortgage debts, taxes, and farming equipment remained at war levels. Almost overnight the plight of the American farmer became desperate, and it was but slightly alleviated with returning industrial prosperity in 1922.

Except for the farmers the post-war depression was comparatively short. It was long enough, nevertheless, to change radically the course of American history. For six years the attention of America had rested upon the problems of Europe. But with the economic depression, the nation definitely turned her eyes again to domestic problems. To veterans, clamoring for recognition, Congress gave monetary appeasement by provision for the disabled and a discharge bonus of $256,000,000. To meet the gloomy agricultural situation it passed the first of a long series of farm bills. In an ill-advised attempt to help industry it rushed through in the late spring of 1921 an emergency tariff.

The problems of industry, agriculture, transportation, power control, and the demands of veterans—these were the economic matters which concerned the American people during the 1920's. To Americans they seemed far more pressing than any international question. The European adventure ended in a battle between the President and a stubborn Senatorial minority in which personal animosities, political expediency, and wartime weariness all played a part. On March 19, 1920, this minority gave the *coup de grace* to the ill-fated Treaty of Versailles and to America's participation in the League of Nations. The Great Crusade had ended.

CHAPTER II

ISOLATION AND LAISSEZ-FAIRE

IF anyone doubted that the Great Crusade had ended, the campaign of 1920 made it crystal clear. Tired of the international turmoil and pinched by the economic recession, the country was ready for political change. This was evident in the elections of 1918, and the next two years tended to accentuate the antagonism to the Wilson Administration. The victory over Germany had been hailed as a great triumph for civilization; but the glories of the conflict did not breed a nostalgia, as in 1861–1865 and in 1898, which military heroes could capitalize to their political profit. The World War had been undertaken in a spirit of grim duty; now that it was over, most people desired to forget it and to return as quickly as possible to the good old days. "There's not enough money in the world," observed Harry Daugherty acutely, "to buy the nomination for a man with epaulettes on his shoulders in 1920."

Not only was this true, but all the resentment

of wartime hardships, all the rancor of German-American and Irish-American groups, all the disillusionment of post-war days, were directed against the party in power and to some extent against the broken statesman who was still its leader. Little prestige was the Democratic Party to obtain from its control of the Administration during the greatest war yet seen, a war in which America's participation had been the determining factor. Little credit was it to gain from the fact that the war had been carried on with greater efficiency and probity than any in our previous history. So rapidly, in fact, did wartime idealism evaporate that Republican politicians felt little fear that the American electorate would resent the unfair treatment given the League of Nations. As the Congress which had killed the hope of American participation adjourned, Senator Lodge cried exultantly: "If the President wishes to make a campaign issue of the treaty, the Republicans are willing to meet that issue."

Republican chieftains gauged well the overwhelming demand for a return to pre-war passivity; and there was no lack of candidates for a nomination that was tantamount to election. As the spring of 1920 advanced, two Republicans stood out above other aspirants. General Leonard Wood, former Colonel of the Rough Riders, Governor-General of Cuba, and Chief of Staff, recently a leader in the preparedness movement, had the support of the more conservative of Theodore Roosevelt's followers. He also had behind him a great deal of wealth, notably the millions of Colonel William C. Proctor of Cincinnati, who managed his campaign. The other leading candidate was Frank O. Lowden, a successful Chicago attorney with a distinguished career in Congress and as Governor of Illinois. As son-in-law of George Pullman he commanded a fortune, but his keen interest in agriculture made him the candidate of the farmers. Among the other candidates were Senator Hiram Johnson, supported by radical Rooseveltians (except the Wisconsin followers of the elder LaFollette), Governor Calvin Coolidge of Massachusetts, who had gained national reputation from the Boston police strike, and Senator Warren G. Harding of Ohio. In the Republican primaries General Wood had won pluralities in South Dakota, New Jersey, and Indiana; Senator Johnson had led in North Dakota, Michigan, Nebraska, Montana and California; while Lowden, LaFollette, and Harding each carried his own state.

Of all the aspirants, Harding was the least distinguished. A small-town newspaper owner and politician, he had served two terms in the Ohio Senate and a term as Lieutenant-Governor from 1904 to 1906, but had been defeated for Governor in the Democratic year 1910. Later he achieved some national reputation as Senator from Ohio, 1914–1920, and as chairman of the Republican National Convention in 1916 had delivered the key-note speech at that gathering. A handsome, urbane gentleman, Harding possessed many friends and few enemies. Even among his friends, however, few considered him a leader of more than mediocre abilities; none a statesman. His career in the Senate had been that of a typical party wheelhorse, and his few speeches had been dull, unoriginal, and ineptly phrased.

The Warwick who made Harding President was Harry M. Daugherty. A long-time friend and clever politican with wide acquaintance, Daugherty had put Harding in the Senate only to dream of an even higher destiny for his friend. A modest man, Harding believed that he had already achieved his highest ambition. It was Daugherty who finally convinced him that he must enter the Presidential race, and then only by the plea that he must do so in order to insure reelection to the Senate. When Harding later had to decide whether to file for reelection or take a chance on the Presidential nomination, he chose the bolder course reluctantly and only under great pressure. "I found him sunning himself, like a turtle on a log," said Daugherty, "and I pushed him into the water."

In an old Washington hotel, Daugherty set up modest headquarters. To astonished newspapermen he admitted that Harding's was a long chance, but predicted that after the Wood and Lowden forces had battled to a standstill, political leaders would turn to his candidate. Pressed more closely, Daugherty replied about as follows:

Well, there will be no nomination on the early ballots. After the other condidates have failed, after they have gone their limit, their leaders, worn out and wishing to do the very best thing, will get together in some hotel room about 2:11 in the morning. Some fifteen men, bleary eyed with lack of sleep, and perspiring profusely with excessive heat, will sit around a big table. I will be with them and present the name of Senator Harding. When that time comes, Harding will be selected, because he fits in perfectly with every need of the party and nation. He is the logical choice, and the leaders will determine to throw their support to him.*

Except for the fact that Daugherty was not present at the big table, the prediction was close to the actual event. Daugherty had done his work so well that there was no need of his being there.

When the Republican convention convened on June 8, it made Henry Cabot Lodge, arch-symbol of Republican reaction, both temporary and permanent chairman. In his keynote speech, Lodge

* Paraphrased and combined by Mark Sullivan from quotations in the New York *Times*, June 13, 1920, and Washington *Post*, February 27, 1921. Mark Sullivan, *Our Times* (New York, Charles Scribner's Sons, 1935), Vol. VI, p. 37.

excoriated Wilson and the League, denounced our policy toward Mexico, and objected to an American mandate over Armenia. As for domestic policy, he asserted that necessary economic legislation could never be passed as long as a Democratic free trader with Socialist tendencies remained in the White House. The platform committee encountered little difficulty except for the plank on the League of Nations. Wilson's foreign policy was condemned in part and in whole; the Democrats were criticized for unpreparedness in both war and peace, and for unsound fiscal policies which had brought about the high cost of living. The President was assailed for "unconstitutional and dictatorial" rule, for defeating national economy, vetoing a budget law, and failing to reform taxation. For their part, the Republicans promised to help every interest, particularly agriculture and transportation, and advocated a higher tariff, woman suffrage, a child labor law, strong military forces, and Federal aid to education, conservation, and reclamation. The platform condemned Government operation of railroads.

When it came to preparing a statement on the League, however, the committee wrangled for three and a half days. After all, many important Republican leaders were sincerely committed to the League or some similar form of international cooperation, and it would be folly to drive them into

the Democratic camp. On the other hand, men like
Johnson and Borah were threatening to bolt the
convention unless it was clear in its renunciation of
the League. After one forty-eight-hour session, the
committee agreed to a long statement, largely the
work of Elihu Root, which seemed sufficiently confusing and straddling to catch all Republicans. The
Covenant, they asserted, had "failed signally" to
promote agreement among the nations and to preserve the peace of the world. Furthermore, it contained stipulations "not only intolerable for an independent people, but certain to produce the injustice, hostility and controversy among nations which
it proposed to prevent." The coming Republican
Administration would bring about "such agreements with the other nations of the world as shall
meet the full duty of America to civilization and
humanity, in accordance with American ideals, and
without surrendering the right of the American
people to exercise its judgment and its power in
favor of justice and peace."

It was Friday morning before the nominating
speeches began, and the applause clearly showed
which candidates were strongest. When the ballot-
ing began, Wood with 287 votes and Lowden with
211 stood far in front. Behind them trailed Senator Johnson with 113, Governor William C. Sproul
of Pennsylvania with 84, Nicholas Murray Butler
with 68, Senator Harding with 65, and Coolidge with

28. On the next three ballots Lowden and Wood gained a few votes. At the end of the fourth ballot someone moved an adjournment. It was obviously defeated, but Lodge after a moment's conversation with Senator Smoot declared it carried. At that instant the convention was taken over by a Senatorial caucus which dominated the situation until a choice had been made.

During the afternoon occurred one of the most unusual incidents in American politics. Fearing a deadlock, but realizing that Lowden and Wood had sufficient votes to control the convention, Wood's manager suggested that the two leading candidates discuss the possibilities of dividing the ticket between them. Both consented, but practical politics necessitated that the conference be held without knowledge of the delegates and press. A taxi picked up Lowden and Wood at different places and the two men talked as it drove around the streets of Chicago. However, the main problem—who would take second place on the ticket—was not solved, and the taxi meeting came to nothing.

That night in the Blackstone Hotel suite of George Harvey, Senators Lodge, Smoot, Grundy, Brandegee, Curtis, and others informally decided that the vote should go to Harding. Whether the real boss of the party, Boies Penrose of Pennsylvania, influenced this choice, it is difficult to say. Desperately ill, he roused himself from a coma,

says his physician, asked his secretary the news
from Chicago, and when he heard a deadlock was
impending, gave the terse order, "Call up King and
tell him to throw it to Harding." If this is true,
Penrose was the Warwick and not Daugherty.
Penrose may have been ill in Philadelphia, but the
gathering, as the *Saturday Evening Post* asserted
a few weeks later, "was bossed, none the less, and
for this reason: The convention was made up
largely of sub-bosses and sub-sub-bosses, . . . all
proficient in the work of running things, all amen-
able to orders."

Two purposes dominated the work of the caucus
that night. First of all, a deadlock must be avoided.
Lowden and Wood were both enthusiastically supported, but it was doubtful if either could get the
nomination. Both had been hurt by the amounts
spent in support of their candidacy—amounts so
large, in fact, as to create a scandal. A Senate committee investigating pre-convention expenses had
revealed a war chest for Wood of $1,282,000, about
half of which had been advanced by Proctor, and
one of $414,000 for Lowden, most of it contributed
by the candidate himself. Everyone knew that
many business magnates, distrusted by the common man, were behind Wood. Furthermore, Wood
had advocated compulsory military service, and
the nation had had enough of that. He was too
much of a militarist for a country anxious to re-

turn to the pursuits of peace. Wood's chief appeal rested upon his lifelong friendship with Theodore Roosevelt and the widespread belief that he had been treated unfairly by Wilson in not being sent to France during the war. These, as it proved, were not enough to win the nomination.

Moreover, old-line Senators were enthusiastic neither for Lowden nor Wood, both men of strong personality. During eight years these Senators had taken orders from the White House and they had had enough. They were eager to seize the reins of power and elect one of their own members, a man they could trust. They wanted a President, as one Senator cynically remarked, who would "sign whatever bills the Senate sent him and not send bills to the Senate to pass." Such a man was Harding.

As state leaders returned to their delegations on Saturday morning, the plan was quietly made known. Wood and Lowden were to be given four ballots to develop their strength or prove that they were deadlocked. In the meantime, Harding was to be strengthened and with the fifth ballot rapidly pushed forward. Like clockwork the plan proceeded; after the fourth ballot Lowden and Wood were rapidly disposed of, Harding assumed the lead in the ninth, and was nominated on the tenth. The delegates realized that the whole procedure was a travesty on popular government, but they were worn out, confused, and anxious to get home.

On Saturday morning the Senatorial caucus had also picked a Vice-Presidential candidate, Senator Irvine Lenroot of Wisconsin. He was to be nominated by Senator Medill McCormick. The scheme unfolded smoothly until a delegate from Oregon, Wallace McCamant, obtained recognition and nominated Calvin Coolidge. This unexpected act caught the imagination of the delegates. In a sudden overwhelming revolt against the Senatorial caucus, disgusted delegates gave Coolidge the nomination on the first ballot by a vote of 674½ to 146 for Lenroot. When Coolidge became President, he tried to reward McCamant with a Federal judgeship, but the Senate turned down the nomination.

The Democrats exhibited much less pre-convention interest than the Republicans. Only about 300 delegates went to San Francisco with instructions, and the primaries had revealed little beyond adherence to favorite sons. The candidates in the lead were Governor James M. Cox of Ohio, Attorney-General A. Mitchell Palmer, and William G. McAdoo, former Secretary of the Treasury. Of these three the lanky and forceful McAdoo was easily the ablest, judged by experience and accomplishment. Born and brought up in the South, he had gone to New York to become an important lawyer and head of the corporation that built the first tunnels under the Hudson River. His career as Secretary of the Treasury, Chairman of the Federal Reserve Board, and Director-General of Railroads demonstrated beyond question his capacity to direct large affairs and his tact in dealing with Congress. By his colleagues he was considered a man of great political skill.

Palmer was a tall, suave, quiet man who had enjoyed a successful if narrow career as a small-town Pennsylvania lawyer, as Alien Property Custodian during the war, and as Attorney-General during the last two years of the Wilson Administration. Known as the "fighting Quaker," he had been charged during these two years with enforcement of the Eighteenth Amendment, combating the influence of the "Reds," fighting the high cost of living, and maintaining industrial peace. His methods were harsh, tactless, undiscriminating, and in large part unsuccessful. They lacked the attributes of statesmanship. Cox was the owner of two successful newspapers, in Dayton and Springfield, Ohio; he was a self-made man of progressive stamp, hostile to machine politics, who had served two terms in Congress and was then in his third term as Governor of Ohio. As Governor he had capably dealt with the difficult problems presented by the terrible floods of 1913, the war, and post-war reconstruction. The Ohio Workmen's Compensation Act and a codification of the state school laws were milestones of his adn.inistration. A man of tactful and pleasing personality and an excellent orator, he had much to commend him as a candidate.

In his keynote speech Senator Homer Cummings gave unqualified endorsement to the policies and leadership of Wilson, placed upon the Republicans full blame for the rejection of the treaty, and contrasted the blameless wartime record of the Democratic Administration with that of the Republicans in 1898. Senator Joseph T. Robinson of Arkansas was made permanent chairman.

Unlike the lifeless Republican convention, that of the Democrats presented a real clash of ideas and personalities. At Chicago the delegates never questioned the work of the resolutions committee; at San Francisco a spirited debate, for which William Jennings Bryan was chiefly responsible, took place. When the committee reported a platform without a prohibition plank, Bryan demanded that it adopt a bone-dry resolution. He failed both in this and in a subsequent effort to modify the plank on the League of Nations. In treating foreign policy, the Democratic platform was more liberal than the Republican. It defended the President's Mexican policy, expressed sympathy with Ireland's desire for self-government, pledged independence to the Philippines, and promised greater home rule to Puerto Rico. The League, it asserted, was the "surest, if not the only, practical means of maintaining the permanent peace of the world"; and it advocated immediate ratification of the treaty without reservations impairing its "essential integrity."

Between the Republican and Democratic platforms there was little to choose on domestic questions. One trimmed as cautiously as the other on important social and economic problems. Both called for woman suffrage and child labor laws; both advocated improved transportation, tax reform, and a Federal budget. Neither offered a forthright program of reconstruction. The Democrats even had the effrontery to "resent the unfounded reproaches directed against" them "for alleged interference with the freedom of the press and freedom of speech," adding, "no utterance from any quarter has been assailed, and no publication has been repressed, which has not been animated by treasonable purpose, and directed against the nation's peace, order and security in time of war."

With McAdoo, Palmer, and Cox in the lead, the Democrats required forty-four ballots to pick their candidate. McAdoo, son-in-law of Wilson, was handicapped in the North as a dry and throughout the nation as heir to the policies of a President whose popularity was rapidly waning. Palmer's national fame had come almost entirely from a bitter campaign against alleged "Reds," and he finally gave up the fight on the thirty-sixth ballot.

The choice in the end went to Cox; while the nomination for Vice-President was given by acclamation to Franklin D. Roosevelt, Assistant Secretary of the Navy during the war.

With the Republican Party retreating rapidly to the narrowest tenets of nationalism and *laissez-faire,* and the Democratic Party equally conservative in home matters, the third parties had to uphold what remained of advanced social thought in American politics. Considering the Federal and local persecution of left-wing groups during the war and post-war years, it is a wonder that radical elements were able to operate at all in 1920. In dealing with the Industrial Workers of the World the Government had been particularly ruthless. Charging that they had conspired "to prevent, hinder and delay" various war acts, Federal agents raided their meetings, entered their homes, confiscated their records, and sent hundreds of their leaders to jail. Patriotic appeals cloaked these attacks, but their chief effect was to crush utterly the most militant of American labor unions, and to weaken all radical movements.

Upon the Socialist Party, which for a decade had been steadily gaining members and votes, the war also had disastrous effects. At a special convention called at St. Louis in April, 1917, the majority described the conflict as one of "commercial and financial rivalry," proclaimed its "unyielding opposition" to the war, and assailed "all proposed legislation for military or industrial conscription." The adoption of these planks caused the pro-war Socialists to secede, but the party membership increased from 67,788 to 81,172 between April and June. What little organized opposition there had been to the war—and it was small—had been carried on by the Socialist Party. The stand of the party brought quick reprisals from the Government. Under the Conscription Act meetings were dispersed, Socialist papers denied second-class mail privileges, and many of the leaders arrested. After the passage of the Espionage Act, the Government increased its attacks on the Socialists. For an anti-war speech delivered in Canton, Ohio, in June, 1918, Eugene V. Debs was sentenced to ten years' imprisonment. A few months later, five leading party officers, including Victor Berger, who had been elected to Congress that November, were sentenced to twenty years each.

The usual bane of left-wing movements, however, is internal conflict rather than outside opposition. The party had no sooner recovered from the withdrawal of the right wing than it was faced by opposition from the left. The Russian Revolution gave a tremendous impetus to radical Marxism, and by the autumn of 1918 extremist groups, particularly in New York and Chicago, were organizing for action and demanding overthrow of the existing state, endorsement of Communist movements in Europe, and affiliation with the newly organized Third International. In the face of this rising revolt, the party expelled many of the left-wing groups. Others withdrew in the summer and autumn of 1919 to join the Communist Party and the Communist Labor Party. Within a year the Socialist Party loss was reduced to one quarter of its pre-war membership. The newly formed Communist parties, however, were to fare quite as badly. Showing a ferocity unparalleled in American history, Governmental hostility under the leadership of Attorney-General Palmer quickly drove them underground.

With these events as a background, the Socialists held their nominating convention in May. In addition to the reform program to be achieved by ballot, not by revolution, the party reiterated its intention of keeping hands off the internal affairs of trade unions. It nevertheless commended industrial unionism. The convention also voted adherence to the Third International on condition that it be not required to endorse any "special method for the attainment of the Socialist Commonwealth." Eugene V. Debs, serving his sentence in the Federal prison at Atlanta, was for the fifth time nominated for the Presidency. Declaring that the practice of condemning citizens for views opposed to the party in power was repugnant to democracy, and pointing to the fact that all the other great powers had freed their political prisoners, the convention petitioned for the release of Debs. It also appointed a committee to inform Debs of his nomination. Its pilgrimage to the Atlanta penitentiary was more than a dramatic episode; it was a gesture of defiance to the Palmer-Burleson violators of civil liberties. It was also an evidence of profound respect for their veteran leader, whose warm human qualities, incorruptible devotion, and inspired leadership had been a tower of strength to the Socialist movement.

No political development in 1920 was more interesting than the organization of the Farmer-Labor Party. It was born primarily from a union of two groups, the Committee of Forty-Eight and the National Labor Party. The former was a body of middle-class intellectuals, inheritors of the progressive tradition of 1912, and believers in civil liberties, rights of labor, and a broad program of Government ownership. Their spokesmen were such papers as the *New Republic* and *Nation*. The National Labor Party was composed of rank and file trade unionists who repudiated the traditional political policy of Gompers and the American Federation of Labor. Its leaders—men like Max Hayes, one-time vice-President of the American Federation of Labor, and John Fitzpatrick, President of the Chicago Federation of Labor—were either members of the Socialist Party or thoroughly indoctrinated by its ideology.

The National Labor Party had held its first convention in 1919. When it called a second to meet at Chicago in July, 1920, the Committee of Forty-Eight asked their followers to gather there at the same time. When the "Forty-Eighters" appeared to be getting nowhere, the delegates walked out en masse and joined the trade unionists. There the combined conventions offered the nomination to LaFollette, but refused to accept the type of platform upon which his followers insisted. In the end the nomination went to Parley Parker Christensen, of Utah, one of the delegates to the Forty-Eight convention, with Max Hayes as his running mate. The coalition called itself a Farmer-Labor Party despite the fact that all efforts to win the cooperation of the farmers' Non-Partisan League of the Northwest failed. The platform demanded Government ownership of railroads, mines, and natural resources, lifting the blockade against Russia, withdrawal from participation under the Treaty of Versailles in any imperialistic ventures, and a long program of social reforms.

Accurately the *New Republic* spoke of the "obscure and lifeless intellectual atmosphere" of the campaign, and the day before election characterized it as "one of the most joyless, futile and irritating campaigns in our history." It was obvious that the campaign was arousing little interest. For this there were several reasons. Voters in the first place felt themselves decidedly betrayed. Both nominating conventions, and particularly the Republican, had shown American democracy at its worst. Alice Roosevelt Longworth, looking in on the Chicago gathering, described it as "wormy with politicians—riddled with intrigue." Neither at Chicago nor San Francisco had the common voter much to say with respect to the candidates. This would have been less deplorable if the results had justified the means. They did not; neither Cox nor Harding was able to evoke much enthusiasm. The more intelligent voters clearly divined that they had a choice between one second-best and one third-best candidate.

In comparison with the vigorous, colorful Roosevelt, Wilson, and Bryan, the great political leaders of the two previous decades, the two nominees seemed pale indeed. Roosevelt had died in 1919. Wilson, severely stricken, was confined to his room; and Bryan, his dry plank defeated, quit the convention, and the campaign, with the words, "My heart is in the grave." Under the circumstances, it was difficult to stir up much enthusiasm. What made the situation more disheartening to honest men was that large elements in both major parties supported their candidates at prodigious sacrifice of personal conviction. Harding, a stand-pat Re-

publican of the McKinley and Hanna type, could
evoke no responsive chord in the hearts of Roosevelt Progressives; Cox, a man of progressive leanings, could hardly appeal to conservative Democrats. Some progressive Republicans like Amos
Pinchot threw in their lot with the Farmer-Labor
Party; others announced that they would support
Cox.

The greatest hurdle which both parties had to
face, however, was the League. Political leaders
were pretty sure it was dead, but they also knew
that millions of voters still approved of the ideal.
Cox quickly indulged in a display of principle
which increased the certainty that he would lose.
At first he appeared to shake himself free from
Wilson's special group by eliminating Homer S.
Cummings and placing George White, a Princeton
man but not a particular friend of the President,
in charge of the campaign. But believing strongly
in the League, he made a pilgrimage to the White
House, committed himself firmly to it, and received
the blessing of Wilson. By the time he had finished
his first tour, Cox was convinced that the League
was the chief issue and that the campaign was, in
Wilson's words, to be "a great and solemn referendum." This was an attempt to clarify the battle,
and an honest effort to inject a real issue into the
campaign. But the stand was probably injurious
to him, for so much prejudiced misrepresentation

had been heaped on the League that it was growing more unpopular.

Although Cox was no total abstainer, he promptly announced that the Democrats would uphold the Eighteenth Amendment. This stand was also a liability, as it automatically cut off many large contributions. The Democrats had little to spend at a time when they badly needed money. Cox, who had won political success as an aggressive campaigner and a progressive executive, fought an active campaign. In successive tours he visited most parts of the country, advocating the League, defending the conduct of the war, and roundly denouncing Republican conservatism. But his call to another progressive crusade made little headway. The flaming demand for social justice had largely burned itself out in the Great Crusade, and his speeches fell on dull ears.

The Republicans played their hands better. Instead of urging Americans to keep on with the task of international organization, they channeled all the various resentments against Wilson into votes against Cox. Instead of sending their candidate up and down the country to trumpet for progress, they kept him on the front porch to deliver "inscrutably bland" speeches stressing a return to "normalcy." Unlike the Democrats, the Republicans had no difficulty in filling a large campaign chest. Piously the National Committee announced that contributions would be limited to $1,000, but this was only for the public. Privately it accepted large sums, while after the campaign ended it took a huge gift from oil interests (through the Continental Trading Company) to help make up the deficit. Altogether, the Republicans were believed to have raised about $5,000,000, the largest sum yet expended in a political campaign.

Although Republican victory seemed inevitable, the position of the candidate was no bed of roses. On the one hand stood the anti-League irreconcilables, Senators Lodge, Borah, Johnson, McCormick and Brandegee. On the other were the pro-League Republicans, including ex-President Taft, Charles E. Hughes, Nicholas Murray Butler, and Elihu Root. The Republicans could ignore the latter group and win, but it was not Harding's idea of good politics to endanger party harmony by affronting such highly respected leaders. After speeches so vague and conflicting that it was impossible to know where he stood on foreign relations, Harding decided, with the help of his two literary aides, George Harvey and Richard Washburn Child, to make a gesture toward the pro-League group. In a speech to visiting Republicans from Indiana and Wisconsin late in August, he promised immediately upon inauguration to call a conference to formulate a plan for a world court with teeth in it and a reconstruction of the League into a "world association for conference." His statements were so vague that they meant nothing. But the speech was a straw at which the pro-League Republicans could grasp. Near the end of the campaign thirty-one of them, led by Taft, issued a declaration that there was more chance of securing a League under Harding than under Cox.

When the confusing and lifeless canvass ended, the result was a Republican landslide. Harding polled approximately 16,152,000 votes (61.6 per cent of the whole) to 9,147,000 (34.9 per cent) for Cox. The electoral vote was 404 to 127. Of the minor candidates, Debs polled about 917,000, Christensen 272,500, and the Prohibition nominee, Watkins, a little over 192,000. So sweeping was the victory that the Republicans carried the border states of Maryland, Missouri, and Oklahoma, and for the first time since 1876 cut into the solid South by capturing Tennessee. In the new House the Republicans were to have 307 seats, the Democrats 127, and the Socialists 1. This gave the Republicans a majority of 179, the greatest in the history of the party. In the Senate the Republicans won 10 seats and thus increased their majority from 2 to 22.

If there was any outstanding issue, it was America's attitude toward the League. But, like most Presidential elections, the campaign of 1920 became

too confused to offer a clear-cut decision. That
America had turned from internationalism there
could be no doubt, but whether that meant a repudiation of the League and all its works was
another question. Americans of German extraction
voted against the Democrats because they believed
that Wilson had failed to live up to his promises
to the German people in the Fourteen Points.
Irish-Americans were anxious to rebuke the sup-
posed lack of sympathy for Irish independence;
Italian-Americans were bitter over Fiume. Many
must have voted in protest against the high cost
of living and in resentment of a depression which
had begun to deepen by November.

More than all else, however, it was an anti-
Wilson vote. It was a reaction against the discipline, the suffering, and the disappointments of the
past three years. Wilson, in the words of a veteran
newspaperman, had become "the symbol both of
the war we had begun to think of with disillusion,
and of the peace we had come to think of with
cyncism." Anti-Wilsonian emotion seemed to be
the one force which held together the various fac-
tions of the Republican Party. Reactionaries hated
him for his idealism, and some liberals for his sup-
posed betrayal of it. Prolonged cheers greeted
Henry Cabot Lodge when he shrieked in his keynote speech at the Republican convention: "Mr.
Wilson and his dynasty, his heirs and assigns, or

anybody that is his, anybody who with bent knee has served his purpose, must be driven from all control of the government and all influence in it."

Lodge, a skillful politician, but a testy, petty, narrow man whose public career was often dominated by the most extreme biases and personal hatreds, had no understanding of either the splendid qualities or the enduring achievements of the great President. To many others, as well as Lodge, Woodrow Wilson seemed cold, imperious, unbending, and intolerant, aloof from the problems of the common man. Intimates, on the other hand, found him cordial and considerate, eager for knowledge and advice on public questions, and capable of warm friendships. Shy, sensitive, and high-strung, he was quick to form his own estimate of people, and highly individual in his relations and responses. His sharp antagonism toward greedy plutocrats and selfish politicians was matched by a warm love for humanity and a sturdy faith in the soundness of the people. Wilson's personality, ideals, and political aptitude, of course, are significant chiefly as they are reflected in his accomplishments. These show statesmanship of a high order in the reform legislation of his first Administration, preeminent energy and organization as a war leader, and superb vision in helping plan a new world organization.

Wilson's greatest ambition—the participation of

his country in a League of Nations—was defeated as a result of the elections of 1918 and 1920. But the bitter attacks and partisan estimates of these elections have no connection with his true character or contributions. The words of Herbert Hoover, written almost two decades after Wilsons' death, offer a sounder appraisal:

But at once I may state that Woodrow Wilson will take a great place in American history. Time will wear away the minor shadows and he will stand out as a great warrior for righteousness. He represented fully the idealism of America. He administered a great war efficiently and effectively. Knowing intimately with what he contended, both during the war and at the peace, his moral courage, his intellectual honesty, and the burning idealism which impelled him, I am proud to have served under him.*

* Herbert Hoover, *America's First Crusade* (New York, Charles Scribner's Sons, 1941), p. 63.

CHAPTER III

Nothing could have more accurately foretold the spirit of the Harding Administration than the campaign itself. Scarcely a week after he had been nominated, Harding struck the keynote of his two and a half years in the White House. "America's first needs," he said in perhaps the only words of his that are now remembered, "is not heroics, but healing; not nostrums, but normalcy; not revolution, but restoration . . . not surgery, but serenity." He cherished the impossible dream of leading the nation back to the "good old days" of pre-war America, or to "normalcy." This he would do through the cooperation of all groups and the reasoned common sense of the great masses. For such a rôle Harding was not entirely unfitted. With all his tragic shortcomings, he was personally a kindly, self-effacing, and urbane executive, desperately anxious to do his best for the nation. Despite his ignorance of national and international problems, he might, with far-seeing advisers and honest friends, have accomplished much, even in the conservative revolution of the "reconstruction" years.

Although Harding had made a gesture toward an "association of nations," it was evident before the campaign ended that he had adopted an isolationist position. This was inevitable, for his advisers were Republicans of the Lodge, Fall, Brandegee, and McCormick type rather than Taft, Root, and Hughes. Even more important than advice in influencing Harding was his fear that the irreconcilables might wreck his Administration rather than compromise. In his inaugural address he made his attitude perfectly clear. "While America," he said, "is ready to encourage, eager to initiate, anxious to participate in any seemly program likely to lessen the possibilities of war," it would not desert its "inherited policy of non-involvement" in Old World affairs. "Confident of our ability to work out our own destiny," said the new President, "and jealously guarding our right to do so, we seek no part in directing the destinies of the Old World. We do not mean to be entangled."

Interpreting the election as a repudiation of the League, Harding called for separate peace treaties with Germany and Austria. "There can be no misinterpretation and there will be no betrayal of the deliberate expression of the American people," he declared in a special message of April 12, 1921. Following his suggestion, the Senate of July 2 passed a resolution declaring the war at an end, but reserving all rights and advantages under the treaty. Separate treaties were ratified on October 18. The President's anxiety to promote peace, on the other hand, found expression in the Washington Conference of 1921–1922 which brought limitation of naval armaments and an effort to stabilize the situation in the Far East. Having prevented American participation in the League, the Republicans felt called upon to make this contribution toward world concord. In other fields, Harding's foreign policy differed but slightly from that of Wilson. As far as Mexico was concerned, the watchful waiting of Secretary Hughes was as patient as that of Wilson. In the little Caribbean nations dollar diplomacy operated with the same misguided efficiency under the new Administration as it had under Democrats and Republicans alike in earlier years.

To Harding and the Senate cabal the futile quest of "normalcy" was mainly a desire to return to the good old ways of conservatism. The new Administration might never achieve normalcy, but at least it could throw over the idealism and progressivism of Roosevelt and Wilson. This intention was made clearly evident by the Cabinet appointments. Like most Cabinets, that of Harding represented a combination of personal desire, political expediency, and an effort to please the voters by including several

popular men of high repute. Of these last he found
two: Charles Evans Hughes, named to the State
Department, and Herbert Hoover, to the Department of Commerce. Harding's first choice for the
State Department had been Senator Fall, for whose
abilities he had a grotesquely exaggerated opinion,
and his second was George Harvey, equally un-
suited. But he was warned that he needed a man
of greater prestige and a less isolationist stamp.
The appointment of Hoover, a man of proved ability and of great popularity because of his promi-
nence in war relief work, was applauded by Americans of both parties.

Harding's one thoroughly personal appointee was
his campaign manager, Harry M. Daugherty, who
became Attorney-General. Like Harding, Daugherty was the product of a small Ohio town, and,
like Harding's, his youth had been something of a
struggle. He managed, however, to obtain a law
degree from the University of Michigan. Unsuccessful in his search for public office and little interested in the grinding study of a law practice,
Daugherty found a natural career as lobbyist and
wire-puller. He rarely appeared in court, but his
firm handled many cases for public utilities seeking favors of one kind or another. Ability in this
work had won him a reputation and contacts beyond his own state, but it hardly fitted him for the
high office of Attorney-General. His choice seemed

dubious even to the reactionary and not overly scrupulous Senators who had nominated Harding. The President was adamant, however, and Republican Senators gave in to clear the way for more politically desirable nominations.

Harding's appointment of Albert B. Fall to the Interior Department was likewise a gesture of personal friendship. But Fall was also popular with the Senate, and it is possible that the oil interests had a hand in the choice. The remaining selections were obviously political. Andrew W. Mellon and James J. Davis, both from Pennsylvania, went to the Treasury and Labor Departments at the behest of Penrose and Knox, two of the most powerful Republican Senators. The War Portfolio, refused by General Wood, was given to John W. Weeks, banker and Old Guard Senator from Massachusetts. When Lowden refused the Secretaryship of the Navy, it was given to Edwin Denby, a Michigan politician whose stupidity and neglect of duty helped to bring discredit upon the Administration. The appointment of Chairman Will Hays of the Republican National Committee as Postmaster-General was the expected award for services well rendered. Henry C. Wallace, editor of an agricultural weekly in Iowa, represented the interests of the farmer.

Except for Denby, the Cabinet did not lack ability. What at least two of its members wanted was

common honesty and decency. Perhaps its outstanding characteristic was its almost unrelieved
conservatism. The only member with any progressive background was Hughes, but his career in the
Supreme Court, followed by four years of close
association with big business as a Wall Street attorney, had largely ended that phase of his interests.
Hoover was a humanitarian, but a devotee of clas-
sical economics. The rest were untroubled by any
stirrings of progressivism. Even James J. Davis,
although he started work in a steel mill and still
held a union card, had long since made a fortune
as organizer of the Loyal Order of the Moose and
was now an affluent banker. "From the point of
view of labor," suggests one observer, "Charles M.
Schwab might as well have got the job." It was
decidedly a rich man's cabinet. Vice-President
Coolidge, asked by Harding to sit in the Cabinet,
contributed nothing to swing that body toward
the left.

Quite as significant in emphasizing the conservative tendencies of the Government were Harding's
nominations to the Supreme Court. The death of
Chief Justice White brought the appointment of
ex-President William Howard Taft in his stead
(June 30, 1921). A man of genial temperament
and long experience, Taft was thoroughly conservative in his legal point of view. George Sutherland
of Utah, appointed in 1922 after the resignation

of Justice Clarke, had served twelve years in the Senate without revealing any progressive tendencies. Pierce Butler of Minnesota, chosen the same year to succeed Justice Day, was a reactionary railroad lawyer. With a conservative majority composed of Taft, McKenna, Van Devanter, Pitney, McReynolds, Sutherland, and Butler, only Holmes and Brandeis were left to hold the liberal defenses.

If all parties had not been so eager to return to "normalcy," the nation might have been spared the bitterest period of labor conflict thus far met in its history. Some progress had been made during the war toward a national labor policy, and machinery had been set up to ease and adjust labor conflicts. After the armistice this machinery was unfortunately dismantled. The War Industries Board ended its work on January 1, 1919, the Shipbuilding Labor Adjustment Board in March, and the National War Labor Board in May. Few were interested in preserving them. The President and Congress were too busy fighting over the peace treaty to give much attention to domestic problems. In any event, the Republican majorities were anxious to end the extraordinary war powers of the President. Business longed to return to the era of *laissez-faire,* and labor, distrustful of regulatory boards which had kept wages down while the cost of living mounted rapidly, were anxious to reestablish freedom of action.

As the situation developed, it brought to the surface all the elements of a grim labor conflict. The cost of living in the post-war boom was jumping ahead more rapidly than wages. Employers, in fact, were already attempting to deflate what they believed to be the high wages of the war years. Although the Government had smashed the Industrial Workers of the World, a new crop of liberals and radicals had been produced by the war. Under pressure of left-wing groups, a committee of the American Federation of Labor drew up a reconstruction program later approved by the Executive Committee. The program included the right to collective bargaining, a living wage, an eight-hour day and a five-and-a-half-day week, protection for women and children, consumers' cooperatives, Government ownership of public and semi-public utilities, suspension of immigration, preservation of civil liberties, and many other demands. For the American Federation of Labor it was an amazingly progressive document. But the nation was not in a progressive mood, and employers ignored the program. At the end of the war, organized labor had achieved the strongest position in its history; but it was quickly evident that its power could be maintained only by a severe struggle.

The first wave of post-war strikes broke in the late summer and early fall of 1919. Railroad shopmen, disgusted over the slow progress made by the

Wage Adjustment Board in meeting their demands, began in August to walk out in unauthorized strikes. At the instigation of President Wilson, Director-General of Railroads Hines made new agreements which raised wages. For the moment the situation was quieted, but "outlaw strikes" of various groups of shopmen recurred in the spring and summer of 1920.

Serious difficulty, in the meantime, was developing in the soft-coal regions. Long years of conflict in this area were a natural outgrowth of the operations of one of the most chaotic industries in the nation. Bituminous coal mining had for years been an overexpanded and overcompetitive industry, afflicted by constant price-slashing. The World War had accentuated this situation and left the production both of soft and hard coal in an unhealthy condition. Moreover, neither operators nor workers were adequately organized to handle the problems of the industry as a whole.

In October, 1917, the United Mine Workers had signed an agreement with the United States Fuel Administration to run for the duration of the war, but in no case after April 1, 1920. When the Fuel Administration ceased to regulate coal prices at the end of June, 1919, and prices began to soar for consumers, the miners demanded a 60 per cent increase in wages, a six-hour day, and a five-day week. If no agreement could be made, a strike

order was authorized. When the operators virtually refused to negotiate, the strike call was issued,
effective October 31. On the 24th, President Wilson
issued a proclamation that the country was still at
war and that a strike would prevent aid to our
allies; on the 29th, Attorney-General A. Mitchell
Palmer asserted that the strike was illegal under
the Lever Food and Fuel Act. Palmer's statement
was made despite Senator Husting's declaration
when the Act was passed that he was authorized
by Secretary of Labor Wilson to say that the Administration did not and would not construe the
bill as prohibiting strikes and peaceful picketing.
But Palmer's interpretation aroused little opposition from the public, whose fears of communism,
socialism, and radicalism had been fanned by a
recent vote of the miners for nationalization of
the mines.

Despite these warnings and a telegram from
Gompers urging that the strike order be rescinded,
John L. Lewis, President of the Miners' Union,
allowed it to stand. On the day set, 425,000 miners
quit work. The Attorney-General, on the ground
that the Lever Act had been violated, obtained an
injunction from the Federal District Court of Indiana, ordering the officers of the union to cease all
activities tending to encourage or maintain the
strike in the bituminous coal industry. On November 8 the injunction was made permanent and

the union was ordered to cancel the strike order. The officers obeyed and urged the men to return to work. Most of them remained on strike, but the trouble was temporarily settled in December by the Fuel Administration's proposal for a 14 per cent increase, with a representative commission of three to be appointed to work out within two months the basis of a new agreement. The commission, although it turned down certain of the miners' demands, awarded a 27 per cent wage increase. The award, which by no means covered the rise in living costs since 1917, was to be effective until March 31, 1922.

Meanwhile, labor difficulties for the first time since the great Homestead strike seriously afflicted the steel industry. Except for a few skilled workers, labor organizations in steel mills had virtually disappeared since that bitter defeat of the union in 1892. With a twelve-hour day, a seven-day week, and a twenty-four-hour shift every two weeks, working conditions were a disgrace to American civilization. General living conditions in company-owned or dominated towns were almost as bad. Believing that the time was ripe for another attempt at unionization, labor leaders made successful efforts late in 1918 to organize the steel workers around Chicago. Early the next year a national committee drew up a list of demands, including abolition of the twenty-four-hour shift, a six-day week, an American standard of living, and collective bargaining. When steel officials, led by Judge Elbert H. Gary, refused to negotiate, even at the behest of the President of the United States, a strike was called for September 22. The unions declared that 267,000 men dropped their tools; the steel companies put the figures at 200,000.

Although the strike was ably led by William Z. Foster and won widespread public sympathy, it eventually collapsed. Employers assailed it as an uprising of foreign "Reds," and brought in Negro strikebreakers from the South to man the mills, while state troopers and coal-and-iron police swarmed into the mining towns to intimidate strikers and crush civil liberties. With few exceptions the press sided with the employers. The strikers were weakened by the jealousy of the twenty-four unions interested in organizing steel, by the eventual desertion of the Amalgamated Association of Iron and Steel Workers, by the failure of Gompers and the American Federation of Labor to give more active cooperation, and by company propaganda picturing the violence as caused only by strikers and the strike itself as a conspiracy led by Bolshevists. Foster's early record of syndicalism may have helped to strengthen the latter charge. But the chief fault lay with organized labor, which failed to throw its full strength into the battle. Among the great unions, only the Amalgamated Clothing

Workers with a contribution of $100,000 and the International Ladies' Garment Workers' Union with one of $60,000, offered enthusiastic financial aid.

After the strike was over, a commission of inquiry sponsored by the Interchurch World Movement made a careful and authoritative report on conditions in the steel industry. It found that the average week was 68.7 hours, that the men were grossly underpaid, and that no working machinery for the redress of grievances existed. The arbitrary control of the Steel Corporation, asserted the report, "extended outside the plants, affecting the workers as citizens and the social institutions of the communities." In brief, conditions were "inhuman" and the strike was "justified."

The strikes of the shopmen, coal miners, and steel workers were but the most outstanding of a year characterized everywhere by labor disturbances. At one time or another, New York City saw its harbor workers, streetcar men, clothing workers, and actors on strike. Chicago had strikes in the building trades and its transportation system. Seattle was paralyzed for five days by a "general strike." In Boston more than three fourths of the city's police force walked out in protest against inadequate wages. Altogether, 1919 witnessed 3,630 strikes involving more than 4,160,000 workers. In at least nine of these conflicts 60,000 or more men left their work. It was the most troubled year which American labor had as yet experienced.

In the midst of the widespread disturbances, President Wilson hurriedly issued invitations to representatives of employers, labor, and the public to meet in Washington on October 6 to formulate principles for a "genuine and lasting cooperation between capital and labor." Among those who came to this industrial conference were representatives of the American Federation of Labor, the Railroad Brotherhoods, farm organizations, finance, and commerce. Unfortunately, the hoped-for "cooperation" never materialized. Labor asked for immediate consideration and arbitration of the steel strike. As this implied a recognition of the right to organize steel workers, the representatives of capital opposed it. The conference then took up the problem of collective bargaining, but when no agreement seemed possible, the labor group walked out on October 22 and the conference collapsed. The group representing the public suggested that the President appoint a small committee to continue work on the settlement of industrial disputes. Such a body eventually submitted two reports; but slight attention was ever given to them.

Despite the discouraging outcome of the steel, coal, and shopmen's strikes, the year 1919 was by no means wholly disastrous for labor. Hundreds of lesser strikes were won. The year actually showed an increase of 19.6 per cent in the membership of the American Federation of Labor over 1918, while 1920 revealed a fresh increase of 25.1 per cent. In 1920 organized labor boasted a strength of more than 5,100,000, the American Federation of Labor giving its membership at about 4,079,000. Although the restlessness characteristic of the post-war adjustment was an important factor in the labor difficulties, the desire of labor for higher wages to meet the rising cost of living was the chief cause both of the strikes and the increase in membership. To labor, "normalcy" meant a standard of living at least as high as that of 1914.

Just as 1920 witnessed the greatest increase in the membership of organized labor since 1903, so 1922 showed the greatest decrease yet recorded. The depression of 1920–1921 threw multitudes out of work, and the open-shop drive of the employers' associations smashed hundreds of locals. Resentment against this clear-cut effort to break organized labor and against the attempts of the employer, sometimes abetted by the Federal Government, to reduce wages, brought a new outbreak of strikes in 1922. The depression of 1920–1921 had done something to deflate prices, and employers believed that wages also needed deflation. Labor, quite naturally, had no sympathy with this particular method of returning to normalcy.

Outstanding among the labor conflicts of 1922

were strikes by the shopmen and the coal miners.
The Transportation Act of 1920 had established a
Railway Labor Board with certain powers over
wages and working conditions. In 1920 the Board
had granted an increase of 22 per cent to shop
mechanics. In the following year, however, it re-
voked the earlier national agreements between
workers and management and ordered a general
wage reduction of 12 per cent. The shopmen re-
torted by a strike ballot and a walk-out on July 1,
1922. In this battle they had to fight alone. The
four brotherhoods patched up their difficulties and
continued work, while the maintenance-of-way
men, clerks, and station employees also refused to
participate. Nevertheless, 400,000 were on strike
and service was seriously curtailed.

Harding stepped in at the beginning by a proclamation warning strikers against interference with
interstate commerce. This helped to alienate public sympathy from the strikers, but did not intimidate them. The President then veered about and
struggled for more than a month to effect an agreement. His failure resulted in a different type of
Government action. On September 1 Attorney-
General Daugherty obtained from Judge James
Wilkerson of the Chicago Federal Court (appointed
by Harding) an injunction restraining the shopmen's union from using funds or engaging in activities even remotely connected with the strike. Based

on an alleged violation of the Sherman Act and the Transportation Act of 1920, Wilkerson's amazing order has gone down in history as the most far-reaching decree of its kind ever handed down in a labor case. The strike gradually disintegrated. Most of the workers obtained agreements from individual roads, others went back without agreements. Generally they were forced to accept reduced wages. One result of all this, naturally, was to end any usefulness which the Railway Labor Board might have.

A somewhat similar attempt was made to break down the wartime wage scale in the coal-mining industry. When the wage agreement in the bituminous fields expired on April 1, 1922, the operators refused to renew it and insisted upon wage reductions of from 17 to 40 per cent. Miners, demanding their old scale and a continuation of the check-off, went out on strike to the number of over 500,000 men. They were joined that April by 150,000 more from the anthracite fields. Such a walkout, including men in districts never before organized, was unprecedented. With the largest supply of coal above ground in the history of the United States, neither operators nor Administration officials were at first greatly concerned. As month followed month, however, and a coal famine impended, public interest became acute. Some mine owners in June attempted to resume operations at

Herrin, Illinois, with imported strikebreakers and guards. The excited strikers, after two of their own men had been killed without cause, laid siege to one of the mines, forced its surrender, and shot down nineteen of the captives.

About a month after the "Herrin massacre," Harding ordered the mine owners to resume operations and telegraphed (July 18) to twenty-eight Governors to provide protection. The Governors of Pennsylvania and Ohio called out the national guard, but few strikers returned to work. Many operators were now willing to make district compacts, but John L. Lewis and the officials of the United Mine Workers insisted on an "interstate agreement." In the end such an agreement was signed by about one fifth of the operators, while most bituminous miners returned to work in August on the understanding that a thorough study of the coal situation was to be made by the Federal Government. But many non-union strikers refused to go back, and continued their struggle for better conditions. The anthracite workers also called off their strike in August under an agreement extending existing conditions for a year and inviting Congress to create an investigating commission. On September 22, Congress established a Coal Commission of seven members to study all phases of the industry and recommend legislation.

The commission was an able and liberal group,

headed by John Hays Hammond. It employed at one time 500 persons, worked for eleven months, and spent about $600,000. In the opinion of John L. Lewis its work was a "lamentable failure" and its report a "maze of well-worn generalities" which could have been written by any well-informed mine superintendent in sixty days. This appraisal was eminently unfair. True, miners were disappointed because the commission did not recommend the check-off, complete unionization, or nationalization. But neither did it recommend compulsory arbitration. What it did do was to urge strongly a program of Federal, state, and local control and a wider use of collective bargaining and voluntary aribitration. The commission stressed throughout the public interest and suggested that Federal control be exercised through a coal division to be established in the Interstate Commerce Commission.

By the time the report was filed, the crisis was less acute, and Congress ignored the recommendations. After all, the appointment of the commission had been largely a sop thrown to the miners and a means of ending a strike. In the meantime both bituminous and anthracite miners had patched up short-term agreements with the operators which left conditions about what they had been before the strikes of 1922. For the anthracite miners the agreement established an eight-hour day, a 10 per cent increase, and union recognition without the check-off but with the right to have a union representative present when the men were paid. During the rest of the decade miners struggled unsuccessfully to maintain standards existing after the 1922 strikes. Their failure to make progress was caused in part by bitter factional fights which almost destroyed the United Mine Workers in the bituminous fields.

Organized labor never forgave Harding for the Daugherty-Wilkerson injunction in the shopmen's strike, nor for his telegram to the Governors in the coal strike. The President had obviously been under the influence of the employers during the crisis. But although Harding might look to big business for advice, his labor record as President disturbed him, and he determined to strike a blow for the workers. It was an important blow; an attack upon the twelve-hour day, which meant taking issue with the United States Steel Corporation, one of the strongest corporations in the country, and with Elbert H. Gary, one of the bitterest foes of organized labor to be found anywhere.

Fortunately, some preparatory work had already been done. The steel strike of 1919 had given publicity to the twelve-hour day, the Survey Associates and studies made through the Russell Sage Foundation had established the facts, and William B. Dickson (Vice-President of United States Steel) and a few others were criticizing the harshness of the Corporation's policies from the inside. In May, 1922, Harding wrote to Gary offering his assistance, and called a White House conference to debate the problem. The only result of the conference was a statement admitting the desirability of abolishing the twelve-hour day "if and when practical"; and for most of the steel men the incident was closed. Public attention, nevertheless, had again been focused upon this sore spot in American industry. Harding, in the words of Paul Kellogg of the *Survey*, had "put his foot in the door that had shut on us, and pried it open again."

His efforts largely ignored by the ironmasters, Harding let the matter rest for a time. But when Gary on May 25 stated that "abolition of the twelve-hour day in the steel industry is not now possible," Harding wrote him to express disappointment. He also intimated that on his imminent trip to Alaska he would speak on the twelve-hour day. Since the labor policies of the steel industry were too vulnerable to withstand another attack from high quarters, Gary had his special committee reverse their former stand and issued a letter approving, with qualifications, the abolition of the old system. Accepting these steps as taken in good faith, Harding spoke hopefully in his Tacoma address of the end of the twelve-hour day. On the day before his death the steel industry decided to reverse its long-standing policy. This Harding never knew, but actually it was the President who "had supplied the final impetus to end the inhuman twelve-hour day" in the steel industry. In the words of Samuel Hopkins Adams, it was "the most salient advance of Harding's presidency, the most positive achievement wrought by his own personal effort." *

But in general it was evident that labor, at least from the point of view of the employer, was quickly returning to pre-war normalcy. Strikes rapidly declined in number after 1919; the membership of unions fell sharply, while the legal position attained by labor before the war was being undermined by court interpretations.

With even greater speed the believers in a high tariff hastened to return to the good old days. Because of the war, the moderate Underwood-Simmons tariff of 1913, one of Wilson's great achievements, had never had an opportunity to prove itself under normal conditions. It was nevertheless unjustly blamed for the depression of 1913–1914 and that of 1920–1921. American industry, which had developed tremendously during the war, feared the dumping of cheap European goods, while farmers pinched by deflation clamored for the protection of agricultural products. With manufactures rapidly pushing into the South and other low-tariff

* Samuel Hopkins Adams, *Incredible Era* (Boston, Houghton Mifflin Company, 1939), p. 389.

strongholds, fewer regions were now opposed to high protection. Unable to wait for the Harding Administration, Republicans and high-tariff Democrats threw together an emergency measure only to see it vetoed by Wilson on March 3, the day before he left office.

In an accompanying message sprinkled with economic truths that were to be amply verified during the succeeding decade, Wilson pointed out that the United States had become a great creditor nation. Such a fact, he insisted, made liberal foreign trade policies a necessity. Only by purchasing commodities from Europe could the United States enable her to pay her debts. It was absurd, he suggested, to strike a blow at foreign trade just after the nation had expended billions on a merchant marine and developed other facilities to promote foreign commerce. Furthermore, it was futile to expect a high tariff to lift prices upon cotton, wheat, and corn, of which a surplus was raised in this country.

This message unfortunately made but slight impression. Harding immediately after his inauguration called the Sixty-seventh Congress in special session and demanded higher rates. These were granted without hesitation in an Emergency Tariff (approved May 27), which, it was believed, would save American industry until a more permanent measure could be written. Its chief significance was that it tried to commit American agriculture to high protection and attempted to foster the growth of America's most important war baby, the chemical industry. Hearings on the more permanent measure, the Fordney-McCumber tariff, had already begun and the bill was passed by the House on July 21, 1921. Not believing it high enough, the Senate held it so long that it did not become law until September 21, 1922.

The Fordney-McCumber Act did more than return to the high protective rates of the Payne-Aldrich Act of 1909; it surpassed them. Agricultural products were given high levies, though they were not needed and did not perceptibly retard the decline in farm prices. More significant were the high duties laid on manufactured goods. The tariffs on iron ore and steel rails, dropped in 1913, were reimposed, and those on textiles, especially silk, were increased. As in the emergency tariff bill, chemicals and dyestuffs were amply protected. Wherever the duties were *ad valorem*, they were to be assessed on the foreign value of the goods or their export value, whichever happened to be higher. As a sop to the multitude of Americans who were aghast over this steep protection, the bill embodied a pretense of flexibility. Proponents of the tariff talked much of equalizing "the difference in costs of production in the United States and the competing foreign countries." The burden of effecting such equalization was left with the Tariff

NORMALCY AND NATIONALISM 83

Commission. Upon its recommendation the President was given power to raise or lower duties not exceeding 50 per cent.

The Fordney-McCumber tariff was a somersault to extreme economic nationalism. It may not have been the signal that started the nations on the madly selfish course which was finally to end in another World War, but it undoubtedly contributed. It was a clear announcement that this country had determined to follow a policy of economic as well as political nationalism. Others pursued the same course; in the decade after 1918 some sixty nations raised their tariffs. The business prosperity which America enjoyed during most of the twenties masked the evil effects of the tariff upon the national economy, and especially upon agriculture. In large part we enabled Europe to buy our goods by lending her the money to do it.

The much-vaunted flexibility features inevitably proved a disappointment. Both Harding and Coolidge were staunch believers in a high tariff, and used the Board mainly to raise rates. Down to June 30, 1927, there were fourteen increases and three decreases, the latter on bobwhite quail, paintbrush handles, and such mill feeds as bran and shorts. When the Board showed some signs of independence, Coolidge got rid of Commissioner William S. Culbertson (by appointing him Minister to Rumania) and packed it with high protection-

ists. The ablest member, Edward P. Costigan, resigned in 1928 because he objected to a "manipulation of the commission since 1922" that had helped
wreck its usefulness. Meanwhile, a Senate committee had investigated the commission and thrown a
flood of light on how that allegedly scientific and
non-partisan body had actually worked.

To a great degree, Harding and Coolidge represented the very imperfect American civilization of
the 1920's. Harding's lax, easygoing temperament
harmonized with the general moral let-down of the
"reconstruction years." Coolidge's almost fanatic
worship of big business and all that went with it
made him an ideal spokesman for a business civilization. He perhaps unwittingly described the attitude of the overwhelming majority when he declared that "the chief business of the American
people is business." But however strikingly Harding and Coolidge symbolized the attitude of the
nation, neither formulated any broad plans or assumed any leadership. It would be difficult, if not
impossible, to find eight years of Federal history
in which policies were more clearly framed by department heads rather than by the President. So
far as foreign affairs were concerned, Hughes clearly
assumed leadership. At home, it was Hoover who
formulated the relationship between Government
and business, and Mellon who laid down the fiscal
program. This departmental leadership was lifted

into relief by the fact that Coolidge kept the members of the Harding Cabinet, with the exception of Daugherty, as long as they wanted to stay. No longer were Cabinet members chief clerks, as they had been under Wilson, or as they were soon to be again under Roosevelt. The Administration after 1923, suggests one observer, might fairly be called the "reign of Coolidge and Mellon."

When the name of Andrew W. Mellon was first suggested, probably by Daugherty, Harding admitted that he had never heard of him. Yet it was this frail, self-effacing but able Pittsburgh financier who was to be the dominant figure in two Administrations, just as he was in the Aluminum Company of America, Gulf Oil, and a score of other leading industries. Harding was a little awed by the wizard of finance whose touch turned everything to gold, and Coolidge regarded him with profound respect. Many besides Harding had never heard of Mellon, but newspaper owners who heartily approved of Mellon's policies soon provided the publicity. He was described as the richest man in America (he was undoubtedly the second or third), and the "greatest Secretary of the Treasury since Alexander Hamilton." This characterization was, of course, a wild exaggeration. Gallatin, Chase, and McAdoo—to name but three—met problems far more difficult than any faced by Mellon.

The fiscal problem when Harding and Mellon

attacked it was fairly clear. The public debt had increased from $967,953,000 in 1914, with a per capita distribution of $9.88, to $24,061,000,000 on June 30, 1920, with a per capita distribution of $228. This debt had accumulated in six years, despite heavy wartime taxation. The problem was to ease the tax burden and at the same time reduce the load of debt. What made it peculiarly difficult was the increase in Governmental expenditures, due primarily to soldiers' relief and interest on the war debt.

It was Wilson who laid the groundwork for fiscal reform in his annual messages of 1919 and 1920 by urging economy, an orderly system of Federal budgeting, and a revision of taxation which would put the nation on a peacetime basis. His emphasis upon Government economy was followed by Harding and raised to the status of a religion by Coolidge. "I favor a policy of economy," said the latter in his inaugural, "not because I wish to save money, but because I wish to save the people. . . . Economy is idealism in its most practical form."

A budget law was passed in 1920, but was vetoed on Constitutional grounds by Wilson, who urged Congress to pass it again with proper changes. Harding also urged such a law and readily approved the Budget and Accounting Act (June 10, 1921). It provided that each year the President should submit to Congress a budget with a complete financial statement of the Government. It also called for the establishment of a Budget Bureau to prepare these statements, and the appointment of a new officer, the Comptroller-General, to supervise government accounting and pass on all claims against the Government. This law for the first time introduced a business system into the realm of national finances and brought some definite coordination of income and expenditure. Charles G. Dawes, a Chicago banker, was the first Director of the Budget.

In revising taxation it was Mellon who took the lead, enthusiastically backed by both Harding and Coolidge. The only brake on his plans was exercised by Congress. Asserting in 1921 that the country was "staggering under the existing burden of taxation and debt, and is clamoring for gradual relief from war taxation," he recommended a repeal of the excess profits tax and an immediate cut in the income and surtax from the 65 per cent maximum to 40 per cent, with an eventual reduction to 33 per cent. To make up for the loss of the excess profits tax and high brackets of the income tax, he proposed doubling the documentary stamp taxes, a two-cent levy on bank checks, a license tax on motor vehicles, and a two-cent rate for postcards.

When it was noted that Mellon's reductions would not apply on incomes below $66,000, and that losses would be made up by taxes on the general consumer, the cry was immediately raised that the relief he proposed was only for the rich. The fight against the Mellon program was led by farmers and organized labor, groups that were not prospering in 1921. The battle was taken up by liberals in the Senate, particularly LaFollette, who asserted that Mellon had "brazenly and impudently" laid down the principle that "wealth will not and cannot be made to bear its full share of taxation. He favors a system that will let wealth escape. . . . He ought to be retired from his place for making such a declaration."

In reply, Mellon insisted that taxes had "passed the point where they can be collected" and that industry, in the face of these high levies, was paralyzed and reluctant to embark on new projects. "I have never viewed taxation," he said, "as a means of rewarding one class of taxpayers or punishing another." According to his statement, the country faced merely a practical matter. Nevertheless, his recommendations year after year never included any help for the small man. Taxes, in his mind, always seemed too high for the rich, never for the poor, and his recommendations invariably called for shifting the burden to the poorer classes. It never seemed to occur to the Secretary that an increase of income to the poor through reduction of taxation could have any beneficial economic effect.

Fortunately, the country at the moment was in

no mood to follow Mellon blindly. Congress compromised by repealing the wartime excess profits tax (saving stockholders $1,500,000,000), but raising the corporation tax from 10 to 12½ per cent. Instead of cutting the surtax on incomes from 65 to 40 per cent or less, Congress stopped at 50 per cent, but reduced surtaxes on all incomes above $6,000. On small incomes the tax remained the same. Such was Mellon's program of taxation as inaugurated in 1921, and consistently followed. As the decade went by, further reductions were made in 1924, 1926, 1928, and 1929. Despite them, the public debt was lowered during the Mellon period from $24,061,000,000 in 1920 to $16,185,000,000 on June 30, 1930, with a per capita distribution in the latter year of $134. Whether the continued Treasury surpluses were attributable to economic prosperity or to reduction of taxation in the higher brackets, no one can know. It was Mellon, however, who got the praise.

Just as Mellon largely formulated the fiscal policies of the Federal Administration during the twenties, so Herbert Hoover was responsible for the Government's policy toward business. To Hoover the economic system which flourished under Harding and Coolidge was essentially sound. Speaking in May, 1923, before the United States Chamber of Commerce, he gave his confession of faith. "Our goal in economic life," said he, "is to do this great thing, to preserve individual initiative, an equality of opportunity, and thus a constantly advancing national standard of living. Our economic and social system is fundamentally right. It has produced the largest advance in the standard of living to the whole of our people that has ever been witnessed in history. Its faults are many, but they can be and are being eliminated without destroying its progress." One of the faults, he evidently believed, was the policing of big business by Government in an effort to enforce the anti-trust laws. Hoover ostensibly opposed any "relaxation in the restraints against undue capital combinations, monopoly, price fixing, domination, unfair practices, and the whole category of collective action damaging to public interest." Nevertheless, the policies of his Department of Commerce often fostered these very practices.

Hoover's fundamental policy was cooperation between Government and business through the encouragement of trade associations. In his mind, such associations could serve as a clearing house for trade information, and an agency by which products could be standardized, uniform credit policies established, trade disputes settled, unfair practices eliminated, and other benefits achieved. The gospel of this type of cooperation was spread in a handbook, *Trade Association Activities*, published by the Commerce Department in 1923, and no stone was left unturned to further the idea. In one of his campaign speeches in 1928 Hoover referred proudly to the "enormous growth of associational activities," and told how he had "introduced this relationship between the Department of Commerce and industrial, commercial, and civic organizations of our country . . . in promotion of foreign trade, in the elimination of waste, in furtherance of economic and scientific research, in improvement of homes, and in scores of other activities."

Belief in the highly beneficial effects of trade associations was not universally held. The Department of Justice was suspicious, the Federal Trade Commission criticized certain policies of the Department of Commerce, and in 1921 the Supreme Court ruled illegal a trade association in the lumber industry (American Column and Lumber Co. v. U. S.), and in 1923 labeled one organized by the linseed oil producers a combination in restraint of trade (U. S. v. Linseed Oil Co.). In the latter case Chief Justice Taft observed: "Their manifest purpose was to defeat the Sherman Act without subjecting themselves to penalties."

To this hostile attitude the Secretary paid little attention, and his Department continued to promote certain salient activities of the trade associations. Eventually, the Federal Trade Commission was rendered almost impotent as far as anti-trust activities were concerned. Likewise, the Supreme

Court in 1925 largely reversed itself by declaring two trade associations legal (Maple Flooring Manufacturers' Association *v.* U. S. and Cement Manufacturers' Protective Association *v.* U. S.); and these decisions did much to open the way to the greatest era of business consolidation which the nation had seen since the early years of the century.

With the Treasury and the Department of Commerce both in the hands of men who believed that prosperity was most readily achieved by aiding those at the top, not much could be accomplished in social legislation or the extension of Government control. Progressives, attempting to interest legislators in social insurance, sound labor laws, and the Government operation of Muscle Shoals, found little response. Congress utterly ignored one of Harding's pet projects, the creation of a Department of Public Welfare. The attention of the Western radicals was largely occupied in an effort to do something for agriculture. The motives of Congress in passing the Bonus Bill over the vetoes of both Harding and Coolidge seem to have been political rather than humanitarian. Harding's recommendation in 1922 that the nation join the World Court accomplished nothing but to antagonize the bitter-end nationalists. The nation had definitely set its rudder on a course of conservative nationalism.

CHAPTER IV

THE ADVANCE OF PROSPERITY

By 1923 the nation had apparently recovered from the immediate post-war depression. From then until late 1929 it enjoyed a period of tremendous business activity. Surveying these seven years, the Committee on Recent Economic Changes of the President's Conference on Unemployment commented in 1929 that it was

struck by the outpouring of energy which piled up skyscrapers in scores of cities, knit the 48 states together with 20,000 miles of airways; moved each year over railways and highways more than a billon and a half tons of freight; thronged the highways with 25,000,000 motor cars; carried electricity to 17,000,000 homes; sent each year 3,750,000 children to high school and more than 1,000,000 young men and women to college; and fed, clothed, housed and amused the 120,-000,000 persons who occupy one-twentieth of the habitable area of the earth.*

That the twenties witnessed a dynamic surge of

* *Recent Economic Changes* (copyright by the Committee on Recent Economic Changes of the President's Conference on Unemployment, McGraw-Hill Book Company, Inc., 1929), p. x.

productive effort which often equaled that of the war years was evident. But did it bring prosperity? Many said so, but the benefits were uneven. To wheat and cotton farmers the decade was discouraging. The same was true of coal miners, leather manufacturers, shipbuilders, and workers in cotton and textile mills. Only a part of the nation, it appears, enjoyed this much-vaunted prosperity. The Middle Atlantic, the east North Central, and the Pacific states, an area including less than half the population but somewhat more than half of the national income, flourished. The rest of the country, however, hardly reached a high average level of well-being. In New England manufacturing waned, while the South, the Middle West and the mountain regions suffered from the agricultural depression. Furthermore, unemployment was a gnawing worry even when the boom was at its height. The best years saw an average of a million and a half hunting work, the second-best three millions or more.

Despite the uneven distribution of rewards and the combination in many areas of "boom and bust," a wealth of statistics prove that a real basis for prosperity existed. The total realized income of the nation jumped from about $60,400,000,000 in 1918 to about $89,000,000,000 in 1928, representing an increase in per capita income from about $651 to $745. Life insurance totals amounted to $26,659,-

000,000 in 1917 and $84,801,000,000 in 1927. Bank deposits advanced from $37 billions in June, 1921, to $53 billions in June, 1928. In the ten years from 1914 to 1924 building and loan policies had increased from 3,103,935 to 8,554,352. These statistics must be interpreted in the light of the much slower increase in population. Census figures of 1920 gave the nation 105,711,000 people, and ten years later 122,775,000, an advance of 12 per cent. Although the proportion of national income taken by labor increased slightly, if at all, after 1920, the decade nevertheless brought a rise in the real income of manual workers, and in that of certain salaried groups, particularly teachers, bankers, and Government employees.

In addition to these gains in real wages, other causes contributed to a higher standard of living. Particularly notable were the enhanced public expenditures for social services. Keeping in mind the relatively slow growth of population, the estimated expenditures for free social services by states and cities with a population of more than 30,000 are significant. According to Leo Wolman of the Committee on Recent Economic Changes, these units spent $708,164,000 in 1915 on education, and in 1926 no less than $2,499,000,000. Their expenditures on libraries in the same period rose from $15,467,000 to $35,874,000; on hospitals from $58,005,000 to $144,819,000; and on charities from

$34,347,000 to $58,211,000. If we add such other items as recreation, health conservation, and mothers' pensions, the grand total rose from $859,336,000 to $2,860,935,000. Various sources of information point to a similar rise in the expenditures which make for a higher standard of living. A larger proportion of income, for example, was going into "optional purchases" rather than necessities, and more time into recreation and leisure.

Is there a simple explanation of the speed with which the United States pulled itself out of the depression of 1921 and 1922 and rose to new heights of industrial prosperity? Wesley Clair Mitchell, surveying the work of the Committee on Recent Economic Changes, believed that he had found one.

Since 1921 [he wrote] Americans have applied intelligence to the day's work more effectively than ever before. Thus the prime factor in producing the extraordinary changes in the economic fortunes of the European people during the nineteenth century is the prime factor in producing the prosperity of the United States in recent years. The whole process of putting science into industry has been followed more intensively than before; it has been supplemented by tentative efforts to put science into business management, trade-union policy, and Government administration.*

* *Recent Economic Changes* (copyright by the Committee on Recent Economic Changes of the President's Conference on Unemployment, McGraw-Hill Company, Inc., 1929), p. 862.

Undoubtedly this does much to explain the phenomenon. An acceleration of earlier tendencies rather than a structural transformation furnishes the key to the understanding of the twenties. Put in concrete terms, the nation witnessed in 1922–1929 an annual increase in primary production of 2.5 per cent a year, in manufacturing of 4 per cent, and in transportation of 4 per cent. Labor productivity was nearly 60 per cent greater in the twenties than at the turn of the century; in manufacturing, it increased 35 per cent between 1922 and 1925 alone, and in agriculture at a rate never before equaled.

This increased productivity was made possible by the application of science to technology and management. By 1920 industrialists possessing even the faintest vision understood the need for intensive research and "scientific management." Previous generations, of course, had laid the basis for this. Now they looked to the magic formula of research for new profits and new business. At the end of the twenties, between $100,000,000 and $200,000,000 were being spent annually on this type of work, in research organizations that varied in size from the small and inadequately equipped laboratory manned by a single engineer or chemist to the Bell Telephone Laboratories with 4,000 employees and a budget of $15,000,000. Significant advances since the turn of the century in metallurgy, the development of synthetics, the use of the internal combustion engine, and above all in the application of electric power, had provided a background for this new era of research.

For decades Frederick Winslow Taylor and his disciples had preached the doctrine of "scientific management," but it was left to the 1920's to witness its almost universal acceptance. While engineers and research scientists devised new machinery to save labor, efficiency experts replanned the movements of workmen or rearranged whole factories to increase output. Psychologists and psychiatrists were sometimes brought in to give more scientific attention to job-placing, and personnel managers were added to plant payrolls. For labor, "scientific management" often meant the development of the "speed-up" and "stretch-out" followed by technological unemployment. There could be no doubt, however, that the per man-hour productivity of the workers was increased, while some advance was made in vocational adjustment.

Encouragement in this application of science to technology and management came from Secretary Hoover and the Division of Simplified Practice of the Department of Commerce. Manufacturers were urged to emphasize the standardization, simplification, and interchangeability of machine parts. To obtain greater output the Government pressed manufacturers to reduce the variety of their products. In the paving-brick industry, for example, varieties and sizes were cut down from 66 to 4, and in the sheet steel industry from 1,819 to 261. The Department of Commerce reported that under its auspices in ten years more than a hundred industries had adopted more than a hundred plans for standardization, at an approximate annual saving of a quarter of a billion dollars.

Of all the industries which boomed during the twenties none showed greater increase than automobile manufacturing and its subsidiary, the building of rubber tires. If we take 100 as the index figure for 1914, physical production of automobiles jumped by 1925 to 988 and productivity per man power to 310. For rubber-tire manufacturing the figures were 680 and 311, and in petroleum refining, another industry that had become more and more a concomitant of automobile manufacturing, the physical production had risen to 399 and the productivity of man power to 177. Automobile manufacturing, which thus symbolized the tremendous technical advance of the twenties, was in many ways the key industry of those years. Before the war, motor cars were largely restricted to the wealthy and to the upper middle classes; after it, use of the automobile spread to the lower middle class and the wage earner, tremendously influencing American social and economic life.

It was in the automobile industry that scientific

management and mass production based on an assembly line reached their greatest development. America's contribution to the motor vehicle was not in basic invention (though such devices as Kettering's electric starter were important), but in design, and in bringing cars within reach of the ordinary consumer through mass production. Registered vehicles in the United States increased from 5,945,000 in 1919 to 26,501,000 in 1929. Naturally, the rapidly expanding sales provided work for a host of Americans. Estimates toward the end of the decade put the number of workers directly concerned in the manufacture of motor vehicles and their parts at about one million, and those indirectly supported by the automobile industry at around three million. As the building and servicing of automobiles employ men almost exclusively, it is reasonable to believe that the number of people supported was two or three times the number hired. This meant that the industry was directly or indirectly taking care of a large part of the increase of population (about 1,700,000 a year) during the decade. The development of the automobile alone was sufficient to account for the industrial prosperity of the twenties.

It is true that an appreciable part of the money paid for automobiles was income which in earlier years would have been spent for other commodities, so that the new industry stunted some other lines of business. But the fact remains that enough new activity and wealth were created by the motor car to speed up the whole economic machine. Of the many by-products of the industry which created work and stimulated industry, none was more important than road-building. The wide use of the automobile produced a renaissance in American highway construction reminiscent of the early nineteenth century. In the improvement and construction of roads America spent close to two billion dollars a year during the twenties.

The early history of the gigantic automobile industry is in large part the fascinating record of scores of tinkering mechanics who, without formal engineering education but with mechanical ability often approaching genius, developed internal combustion engines and motor vehicles which literally put the nation on wheels. This was done largely without the aid of bankers. By the twenties, many little companies had disappeared or been merged with giant corporations. The industry had then become relatively stabilized. Out of this early hectic period had emerged three giant corporations which did nine tenths of the business at the end of the decade: the Ford Motor Company, General Motors Corporation, and the Chrysler Corporation.

From its beginnings the Ford Company had been largely a one-man concern, based on the mechanical ability of a Michigan farm boy who built a practical automobile and then pioneered in the field of low-cost cars. His success through mass production and the assembly line won him many followers and strongly influenced industrial technique during the twenties. His ability to build up an immense business and at the same time keep clear (as did Rockefeller) of the grasping tentacles of Wall Street conquered the admiration and envy of many a struggling industrialist. A strong individualist who combined a paternalistic attitude with a rough labor policy, Ford seemed unbeatable in his own field, though most of his occasional sorties into politics, sociology, and international relations were ridiculous failures.

Perhaps the most brilliant figure in the automobile world of the twenties was Walter P. Chrysler. His early years had been spent in railroad machine shops, and he became a mechanic of unusual ability. Equally remarkable was his managerial capacity. Chrysler was not a pioneer in the automobile industry; it was not until 1910 that he turned to automobile manufacturing as works superintendent of the Buick plant at Flint. In the early twenties he left Buick to rehabilitate the Willys-Overland and Maxwell companies, and he used the latter to establish the Chrysler Corporation, eventually gaining control of the Dodge Corporation.

Ford and Chrysler were mechanics, production

men, and executives of a high order, but William
C. Durant, the most spectacular figure of the industry, had qualifications of a very different character. He was essentially a supersalesman whose
temporary success was based on his fervent belief
in the future of the automobile—a daring promoter
and speculator. His chief claim to fame lay in his
organization of General Motors. Making a fortune
almost overnight as a wagon manufacturer, Durant
secured control of the then tiny Buick factory.
When he turned to Wall Street for financial backing he found that New York bankers had little
faith in the future of automobiles. However, he
finally interested Pierre Du Pont in his project,
and with the Du Pont millions and a score of able
engineers General Motors quickly became one of
the "big three." Durant's grandiose schemes almost wrecked General Motors in the depression of
1921 and he resigned the presidency. His later
efforts to manufacture the Durant car failed, but
he was the hardiest entrepreneur and the most dynamic personality of the early days of the industry.
More than Chrysler, more than the meteoric Dodge
brothers, he foresaw the enormous possibilities of
the automobile.

But the automobile was by no means the only
new commodity that found avid buyers. The market for radios also spread downward from the well-
to-do through the upper middle class to the poorer

farmers, clerks, and wage earners. A rapid expansion in the use of radio came after stations WWJ of Detroit in August, 1920, and KDKA of East Pittsburgh in November, 1920, introduced commercial broadcasting. At the opening of the decade a few wireless cranks were trying to catch programs by tickling a piece of galena with a tiny wire. By 1928 more than seven and a half million radios were in use. In 1921, manufacture of radio apparatus (including tubes) was valued at approximately $10,648,000; by 1929 this figure had skyrocketed to $411,637,000. Still another new industry, its potentialities far greater than its immediate importance, was the manufacture of airplanes. Although their commercial value was still limited, nevertheless 6,482 airplanes were constructed in 1929 at a cost of $46,848,000.

Next to the automobile, the most important industrial advances were registered in the manufacture of electric machinery and appliances. The value of these products increased almost threefold, from $809,590,000 in 1921 to $2,334,246,000 in 1929. The growth of this industry is especially interesting because it represented a significant development in luxury purchases. Between 1923 and 1928 the number of such household appliances as electric flatirons, washing machines, vacuum cleaners, and heaters approximately doubled; the number of ironing machines tripled, the number of toasters quadrupled, and the sums spent for electric sewing machines tripled. Far more impressive, however, was the almost insatiable demand of Americans for iceless refrigerators. Along with the automobile and the radio, this convenient new device represented the American ideal of luxury-purchase, and like them it moved rapidly from the status of a luxury to that of a necessity. The number in use at the beginning of 1923 was 27,000. Five years later there were 755,000.

Although the automobile, radio, and household electric appliance were among the principal hallmarks of means, perhaps the broadest display of luxury-buying came in women's apparel. The growing number of women wage earners, the increased sums available for nonessentials, and the vogue for short skirts created a demand for silk and rayon. Manufacturers of cotton stockings turned to silk or went bankrupt, while makers of cotton underwear shifted to rayon or faced the same fate. In stockings, silk soon almost completely displaced cotton or wool. The revolution in women's underwear was not quite so rapid, a survey in 1926 showing that 36 per cent of the garments sold were rayon, 31 per cent silk, and 33 per cent cotton. From one viewpoint this represented only a change in the type of manufacturing. From another, it represented either more prosperity or else the spending of a greater proportion of income for luxury.

If the greater productivity of machines and labor was the secret of the current prosperity, and the purchase of luxury commodities its most obvious result, nothing better links the two than the remarkable development of electric power. Research, invention, and scientific management all stimulated industry; but this added power also helped make possible the greater production of manufactured goods. In pre-war years the United States was producing 14.4 billions of kilowatt hours. By 1920 this had been raised to 43.3 billions, and in 1929 to approximately 96 billions. Research engineers had made this possible by building ever-larger generators and devising more efficient methods of transmitting energy. The falling cost of electrical energy, along with its greater cleanliness and convenience, caused manufacturers to adopt it in place of steam. In 1914 only 33 per cent of the power used in factories was electric. After that date practically all the increase in factory power equipment was in electric motors operated from central stations. By the end of the decade electricity provided three quarters of the power used in American industry.

An equally significant story was the increasing use of electricity for domestic purposes. Rapid urbanization, higher incomes, declining rates, and the improvements of lamps and electric household appliances accounted for this. From the beginning of 1913 to the end of 1927, the number of customers using electric light and power increased 465 per cent. While only 16 per cent of the population in 1912 lived in electric-lighted dwellings, in 1927 at least 63 per cent did so. In the latter year only one third of the current produced was sold for domestic purposes, but that third represented a remarkable addition to the well-being of the American people. It was an advance which the New Deal years were to continue with Federal encouragement in rural areas.

Future students seeking the keys to American economic history between the two world wars will undoubtedly find one of them in the expansion of electric power. Indeed, technicians have declared that these two decades marked a transition from the "machine age" to the "power age." The power age, suggests one engineer, "broke the shackles of belts which tied machines to the driving shafts; it fused machine-tool, transmission and motor into one self-contained production unit, and emancipated this unit from the countless limitations of manual operation." If man's economic advance is written in terms of his search and conquest of power, then his entire progress "since the world began, was merely the tuning of an orchestra before the start of the concert." * Electricity was the

* Walter N. Polokov, *The Power Age* (New York, Covici Friede, Inc., 1933), pp. 85, 87.

most powerful and efficient servant which mankind had yet subjected to his needs, and the factory power plant or public utility central station became the life center of many communities. Yet not all of the effects of electric power were good. The number of workers failed to keep pace with increase in the use of power; technological unemployment was accentuated. While the "power age" opened limitless opportunities for the benefit of mankind, such benefits could be achieved only by an economic and social philosophy adjusted to a new economic era. Except in the sphere of technology, few leaders in the 1920's had any real comprehension of the significance of the new "power age."

American boom periods have ordinarily been characterized by intense speculation in transport facilities and real estate development. The flush years of the 1920's were no exception. Just as in earlier booms the construction of canals and railroads had nourished industrial activity and brought a fever of land speculation, so now the building of automobiles and the widespread improvement of highways effected the same result. Just as the building of canals and railroads in earlier years revolutionized land values and opened the way for speculation, so new roads and motor traffic enhanced land values. Canalization of rivers, and a little later the rapid development of air transportation, also undoubtedly had some influence on land prices; but these factors were slight in comparison with improved roads.

The movement for better highways went back to the bicycle craze of the 1890's and the introduction of rural free delivery in 1896. Progressing steadily under the influence of the automobile, it was stimulated by the Federal Aid Highway Act of 1916. In this legislation the Government reverted to the old policy followed in building the National Pike. That is, it assisted the states to lay interstate highways and connecting secondary roads, paying half the cost. The American road system at the opening of the First World War was still in a backward stage. Few well-paved roads existed, and these were mainly local or county-built, planned only with reference to local needs. All this the automobile rapidly changed. The old macadam and asphalt surfacing gave way to better types. Under the spur of the Federal Government, state and regional commissions and planning boards began to integrate the nation's highway systems. As the old thoroughfares rapidly deteriorated under the friction of passenger cars and motor trucks, it became necessary to improve them in all sections. The total of concrete roads, for example, increased from 7,000 miles at the end of 1918 to 50,000 in 1927, and this figure was doubled during the next five years. Conservative estimates during the late twenties put the annual expenditures for roads at between $1,400,-000,000 and $2,000,000,000. Within a decade after the war the United States was transformed from a land of poor roads into the nation with the world's finest system of highways.

But the fever of road-building was far from being the only explanation for real estate speculation. The fact that the value of farm land rose again in New England and New Jersey was as largely attributable to the development of dairying, poultry raising, and truck farming near urban areas as it was to automobiles or improved highways. Similarly, the real estate boom in many cities was founded on industrial expansion rather than improved roads. Without its subtropical winter climate, Florida could not have attracted the multitudes who flocked to its lakes, groves, and strands. Nevertheless, it was the automobile that facilitated transportation and gave an impetus to the Southward movement of population. A few farsighted capitalists, notably Henry M. Flagler, who built a railroad along Florida's east coast, and Henry B. Plant, who built one to the west coast, had perceived the future possibilities of those areas; but little interest was taken in central or southern Florida until the twenties. As late as 1920 fewer than a million people lived in the state. Then, just about a century after the United States had forced Spain to cede us the region, the American people suddenly awoke to its beauties. Balmy winters, accessibility to the thickly populated sections of the Northeast, firm sandy roads, citrus orchards, and glorious beaches combined their allurements. Automobiles appeared in myriads. The real estate promoters did the rest.

When the winter migration set in, it was the "flivver" and the Buick rather than the Pullman that carried the flood of settlers and winter tourists. Many a citizen who had never been a hundred miles from home packed his family and belongings into a Ford, and set off for the land of sunshine. The migratory habits of Americans, submerged with the passing of the frontier, again rose to the surface. During several seasons of the middle twenties the winter tourists outnumbered the entire permanent population of Florida. Not alone the winter sunshine, but the dream of easy wealth brought many. People who had never played penny ante at home plunged into the business of buying and selling Florida real estate. "Developments" never destined for agriculture, home sites, or any other useful purpose, sprang up on every hand. Thousands of real estate agents were reaping fortunes. When the boom crashed in 1926, all was not lost. Many remained to develop the growing of vegetables and citrus fruit. Others invested in hotel property, helping to create a great winter playground. Between 1920 and 1930 the permanent population of the state increased by half a million or 51.6 per cent. Miami, Florida's leading city, more than tripled in population during this decade.

While Florida's boom was spectacular, that of California was more substantial. The population of California increased during the decade by 2,250,000 or 65.7 per cent. When Taft was President, California had been the twelfth state; when Hoover entered the White House, it was sixth. Like Florida, it enjoyed a large migration of winter tourists, but a greater number came to stay, for the Pacific coast offered larger economic opportunities. The center of the boom was in southern California and particularly around Los Angeles. This city leaped from a population of 319,000 in 1910 to more than 1,238,000 in 1930. Suburbs were laid out and filled almost before the buildings could be constructed, and most of the development proved permanent. For the "realtor," it was indeed a golden age.

Miami and Los Angeles indicate that the land speculation of the era was primarily urban. Earlier booms had, of course, brought an active expansion in the value of urban real estate, but in general they were essentially a rural and frontier phenomenon. Not so with the twenties. The prosperity of this decade was an urban prosperity. During the ten years the population of the nation grew by about 17,000,000. Dwellers on the farms, however, decreased from 31,614,000 in 1920 to 30,169,000 in 1930, in a net migration of about 600,000 people a year.

Urban prosperity and the growth of towns at the expense of the country did not alone account for the boom in land values and in city construction. A shortage of houses had naturally resulted from curtailment of building during the war. Normal increase in population demanded about 400,000 additional houses a year, at this time chiefly in the cities. Savings were available for building purposes; interest rates on mortgages had declined; and the country had fluid new arrangements for financing construction. In short, all the ingredients for a building boom were at hand. Construction in the late twenties (including roads) was at the rate of seven billion dollars annually, of which about five billions were spent through private initiative. Prices were high, but, considering the decade as a whole, perhaps not unduly inflated; and while a certain amount of the construction was shoddy, much of it was solid work. Furthermore, the architectural standards in both city skyscrapers and suburban homes marked a great advance over earlier decades. About one third of the construction in the twenties took place in New York City alone, where the skyline changed with tremendous speed as one skyscraper followed another. The climax was reached in 1931 when the

Empire State Building, towering 1,248 feet above the street, was completed. With New York setting the style, it was not long before many a little city was hastening to put up its own quite unnecessary skyscraper.

But spectacular booms in special areas must not be allowed to distort the picture. As we have said, the most prosperous areas of the nation were the Middle Atlantic states, the east North Central states and the Pacific states. These groups surpassed the others both in growth of population and of per capita income. In the Middle Atlantic states this prosperity apparently arose less from manufacturing development than from expansion in transportation, banking, construction, trade, and unclassified industries. Perhaps the most notable industrial growth here lay in the manufacture of electrical equipment. Prosperity in the east North Central area, largely confined to urban districts, came primarily from industrial expansion, notably in the manufacture of motor vehicles. On the Pacific coast the increase in per capita income seems to have come less from agriculture and manufacturing than from a shift in the residence of persons receiving high incomes.

While the greatest advance was largely centered in these regions, other areas about held their own or slightly declined. In New England, which derived only 5 per cent of its income from agriculture, prosperity rested largely on manufacturing. Metal manufacturing held its level, but there was a notable decline in footwear and in cotton. Shoe factories tended to shift westward; cotton factories to the south. In the west North Central, where one third of the income was drawn from agriculture, the rural depression was heavily felt. The South Atlantic states from Maryland to Florida revealed a considerable decline in agricultural income per capita and a slight decrease in manufacturing income. But for the agricultural expansion in Florida, the showing would have been worse.

When Sinclair Lewis wrote of the typical American businessman, he selected George Babbitt, real estate promoter of Zenith. This was historically sound, for the occupation and exploitation of land was America's chief business for three centuries. During the twenties, however, the real estate salesman was in danger of being outstripped by promoters of a hundred other commodities. Behind the salesmen were the advertisers, evangels of the new prosperity. After all, family incomes were increasing. Manufacturers, likewise, were turning out new commodities—automobiles, radios, iceless refrigerators, and scores of new gadgets. Consumers must be made to want them and persuaded to buy them. If they had no ready money, then a way must be found to extend credit.

High-pressure advertising and salesmanship flourished as never before. While population increased during the decade by 12 per cent, the paid circulation of newspapers and magazines rose almost a third. Even sharper was the growth in space and expenditures devoted to advertising. Between 1921 and 1927, expenditures for advertising in magazines almost doubled. By the late twenties, radio advertising was beginning to make real headway, for annual expenditures in that field were estimated at about $7,000,000. But this was still a relatively small sum; the total advertising expenditures of the nation for 1927 were estimated at about $1,500,000,000.

Not only were advertisers spending more money, but they were doing it in a different way. As competition grew more strenuous, methods changed. Huge national campaigns were launched, coordinating newspapers, magazines, and the radio. In artistic design and persuasiveness a marked improvement was registered; in ethics and helpfulness to the consumer, a decline. Advertisers spent less energy in demonstrating the superiority of their goods and more in trading on the frailties of human nature. As the average person wished to look young and handsome, be popular, and get rich quickly— or at least keep up with the Joneses—advertisers capitalized these ambitions. In many instances advertisements bore little or no relationship to the commodity or its quality. Advertising also became more frank. Bodily functions, personal hygiene, and fear of disease were mercilessly exploited in the promotion of sales.

To follow up advertising, salesmanship was emphasized as never before. Judged by standards of the 1920's, the business of selling before the war was in a haphazard and chaotic state. As the twenties progressed, ideas of scientific management began to receive attention in sales departments as well as in factory production. An examination of business magazines, for example, shows that half again as many articles on such subjects as the selection, training, and remuneration of salesmen appeared in 1927 as in 1925. Much of the new interest was devoted chiefly to whipping up greater sales pressure. Some companies, however, attempted to obtain men with technical knowledge as well as persuasive power. Whatever the direction of the drive, it had its effect. Sales resistance was low, and the salesman flourished like a green bay tree.

The purchase once made, the more difficult problem of paying for it followed. But the decade was also equal to this. As the cost of an automobile, an electric refrigerator, or even a radio was far beyond the immediate ability of most consumers, various methods of installment buying were promoted. While "personal loan" companies extended their operations, corporations set up "finance companies" to provide credit to pay for their commodities, and banks established departments to care for this kind of business. Installment selling itself was not new, having been applied long before to sewing machines, books, pianos, and furniture. After 1921, however, it increased greatly in volume. A change in psychology was involved. People who in earlier years would have gone to any extreme to keep out of this type of debt, now took it as a matter of course and mortgaged their income for years ahead.

By the end of the decade, one seventh or one eighth of all retail trade was carried on through installment buying. It was by this method that retailers disposed of 75 per cent of their radio sets, 60 per cent of automobiles and furniture, and 50 per cent of electrical household goods. In the end, few commodities could not be bought "on time." During the depression the system was even extended to European and domestic travel on a basis of "pay after the trip is over." Installment buying, which had amounted to not more than a billion dollars in 1910, had grown to seven billion by 1929. Whether the added costs of advertising, selling, and financing were compensated for by wealth produced through increased production, it is impossible to determine. Certainly, the business activity of the decade was increased.

It remains to say a final word upon the status

of our foreign trade during the boom twenties. Unquestionably the economic well-being of the nation depended in no small part upon healthy activity in this field. Exports of merchandise grew from $3,832,000,000 in 1922 to $5,241,000,000 in 1929, and imports from $3,113,000,000 to $4,399,000,000. This meant that our visible exports accounted for about one tenth of the domestic production of our exportable commodities. Furthermore, the physical volume of imports and their value were both increasing more rapidly than of exports. If the real goal of economic effort is to secure goods for meeting human wants, this extraordinary increase was a favorable sign.

But when examined more closely, the situation with respect to foreign trade appeared less encouraging. The proportion of domestic production going into the export trade seemed to be definitely dependent upon our heavy loans overseas. American investments abroad increased by four billion dollars between 1922 and 1927, and the future safety of this sum was highly dubious. Furthermore, the extreme difficulty of exporting to countries with high tariff walls was inducing American firms to establish branches in foreign lands. It is also interesting to note that next to cotton, the most important export was machinery. Increasing shipments of machinery and capital to set up rival factories abroad boded no good for the future of

American foreign trade, or, indeed, for American production.

Such considerations take us back to the general question of the extent of American prosperity during the twenties. In a little book, *Prosperity: Fact or Myth*, finished just before the crash of 1929, the popular economist Stuart Chase attempted to strike a balance. Before we could boast of prosperity, he insisted, it was necessary to exclude all states not included in the Middle Atlantic, east North Central, and Pacific sections. Within these prosperous states, many citizens must be left out of the picture of success—farmers, the small businessman, the independent storekeeper (hit by the chain stores), the wholesaler, and many professional men and women whose income had failed to keep pace with the new standard of living. Likewise untouched by prosperity were the unemployed. Technological unemployment, it was estimated, had overtaken some 650,000 since 1920.

On the debit side must be reckoned the sick industries—coal mining, textiles, shipbuilding, leather, railroad equipment, and the boot and shoe industries. Nor were the railroads in a healthy position, for they were rapidly losing both freight and passenger business in middle-distance hauls. Observers could not overlook the excessive number of businesses and little banks that had succumbed during these years. Finally, millions of unskilled toilers had been teetering on the edge of a bare existence at the opening of the era, and their position in 1929 was only a little less precarious than before.

On the credit side stood a 20 per cent increase in the national income per capita between 1922 and 1928, a 30 per cent increase in physical production, and a 100 per cent increase in the profits of the larger corporations. The expansion in housing and in educational facilities was increasing faster than population; there was an increase in the average health and longevity, and a per capita advance in savings and insurance. Important for the wage earner was a five-hour decline in the average working week and a slowly rising wage scale as against a fairly stationary price level. Finally, American industry had an increasingly alert and intelligent management, which helped to stimulate an ever-growing productivity per worker.

With the ledger open and the debits and credits before the eye on opposite pages, how may we add up the results? As evidenced by the usual business barometers, such as corporate profits, new capital, bank clearings, life insurance totals, and foreign investments, remarkable gains had been made. An unquestioned advance also took place in the flow of commodities and services, and an increase in the tonnage of consumer goods distributed among the population. What about prosperity measured in the more abundant life, and in terms of economic peace and security? Taking $2,000 a year as a rough estimate of a decent standard of living, the National Bureau of Economic Research found that in 1918, during the height of the war boom, 85.9 of all the gainfully employed received less than $2,000, and 72 per cent received less than $1,500. Eighty per cent of American families were living below the standard of health and decency at the beginning of the decade. Probably two thirds of the families were still below it when the boom faded into depression.

As to advances in economic security and peace of mind, they seemed to be slight. Technological improvements imperiled jobs; time studies and the "speed-up" were reducing the work life of the average wage earner. The typical American in the prosperous section might save more, and even buy more life insurance, but the period between the loss of a job and public charity was for most workers but slightly extended. Income of middle-class groups was not increasing as fast as that of skilled workers, and for most professional people it was inadequate. The independent merchant was in constant jeopardy from the expansion of the chain stores. Even the most encouraging aspect of the twenties, the extraordinary technical progress resulting in greater productivity, often entailed loss of jobs, unemployment, and misery.

Certain broad aspects of this decade which do not lend themselves to statistics, but which are of cardinal importance, must be reckoned with in any survey. Gains and losses in cultural and moral fields are sometimes intangible, and easily lead to generalizations difficult to prove. Many students of American civilization have denounced the decade as strengthening the crasser, seamier elements in American life. Instead of developing her cultural values, America, they insist, surrendered as never before to material standards. A decline in respect for the scholar, the artist, and the spiritual leader became visible, while the times glorified the businessman. The speed-up of energy necessary to accumulate the luxuries of the decade gave men little opportunity to pursue an interest in arts, and the determination of standards and tastes shifted more than ever to women. Studies like the Lynds' *Middletown* showed a declining interest in literature and the arts among the plain people. Even the millionaire had changed. The barons of the gilded age had ransacked Europe for treasures of art and literature. The *nouveaux riches* of the Coolidge boom contented themselves with Spanish mansions in Florida or California, or continued to give their full attention to making more money.

In brief, the twenties were charged with fostering a businessman's civilization of which the industrial captain and the successful money-maker were con-

sidered the finest flower. That the period revealed
an undue emphasis upon materialistic values most
students, and most intelligent observers who lived
during the decade, have agreed. Although the
tendencies strong in the twenties were not new in
American history and had always flourished during years of prosperity, it is doubtful if material
success was ever worshiped more unreservedly.
Nevertheless, it should not be forgotten that the
nation's educational and cultural equipment—
libraries, schools, scientific laboratories—increased
disproportionately to either population or wealth.
America was at least investing in culture. Nor was
materialism wholly triumphant. Not since the Civil
War had a decade shown a greater amount of distinguished writing; at no time had there been a
greater advance in architecture. Science throve
mightily, while these years presented credit items
even in the spiritual and aesthetic realms.

Those who dominate the economic and social life
of a nation are bound in the long run to dominate
its government and its political ideals. The United
States in the twenties was a perfect demonstration
of this fact. America's political leaders after 1923
were Mellon, Hoover, and Coolidge. The first two
stepped from highly successful business careers to
important political stations. Coolidge, with a life
career in politics, was as firm a believer in *laissez-
faire* economics as the most conservative business

chieftain. He entertained more extensively than any earlier President save Theodore Roosevelt, but his guests were almost entirely limited to leaders of industry and finance. The economic views and ideals of all three men were those which had flourished a half century earlier.

Under the circumstances, the political lag of the twenties is understandable. The policies of Mellon, Hoover, and Coolidge were chosen to help the businessman, and legislation was pointed to this end. In particular, they sought to reduce Government controls wherever possible. Social legislation and other aids to the workers were neglected. Only political expediency forced the passage of a modicum of legislation for agriculture. Realistic new approaches to Government problems were neglected. Critics of this policy of drift received the one answer—prosperity. It was prosperity which gave prestige to the Coolidge policies, and as long as it lasted there was little opportunity for change.

CHAPTER V

SOCIAL CONFUSION

ECONOMIC expansion may be the most important
factor in the interpretation of post-war America,
but it is only one of many significant influences
which played upon these years. At the other extreme, historians who attempt to explain the 1920's
merely in terms of a reversion to political nationalism and economic *laissez-faire* have likewise missed
essential factors. In many ways the decade was
one of the most amazing in American annals. Peer-
ing beneath the advancing prosperity and the rising
standard of comfort, we perceive a confusion of
ideas, an uprooting of ancient mores, and a revolution in ways of living. On the one hand stood
religious Fundamentalists, economic reactionaries,
and moral philosophers of the Victorian school
struggling desperately to lead the nation back to
the simpler ways of the pre-war era; on the other,
the many influences tending to disintegrate the
older American civilization. For a time the victory
of reaction and intolerance seemed assured, but in

the long run it failed. A confused interweaving of old and new made the decade indeed an "incredible era."

To explain America of the twenties the historian inevitably goes back to the World War. The inanition and disillusionment which followed this costly struggle account for much. The movement for a broader social justice which dominated the first fifteen years of the century and culminated in the World War had kept the nation for years on a plane of high idealism. Suddenly in 1919 the foundations of American idealism seemed to collapse under a wave of cynicism. A war fought to save the world for democracy and to abolish all wars had ended in a peace which laid the foundations for new autocracies and future conflicts. A nation which had made heavy sacrifices to aid Europe found itself the target of bitter criticism from abroad. To the four million young men who had been uprooted from their normal surroundings the Prussianized discipline of army life was distasteful. Those who went overseas found actual warfare a grueling ordeal and French civilization a disappointment. They returned to a nation anxious to forget the war. It was America's most disillusioning experience.

The war, however, was not the only influence which tended to create the frustration and restlessness characteristic of the decade. While millions of boys felt the disintegrating influences of separation from their homes, American women were also experiencing new impacts. To the increased economic independence which the war had promoted, the Nineteenth Amendment added political equality. A rising standard of living and a hundred every-day conveniences had lessened household drudgery for millions. This new independence, combined with the irresponsibility of life in crowded urban environments, the relaxation of religious restraints, and the influence of an untrammeled and sometimes even licentious literature, produced the changed morals and mores of the times.

While older codes of behavior were breaking down, prosperity and a perfected technique in advertising, installment buying, and sales pressure tended to make prudence and thrift seem old-fashioned. At the same time, the rapid expansion of the automobile was converting America into a nation on wheels and increasing the restlessness so characteristic of the decade. Cocksure as many Americans were of their economic prosperity, not a few questioned the soundness of the developing civilization. Some leaders might encourage the new tendencies by a superior attitude toward the past, but others, of whom H. L. Mencken and Sinclair Lewis were the most famous, devoted their talents to "debunking" the shallow features of the period. Many sober citizens were deeply disturbed by the current political corruption, which in itself tended to undermine the national morale.

Of all the influences tending to weaken the moral fiber of the nation, none was stronger than certain unexpected consequences of the prohibition of alcoholic beverages. Advocates of prohibition insisted that it had enormously reduced the consumption of liquor, arrests for drunkenness, and deaths from alcoholism, and had increased deposits in savings banks and greatly improved the condition of the poor. Opponents could see only the corruption and lawlessness that followed its adoption. The demand for national prohibition had sprung up as a result of long agitation by temperance groups supported by most of the Protestant churches. It had gained impetus from the obvious fact that the automobile and other complex appliances had created a highly mechanized society in which drunkenness was an anachronism. Finally, it had been speeded by the World War, which centralized authority in Washington and justified Federal restrictions on the use of grains in the manufacture of beer and hard liquors.

To the prohibitionist the drinking of alcoholic beverages had become a moral issue, and he would accept no compromise. Backed by the Anti-Saloon League, one of the most efficient of all pressure groups, prohibition had conquered eleven states by the end of 1914. During the next four years the movement spread so rapidly that by the end of 1918 eighteen more states had been added to the "dry" area, while local option was in effect in others. Despite this rapid advance, at least one third of the population still lived in "wet" territory. These regions, mainly around the great cities of the Northeast and the northern Mississippi valley, were as strongly committed to alcoholic beverages as prohibitionists were opposed. Finding it impossible to capture these strongholds by state laws, prohibitionists turned to Federal action. While temporary war restrictions were being extended, a joint resolution proposing the Eighteenth Amendment was passed by the House on December 17, 1917, and the Senate on the following day. Accepted by two thirds of the states on January 16, 1919, the Amendment was proclaimed on January 29. It forbade the "manufacture, sale, or transportation of intoxicating liquors" and was implemented by a National Prohibition Act (Volstead Act) passed in October, 1919. Vetoed by Wilson, this measure was repassed over his veto on October 28, 1919. Under the Volstead Act, intoxicating liquor, following an old decision of the Bureau of Internal Revenue, was defined as any liquor containing more than one half of one per cent of alcohol.

Whether in a more sober era national prohibition might have succeeded it is impossible to say. In the hectic decade of the twenties it was doomed from the start. The liquor interests, seeing the value of their vast property ruinously diminished without compensation, were determined not to give up. Immigrants, accustomed to wines and beers and utterly oblivious of any moral implications, resented this interference with their normal habits. Many Americans previously indifferent to the Bill of Rights began to talk about the personal liberty of which they were now deprived.

While the Bohemian intelligentsia of Greenwich Village made it a point of honor to defy the Amendment, the wealthy rendered open law-breaking fashionable. Only the stolid church-going bourgeoisie of the earlier prohibition areas continued to take the law seriously, and they were considered old-fashioned by their children, who felt that no dance was complete without a circulating hip-flask. Otherwise serious-minded adults exchanged recipes for home-brewed beer and "bath-tub gin."

With millions of people openly flouting the law, the violation of the Volstead Act grew into the proportions of big business. Profits were tremendous and the methods of evading the law numerous. They included, in addition to ordinary illegal brewing and distilling, the redistillation of industrial alcohol, the misuse of permits for using industrial alcohol, the abuse of druggists' prescriptions, and smuggling from Canada, Mexico, the West Indies, and Europe. After a decade of attempted enforce-

ment, the Director of the Prohibition Bureau estimated that the illicit production for the fiscal year
ending June 30, 1930, amounted to almost 40 per
cent of the legitimate withdrawals in 1914.

It was not the individual home brewer and moon-
shiner who were mainly responsible for law-breaking and political corruption, but the groups of
smugglers, illicit brewers, bootleggers, and hijack-
ers, who divided the country among themselves
and monopolized the illegal traffic, the yearly
profits of which ran into hundreds of millions. That
these profits were great enough to undermine enforcement was obvious to all. Whiskey, for example, which had been loaded at St. Pierre at a
cost of $8 to $20 a case, depending on quality,
was later sold in New York at from $72 to $120 a
case, and in the meantime had been "cut" to one
third of its strength, allowing the smugglers and
bootleggers three cases for one imported. Expenses
for distribution and political corruption were heavy,
but the profits were, nevertheless, tremendous.

Facing the widespread opposition to the law and
the powerful underworld rackets which defied it,
enforcement officers worked under heavy handi-
caps. From the start, prohibition enforcement was
a football of politics, handicapped by political
squabbling in the halls of Congress, by political
appointments to the enforcement service, by political quarrels among Federal agencies and between

Federal and state authorities. Small wonder that a spirit of "Oh, what's the use?" developed, under which even honest officers gave up the struggle.

In the first place, enforcement officers worked under the handicap of insufficient support; Congress was never willing to appropriate adequate funds. When John F. Kramer, the first Prohibition Commissioner, an honest and sincere official, made his initial announcement to the press, he spoke with amazing confidence.

The law will be obeyed in cities, large and small, and in villages, and where it is not obeyed, it will be enforced. . . . The law says that liquor to be used as a beverage must not be manufactured. We shall see that it is not manufactured, nor sold, nor given away, nor hauled in anything on the surface of the earth or under the earth or in the air.

That such a promise would never be fulfilled must have been obvious after a few weeks. Congress, it is evident, had passed the Prohibition Amendment and the Volstead Act in part to be rid of a politically annoying issue. It felt that it had done its duty and wanted to be left alone. The prohibition forces, fearing that the nation might think the Amendment a failure, for some time acquiesced in letting Congress alone. Nor did the White House at any time care to make an issue of prohibition or bring real pressure to bear upon the legislative branch.

Between 1919 and the passage on March 24, 1924, of the "Emergency Beer Bill" (Willis-Campbell Act), a measure forbidding the prescription of beer as a medicine and limiting prescriptions of spirituous and vinous liquors, Congress had done virtually nothing about the matter except make the annual appropriation. The Anti-Saloon League had suggested that $5,000,000 a year was ample. Congress had done better than this, appropriating during the first five years an average of slightly less than $8,000,000 annually. This, as it turned out, was but a tiny fraction of the amount necessary to enforce prohibition—if it could be enforced at all. In 1924 the Prohibition Bureau had on its payroll 3,374 employees whose business it was to prosecute 40,000 prohibition cases in the Federal courts, guard 18,000 miles of seacoast and border, safeguard against diversion 57,000,000 gallons of industrial alcohol, and, with what help it could obtain from state and local officials, prevent the manufacture of intoxicating beverages in 20,000,000 homes. In New York City at the end of 1925 there were only 17 inspectors to keep check on 1,200 drugstores and to investigate a million prescriptions issued every year by 5,100 doctors. Rather than provide funds for an adequate personnel, Congress, as the years went by, usually preferred to pass another act.

Even with an inadequate budget, the Prohibition

Bureau could have accomplished more had it not been packed from the top down with worthless political appointees. The incompetency and often dishonesty of its personnel arose primarily from the failure of Congress to put the Prohibition Bureau under civil service. "When the Volstead Act was passed," admitted the Secretary of the League, "neither the Anti-Saloon League nor any other agency could have gotten into that law a civil service provision, and for the League to have forced the issue would have been to jeopardize the passage of the bill." By 1927 the situation became so bad that Congress finally put the Bureau under the classified civil service, but only after bills to accomplish this had languished in Congress for six years. When civil service was thus finally introduced, some 1,500 enforcement agents already on the payrolls failed to pass the examinations.

Inefficiency was fostered also by administrative division of authority in supervision and prosecution. When the Volstead Act was first passed, a Prohibition Bureau was organized as part of the Bureau of Internal Revenue of the Treasury Department, which already exercised control over licensed manufacturers and distributors. Thus the prohibition officers investigated and detected offenders, while the duty of prosecuting remained with the Department of Justice. Not until 1930 was the prohibition work of the Treasury Department transferred to the Department of Justice. Authority was also divided in a deplorable way between Federal and state administrations. Federal officials received little help in many sections where the law was openly violated. The "Maryland Free State" never passed an enforcement act, while New York repealed her "Baby Volstead Act" as early as 1923. In many states a majority of the citizens opposed prohibition, and the police were hence under no pressure to cooperate with Federal authorities. Indeed, it used to be said that the best way to find a speakeasy in a strange town was to ask the first policeman encountered. Effective state and local enforcement also required more funds than the authorities were willing to allot. After all, ran the general sentiment, it was a national act; let the Federal Government enforce it.

Over the entire program hung a cloud of corruption. Out of the vast profits of the illegal liquor business generous chunks were allotted to corrupt local, state, and Federal enforcement officials. The slime of graft touched all ranks, from the policeman on the beat to high national functionaries. A grand jury investigation in Philadelphia in 1928, though merely scratching the surface, brought about the dismissal of three inspectors, ten captains, and two district detectives. In New York City, Tammany Hall, the ruling political machine, was reduced to the status of an agency to protect gangsters and racketeers operating primarily in the illicit liquor business. Little fellows were often caught and prosecuted, but the important operators usually escaped. Al Capone, however, the head of a gang which for years controlled the "beer racket" in Chicago, finally went to jail; not because he violated the Volstead Act, but because he evaded the income tax.

The career of "Scarface" Al Capone, in fact, gives some idea of the opportunities afforded the under-world by prohibition as well as the inadequacies of enforcement. Capone served his apprenticeship among Chicago gangsters who operated in prostitution, but with the advent of prohibition he followed his boss, Johnny Torrio, into the much more profit-able beer racket. The careers of leaders in "big-shot" racketeering were notably short, and Torrio, after being severely wounded and serving time in jail, retired in favor of Capone. The new chief quickly expanded from beer and liquor into slot machines, laundries, and other activities, at the same time gaining control of certain labor unions and city and county officers. Gross return from his various rackets, it was believed, ran into several million dollars a month. So rich was the prize that rival gangs of greater or less strength were con-stantly attempting to "muscle in" on Capone. In the seven years after 1920 more than two hundred and fifty men were killed in the gang warfares of

Chicago. Since most of the murders were done by unknown gunmen from the outside, the police were never able to pin any of them on Capone, but they believed that he was frequently responsible. "Scarface" Al himself escaped death more than once by pure luck.

Capone tried at various times to stabilize the rackets by urging rival gangs to call a truce. About 1927 he divided Chicago into two areas to be run by separate gangs and retired to a Florida mansion. But he was no sooner gone than new rivalries broke out, culminating on St. Valentine's Day, 1929, when gunmen employed by Capone's former gang lined up seven of their rivals in a beer-truck garage and mowed them down with machine guns. Capone's efforts to lead the life of a "retired gentleman" in Florida, at the same time keeping his fingers on the underworld, finally ended in 1931 with an eleven-year term for income tax evasion. His career differed from that of other racketeers only in the size of his operations and his success in dodging the almost inevitable bullet from a rival gorilla.

Under Attorney-General Daugherty prosecution of liquor offenders got off to a bad start. Although the Federal Government in less than two years (1921–1923) instituted 3,500 civil and 65,760 criminal actions, winning 2,314 of the former and 43,905 of the latter, the offenders were for the most part unimportant. The big racketeers, who knew how to make arrangements with the right people, usually escaped. Nearly 10 per cent of those who served in the Federal prohibition unit, it is estimated, were dismissed for malfeasance in office. Many other guilty officials were never discovered.

The breakdown of the Eighteenth Amendment, as exemplified by political corruption, underworld racketeering, and defiance of the law by millions of otherwise reasonable citizens, was but one phase of the social and intellectual confusion of the decade. With European civilization reeling under the terrific blow of four years of war, and with society everywhere affected by the impact of technological changes, new religious, economic, and political concepts took deep root. Against these concepts upholders of the existing civilization, such as it was, struck back fiercely. In a decade characterized by rapid changes in the ways of living, America witnessed the anomaly of a blind and bitter reaction.

What were the forces which made this an era of intellectual reaction? In the first place, the nation experienced a normal swing back from the era of the muckrakers and the great crusade. It witnessed a natural revulsion against the moral letdown of the war and the disturbing changes. Protests arose against the rising aggressiveness of labor as exemplified in the steel, rail, and coal strikes of the post-war years. Many conservative citizens were quick to attack those who questioned the beneficence of the American scene or the perfection of its Government.

That the nation was honeycombed with the Communist ideas of the Russian Revolution seemed clear enough to the conservatives of 1919. The Socialist Party, pacifist and internationalist in its point of view, had opposed the war. Its leader, the mild and lovable Debs, had referred to Lenin and Trotsky as the "foremost statesmen of the age," and to the Supreme Court as "bepowdered old fossils who had never decided anything." Now the Socialist Party was being smashed by a more radical group, the Communists, who held that the American Government should be overthrown by force. The Communists, it was believed, had already launched their nefarious campaign by attempting to strike down upholders of law and order, as in the bombing on June 2, 1919, of the Washington home of Attorney-General Palmer. Was it not true that Northwestern farmers were responding to Socialist tenets promulgated by the Non-Partisan League? Was it not true that conservative Railroad Brotherhoods were demanding the Plumb Plan, while the more radical United Mine Workers were advocating nationalization of the mines? Was it not true that in Boston even the policemen had struck? To upholders of the old ways, the nation was obviously in great danger.

In ruthless efforts to prevent criticism or halt the development of new ideas, conservative groups had already received some training during the World War. Shortly before America's entry, Woodrow Wilson had prophesied that if war should come, "Conformity will be the only virtue. And every man who refuses to conform will have to pay the penalty." He described accurately what was about to happen. The Espionage Act of June 17, 1917, as amended in May, 1918, was an Administration measure. Even under the leadership of the liberal President, the Constitutional guarantees of free speech, free press, and free assemblage were sadly impaired by legislation and were violated innumerable times. Under Attorney-General A. Mitchell Palmer nearly 2,000 men and women went to prison for terms up to twenty years, while Postmaster-General Burleson excluded from the mails *The Masses, The Milwaukee Leader*, an issue of the *Nation*, and many books and pamphlets. Whatever the excuses for violation of the Constitution during the war, none existed after hostilities had closed; yet as late December, 1919, Wilson urged more legislation to curb the Communists. There might have been some justification for a wartime law to punish active interference with the national defense, but after the conflict was over there was none for using such a law to destroy pacifists and economic dissenters.

It was in 1919 and 1920, months after hostilities had ceased, that the Federal Government descended to the depths of greatest intolerance. It is true that the President was stricken with illness during this period, but there is no evidence that he ever tried to stay the hand of his Attorneys-General, Gregory or Palmer, of Postmaster-General Burleson, or of Secretary of Labor William B. Wilson. The ruthless wartime destruction of the left-wing labor movement by the wholesale arrest of leaders of the Industrial Workers of the World, the imprisonment of Socialist leaders, and the incredibly harsh treatment of conscientious objectors remain a dark blot on the Wilson Administration. Far worse were the Federal policies in the months after hostilities had closed. Wilson refused to listen to pleas for clemency for political prisoners. With more of the milk of human kindness, Harding, even before his inauguration, began steps to free Debs from prison. He did not, however, do much toward the release of 1,500 other political prisoners. It was more than a decade before a blanket amnesty issued by Roosevelt in 1933 restored them to citizenship and civil rights and closed this chapter of the war.

With public antipathy toward Bolshevism and radicalism deeply aroused, it is not surprising that the states followed the same road. Criminal syndicalist laws of one kind or another were passed in thirty-two states, and laws punishing the display of the Red flag as a political emblem in twenty-eight. Innumerable city statutes and ordinances were enacted covering disturbance of the peace, parades, street meetings, and distribution of literature; their purpose was to curtail the activities of radical groups, and their effect, to deny freedom of speech, press, and assemblage. Nor is it surprising that private organizations like the Ku Klux Klan and the American Legion should have taken upon themselves the duty of fighting "Reds," or that other organizations of citizens should have attacked gatherings of labor or radicals. Typical of such incidents was the storming by a mob of soldiers, sailors, and others, of the offices of the Socialist New York *Call*, where a reception was being held on May Day, 1919, and the smashing of the furniture and the clubbing of men, women, and children gathered there. Another more famous incident occurred on November 11, when American Legion members clashed with members of the Industrial Workers of the World at Centralia, Washington. The Legion account was that I.W.W. men fired wantonly into a veterans' parade; the I.W.W. story was that the Legion, without provocation, had attacked a labor meeting and the workers had fired in self-defense. Blood was shed on both sides. After a prosecution which was variously attacked and defended, sentences of from twenty-five to forty years were imposed on seven I.W.W. defendants.

A thousand incidents might be cited as illustrations of the "Red hunts" of 1917–1920. Two or three will be sufficient. Victor L. Berger, Wisconsin Socialist and publisher of the *Milwaukee Leader,* was twice denied membership in Congress, although legally elected. On January 7, 1920, the New York Legislature refused to permit the seating of five duly elected men, for no other reason than that they were Socialists. The anti-radical movement in New York State was kept at white heat by the Lusk Committee, whose own activities were often far more illegal than any attempted by the Socialist Party. The climax of the Federal activities against extremists was reached in repeated raids upon radical headquarters and the arrest and deportation of aliens, particularly those suspected of radical leadership. On December 29, 1919, some 249 were shipped back to Russia via Finland on the *Buford.* Widely applauded by the reactionary press, Attorney-General Palmer determined upon a nation-wide round-up. His agents on New Year's Day, 1920, swooped down upon Communist headquarters and raided meetings of various kinds, arresting more than 6,000 suspected alien radicals. Most of these were illegally held incommunicado, without benefit of counsel. Of more than 6,000 arrested it was discovered that only three were armed, and many were neither radicals nor aliens.

Symbolic of the political reaction in the 1920's was the case of Nicola Sacco, a shoemaker, and Bartolomeo Vanzetti, a fish peddler, two Italian anarchists accused of murdering a shoe factory paymaster at South Braintree, Massachusetts, in April, 1920. The evidence upon which they were convicted seemed so flimsy, and the judge who presided so biased, that liberals and radicals throughout the world (to say nothing of many conservatives) looked upon the trial as an illustration of the way in which innocent men might be railroaded to death because they were radicals. This attitude was strengthened by Felix Frankfurter and other legal scholars, who gave wide publicity to the weakness of the prosecutor's case. Men and women, convinced of the innocence of the pair and stirred by the nobility of Vanzetti's writings, kept the case open for seven years, but Massachusetts law made it impossible to obtain a new trial. Under liberal pressure the Massachusetts Governor finally asked a committee of three prominent citizens, headed by A. Lawrence Lowell, President of Harvard, to go over the evidence. They reported that they could see no reason for changing the verdict, and the two men were executed amid world-wide protest on August 23, 1927. For many Americans this was the blackest day of the decade.

Despite the tragic conclusion of the Sacco-Vanzetti case, the long-continued efforts to save these men proved that liberalism had by no means disappeared. The survival was evident also in the continued agitation for the release of two radical labor leaders, Warren K. Billings and Thomas J. Mooney. Billings had been condemned to life imprisonment and Mooney to death for allegedly planting a bomb during a San Francisco preparedness parade in 1916; explosion of the bomb had caused the death of eight persons. Under pressure from President Wilson, the California Governor commuted Mooney's sentence to life imprisonment. The conviction of Mooney and Billings was recognized as a triumph of the anti-labor movement in San Francisco, and each new investigation indicated that perjured testimony and mass hysteria had played a large part in the conviction. Organized labor and liberals of all types made the freeing and vindication of Mooney and Billings a major objective throughout the twenties. It was not until 1939, however, that Governor Culbert L. Olson had the political courage to free them.

When Theodore Roosevelt early in the war popularized the phrase "one-hundred-per-cent Americanism," he could hardly have envisaged the numerous forms it would take. Before Americans had recovered from their undiscriminating nationalism and had ceased shuddering at the specter of Bolshevism, they had turned their backs on the League of Nations and the World Court, erected high trade barriers against Europe, ended large-scale immigration, waged official and private war upon radicals, and attempted to regiment many processes of intellectual life. The United States in the twenties may still have been the "home of the brave," but many questioned whether it was any longer the "land of the free." A natural rebound from pre-war liberalism, accentuated by post-bellum weariness, accounted for many of the restraints. On the nationalistic side, the reaction was strengthened by the bitter criticism of some Europeans who minimized the American war effort and denounced the United States for deserting the League and attempting to collect at least a part of the war debts.

One of the earliest results of the swing toward nationalism was the tightening of immigration restrictions. For many years various groups, particularly organized labor, had clamored for some sort of selective basis. This demand, originating in the 1890's, grew stronger during the first decade of the century, a decade in which 8,795,000 immigrants arrived on American shores. Of these millions, more than 70 per cent came from Southern and Eastern Europe. In the hope of checking the overwhelming tide, Congress had excluded various types of undesirables, but with little effect. A literacy act was first passed in 1897. Vetoed by Cleveland, it was later reenacted only to be vetoed again, once by Taft and twice by Wilson. It was finally passed over Wilson's veto in 1917, but failed completely to stop the flow.

When the war ended, the demand for further restriction became overwhelming. Immigration since 1900, it was felt, had been too rapid to be easily absorbed. Many "hyphenated Americans" had shown a dubious loyalty during the war years, and now America seemed in danger of a new flood from war-stricken Europe. To the old demands of organized labor were added those of various "patriotic societies." Nor did employers any longer oppose restriction, for there was practically no labor shortage in the prosperous years of the middle twenties. Under these circumstances, drastic immigration legislation was inevitable. The literacy test having failed, Congress moved on to restriction by quota. An act was passed in the closing days of the Sixty-sixth Congress, only to be pocket-vetoed by Wilson. Early in the Harding Administration, the Emergency Quota Act of 1921 was quickly passed, limiting immigration in any one year to 3 per cent of the number of each nationality living in the United States in 1910. The life of this Act was to be one year, but was later extended for two more.

Although the Emergency Quota Act somewhat cut down the inflow of immigrants, the tide began to mount again by 1923. Furthermore, this legislation did not favor the immigration from Northern and Western Europe as much as its proponents had hoped. Congress was determined not only to reduce the amount of immigration, but also to control the type. The result was a new law in 1924 changing the quota to 2 per cent of any nationality residing in the United States in 1890. Canadians and immigrants from the independent countries of Latin America were exempt, as were travelers, merchants, and seamen, but Japanese were debarred. The quota scheme of the Immigration Act of 1924 was to remain in effect only until 1927, when the base was to be made "that proportion of 150,000 which the number of persons of a given national origin residing in the United States in 1920 bears to the country's total population in 1920."

When Government scientists attempted to determine the "national origins" of the American people they found the task virtually impossible. Congress, however, insisted that some apportionment be made, and after delaying application of the Act until 1929, the "national origins" quota was put into effect. Under the new law, Great Britain and Northern Ireland were favored, and Southern and Eastern Europe were little affected, while immigration from Germany, Scandinavia, and Southern Ireland was lowered. By the end of the decade the long battle for immigration restriction had proved more successful than its exponents had ever hoped.

Between the quota system and the depression which began in 1929, immigration for a time virtually ceased. During certain years in the 1930's more aliens left America than came in.

No organization in the country was more powerful in developing anti-alien feeling, racial antagonism, and religious intolerance than the Ku Klux Klan. It represented the reaction of the twenties at its worst. Although it took the name and accoutrements of the best-known of the secret organizations founded after the Civil War to maintain the political, economic, and social supremacy of the Southern whites, the Klan in reality was a revival of a much earlier nativist movement. A protest against alien races, creeds, and social ideas, it pledged itself to preserve "native, white, Protestant" supremacy, and manifested a truculent hostility toward the Negro, Jew, and Catholic. "Americanism, to the Klansman," wrote Imperial Wizard H. W. Evans, "is a thing of the spirit, a purpose and a point of view, that can come only through instinctive racial understanding . . . few aliens can understand that spirit." The Negro, unlike the Jew or Catholic, was "not a menace to Americanism"; he was "simply racially incapable of understanding, sharing or contributing to Americanism."

Founded in 1915 by William J. Simmons of Atlanta, a man of glib eloquence but slight organizing ability, the Ku Klux Klan numbered a bare 5,000 by 1920. In that year the struggling society was rescued from oblivion by two professional publicity experts, Edward Young Clarke and Mrs. Elizabeth Tyler of Atlanta, long associated with the Southern Publicity Association. Under their direction, a better financial management was installed and a nation-wide membership program was launched. That commercial motives played no small part in the sudden growth of the Klan there can be no doubt. The membership fee was ten dollars, of which four went to the local solicitor (Kleagle), one dollar to the state sales-manager (King Kleagle), fifty cents to the district salesman (Grand Goblin), and the remaining four dollars and fifty cents to the main office at Atlanta, where the promotion department, headed by Imperial Kleagle Clarke, came in for a goodly share. Under clever promotion the Klan grew within a year from a few thousand to nearly 100,000 members.

The Klan was no sooner well launched than its evils became apparent. According to the New York *World*, which early inaugurated a crusade against the organization, its lawless activities during the year from October, 1920, to October, 1921, included four killings, one mutilation, one branding, forty-one floggings, twenty-seven tarrings and featherings, five kidnapings, and numerous parades of masked men carrying intimidating placards. These early exhibitions of violence, it is interesting to note, were rarely directed against Negroes, Jews, or Catholics, but rather against persons believed to have violated accepted codes of morals. The Klan officially denied any connection with such crimes, but since they were ordinarily perpetrated under the mask of Klan paraphernalia, most Americans held the organization responsible. Public denunciation, led by the *World* and a few other newspapers, was sufficiently vigorous to bring about a Congressional investigation in 1921. For the moment, unfortunately, this seemed to have no effect except to provide publicity upon which the Klan throve.

At one time the organization was alleged to have grown at the rate of 100,000 a week, and at the height of its power in 1925 it claimed a membership of 5,000,000 or more. Probably it never had more than 4,000,000. Neither skillful promotion nor the opportunity for masked men to pay off a grudge or take the law into their own hands, however, fundamentally explains this rapid growth. The Ku Klux Klan appealed to the simple and ignorant, particularly in the rural and Protestant South and Middle West. It drew thousands who believed that Catholics were plotting to bring the Pope to America, assume political control, and crush Protestantism, and other thousands who held that the Jews were involved in a great international conspiracy to dominate the world's economic life. Many Southerners, disturbed by the restlessness of Negroes and the migration of 600,000 colored folk to the North between 1917 and 1925, saw in the Klan an instrument to keep them in submission. Many business and professional men were intimidated into joining. Others went in to share the great financial bonanza which the Klan was yielding. Many members, of course, held a sincere belief that American traditions and ideals were endangered. "Even granting . . . that Clarke and his assistants were merely commercializing hates and prejudices," wrote a careful student of the movement, "it is well to remember that men joined the Klan because it appealed to their patriotism and their moral idealism more than to their hates and prejudices." * To one historian, the chief source of the Klan's strength "seems to have been that it was all things to all men." † In communities where cooperation with Europe was unpopular, it would denounce the League and all its works; in communities where prohibition was approved, it waged war on the bootleggers. It allied itself everywhere with popular local issues.

That the interpretations just given are sound is

* J. M. Mecklin, *The Ku Klux Klan* (New York, Harcourt, Brace and Co., 1924), p. 13.

† P. W. Slosson, *The Great Crusade and After* (New York, Macmillan Co., 1931), p. 308.

substantiated by a survey of the regions where the Klan was most powerful. Certain groups may have been primarily interested in "keeping the Negro in his place," but the center of the Klan's strength was never in the older South. Its first great successes were attained in the area west of the Mississippi that includes northern and eastern Texas, Arkansas, Oklahoma, and northern Louisiana. From this region it quickly jumped to the Sacramento Valley and other parts of California, long accustomed to men who took the law in their own hands. It then moved into Oregon, where it rapidly became powerful in state politics. Its last great success was in the Middle West, particularly Ohio and Indiana, by no means the least civilized states of the nation.

Perhaps the most amazing story of the Klan has to do with Oregon. Imported from California in 1921, it grew with such rapidity that within a year it had a membership of around 100,000. Few communities did not possess a Klan organization. The outside observer found it difficult to understand this growth. Eighty-five per cent of the people of Oregon were native whites. Only 3 per cent were Negroes and 5 per cent Orientals; only 1½ per cent were illiterate. The Klan began in Oregon with the avowed purpose of assisting the enforcement of prohibition. It was undoubtedly spread by the able salesmanship of the local

Kleagles, but the chief factor in its growth appeared
to be a persistence of the Know-Nothingism and
anti-Catholicism which the population had imported from their original homes in the East and
Middle West. With able leaders and a large membership, aided by two auxiliary women's orders
(Ladies of the Invisible Empire and the Royal
Riders of the Red Robe), the Klan became a power
in politics. When Republican Governor Ben W.
Olcott on May 13, 1922, issued a proclamation condemning it because of night-riding outrages, it
threw its power behind his Democratic opponent
in 1923 and ousted Olcott from office. Its influence
reached a climax when it pushed through a school
bill compelling parents or guardians, with minor
exceptions, to send all children between eight and
sixteen to the public schools. The law was declared
unconstitutional in 1925 (Pierce, Governor of
Oregon, *et al. v.* Society of Sisters, 268 U. S. 510);
but even before this decision the more intelligent
citizens were revolting against the political domination of the organization and its demoralizing
effects.

Americans who believed that political, religious,
and social tolerance was the true national tradition
deplored the rantings of the Klan. Sober citizens
looked askance at its growing political power, and
all decent persons were sickened by the revelations
of killings, mutilations, floggings, kidnapings, and

other crimes perpetrated by the organization. Although resentment against the Klan was growing for many reasons, it was probably the excesses of the organization and its leaders in the political field that brought about its downfall.

Nowhere were the revelations more shocking than in Indiana, where the Klan reached its greatest Middle Western power. In this supposedly advanced state a certain David C. Stephenson, master salesman and "rabble rouser," lured about 200,000 Hoosiers of one type or another into the organization. Rural Indiana, it appeared, was a fertile ground for the seeds of prejudice and hate. Ranting orators had no difficulty in whipping poor and ignorant men into a frenzy over nonexisting dangers. Credulity seemed to have no limits. When a Klan orator declared to a crowd at North Manchester that for all they knew the Pope might descend upon the town any day, possibly "even be on the north-bound train tomorrow," a mob of 1,500 persons marched to the station to safeguard the community from this impending danger. While many joined the Klan to protect America from Catholics, Jews, and Negroes, others found in the hood and robe a compensation for frustrated ambitions and an opportunity for excitement. And with his organization rapidly growing, Stephenson took the Klan into politics. His followers seized the Republican machine, nominated and elected their candidates to state offices, and captured the city government of Indianapolis. So powerful had the Klan become that both United States Senators from Indiana were forced to adopt a friendly attitude toward it.

It is probable that only a political fight between Stephenson and his rival for state control of the Klan saved Indiana from the legislation it had promised—legislation abolishing private schools, establishing segregated Negro districts in cities, requiring New Testament instruction in the public schools, forbidding alien landholding, and setting up other group restrictions. It was likewise only the political and personal immorality of Stephenson and certain of his followers that saved the state from a considerable period of Klan domination. Stephenson, after abducting a girl and terrifying her into suicide, was himself sentenced to life imprisonment. His hand-picked Governor, Ed Jackson, was indicted for bribery, as were several members of the Indianapolis government. One of the leading Klan orators, Judge Clarence W. Dearth, was impeached for oppression in office. Governor Jackson was saved from conviction only by the statute of limitations. Although a majority voted for conviction on five counts against Judge Dearth, the two-thirds vote necessary to unseat him was not obtained. This was the first time in ninety-two years that an Indiana judge had been ordered before the bar of the Senate for trial, and it was a sobering experience for most citizens.

The shocking situation in Indiana brought a reaction. Scandals in other states likewise revealed the Klan as an organization whose clever leaders preyed on the superstitions and resentments of the multitude to obtain easy money or political power. Wizard Evans attempted in 1928 to save it by abolishing masks, changing its name, and instituting other reforms, but the membership rapidly declined and its power was broken.

The rise of the Klan was merely symbolic of the chauvinism and intolerance rampant during the twenties. Just as racketeers used it to obtain wealth and power, Northern politicians used the "Red menace" and similar issues to win popularity and votes. Indeed, this was one method employed by Coolidge and Dawes in 1924 to divert the voters from the corruption of the Harding Administration. Mayor William H. Thompson of Chicago, for example, sought to maintain his political popularity by twisting the lion's tail and periodically saving his great city from King George. Both Mayor Thompson of Chicago and Mayor Hylan of New York sponsored investigations into American history textbooks, not for their economic radicalism (they contained none), but to ascertain whether some writers had failed to be critical enough of Great Britain. Even the American Legion sponsored a specially written volume for junior high schools to teach history in the proper way—a way which professional historians had presumably not followed. Little was accomplished by the textbook investigations except to convince authors that they must be careful to mention Revolutionary heroes of Irish, German, Polish, and other nationalities.

More serious was the general drive against freedom of education. Led by the Hearst and McFadden publications, and pushed on by such organizations as the Daughters of the American Revolution, the Veterans of Foreign Wars, and the National Civic Federation, an impression was developed that American colleges were full of radical teaching. Even Vice-President Coolidge expressed such a belief in a series of *Delineator* articles published in 1921 under the title "Enemies of the Republic." Influenced by this hue and cry, college presidents sometimes ousted "radical" professors or kept liberal lecturers off their campuses. Between 1917 and 1931, the legislatures of thirteen states passed laws requiring every teacher to take an oath to support the Constitution. This, it was apparently believed, would end any possible suspicion on the part of the teachers that there could be any flaws in the social, political, or economic system.

While economic reactionaries were sniping at American education from one direction, religious Fundamentalists were attacking it from another.

Just as economic and political America had felt the refreshing breeze of liberalism during the first fifteen years of the new century, so the churches had been touched by a broader vision. Under the impact of science many religious leaders had become less dogmatic, more inclined to cooperate with Christians of other denominations, and more convinced of the importance of the "social gospel." So rapidly had social and theological liberalism advanced in Protestant Christianity that it was bound to fall within the compass of the general post-war reaction.

In this battle against religious liberalism, the Ku Klux Klan worked hand in hand with Fundamentalists. While the Kleagles and Goblins blew the religious bigotry of the rural South to white heat, Fundamentalist clergymen led by William Jennings Bryan brought pressure to bear upon state legislatures to ban the teaching of evolution in public schools and state universities. "Power in this country," insisted Bryan, "comes from the people; and if the majority of the people believe that evolution breaks down a religious faith and threatens Christianity, they have a right to demand that it be suppressed or at least confined to a little group of research men who may study it as a theory not yet proven." Bryan and his followers were successful in Tennessee (1925), Mississippi (1926), and Arkansas (1928). Efforts to obtain similar laws in Louisiana, North Carolina, and Virginia failed after bitter fights, the result being largely due to the opposition of the South's most enlightened newspapers. It was a combination of Ku Kluxers and Fundamentalists that in Oregon carried a referendum compelling all children to attend public schools; only to see their law annulled, as we have noted, by the Federal Supreme Court.

The lengths to which the religious reaction had gone were first advertised to the nation by the trial of John I. Scopes, a high school teacher of Dayton, Tennessee, on the charge of teaching evolution. With William Jennings Bryan defending the law and Clarence Darrow leading the counsel for the defense, the country was treated to the amazing sight of a great Democratic leader and a famous liberal lawyer debating the veracity of the Biblical account of the creation. The trial unfortunately dealt but slightly with the great problems of Constitutional rights, academic freedom, and the relation of church to state. It did, however, thoroughly deflate the rampant Fundamentalism of the twenties. The fact that such a spectacle could take place in America of the twentieth century humiliated thoughtful observers.

While many Northerners smiled over the "monkey trial" in Tennessee, they had to face in their own section another absurd type of activity. This was the continual attack of "professional purists" upon art, literature, and the scientific approach to sex education. Such organizations as the New York Society for the Suppression of Vice and the Boston Watch and Ward Society, aided by the customs officers of the Treasury Department and by the Post Office Department, took the initiative. Although some obscenity was suppressed, these organizations became notable chiefly for their efforts to ban certain books of high literary value and little or no real licentiousness, while the circulation of obviously pornographic magazines went on virtually unchecked. Organizations of this type were also conspicuous for their opposition to decent sex education. Censorship of books, moving pictures, and art exhibits was by no means limited to the twenties, but it is doubtful if it has ever been more stupidly exercised than in this period.

CHAPTER VI

POLITICAL CORRUPTION

INTO the milieu of post-war moral disintegration and intellectual confusion, political corruption fitted harmoniously. As in the so-called "reconstruction" days of the Grant Administration, with its Black Friday, its Credit Mobilier, and its Whiskey Ring, the Harding Administration had its Ohio Gang, its Teapot Dome, and its scandals in the Veterans Bureau. Nor was the political corruption limited to the Federal Government. Various states had their raffish figures, like "Pa" Ferguson in Texas, Huey Long in Louisiana, and Frank Smith in Illinois; while not a few municipal governments throughout the nation were struggling with graft quite as flagrant as that practiced by Boss Tweed and his henchmen of an earlier day.

Though such corruption flourished far and wide, it was perhaps most obvious in New York, Chicago, and Philadelphia, the nation's largest cities. Philadelphia, a city which Lincoln Steffens described in 1903 as "corrupt and contented," had evidently changed its ways but little two decades later. Its political life was controlled by the Republican machine under William S. Vare, Congressman from 1912 to 1927. Elected to the Senate in 1926, he was eventually refused admission on the ground that he had literally bought his seat. While Vare gave most of his attention to Federal politics, his henchmen let vice flourish in the town. Twice, however, some responsible citizens were sufficiently aroused to demand reform. The first effort was in 1924–1925, when they borrowed Brigadier-General Smedley D. Butler from the Marine Corps in a futile effort to cleanse the city of bootlegging, gambling, and prostitution. The second was in 1928, when a Grand Jury investigation, probing the background of what proved to be a gang murder, revealed the ramifications of the Philadelphia bootlegging industry.

It was high time for action.

The information which we have described so far [said the jury in its presentment] is amazing in character and almost unbelievable in its significance. It clearly shows that there has existed in the county of Philadelphia during the last several years and up to the present time a group of lawless men who have violated the law upon a wholesale scale. They have with the benefit of legal advice created an organization which has systematically flouted the law with the corrupt connivance of police officials, high and low, resulting in the enrichment of its members to the extent of millions of dollars.

This was a conservative statement. The investigation showed that illegal liquor interests had established an inner government with an inner law, under a chief arbiter before whom attorneys practiced and whose decisions were enforced by the industry's own police, that is, gunmen. The streets of Philadelphia, observed Judge Edwin O. Lewis in 1928, had been made a battleground for gunmen. That the illicit manufacture and distribution of intoxicating beverages amounted to big business was shown by the fact that one Philadelphia bank had on deposit $9,500,000 of bootleggers' money, while another had $2,000,000.

Deep-rooted and pervasive as were graft and corruption in Philadelphia, they existed in the quiet manner so characteristic of that city's life. In Chicago, however, dishonesty was brazen. Except for a brief respite in 1923–1927, when Mayor William E. Dever made an earnest effort to enforce the law, the Chicago administration was headed by William H. Thompson (Mayor, 1915–1923, 1927–1931), advocate of a "wide open" town. Corruption in the courts and among the police effectively blocked the efforts of Dever, but Thompson was nevertheless gladly welcomed back by the underworld and all the types of shady business. During the Dever administration Capone and other gangsters moved their headquarters to the suburb of Cicero, but with Thompson's return they were back again in Chicago.

An "open town" during the Thompson regime meant a free rein to bootlegging, gambling, and prostitution—operating, of course, with the co-operation of police and officials. In addition, it implied widespread robberies and racketeering. So lax were the Chicago police that holdups were almost a matter of course. Racketeering, which took many forms, was mainly concerned with the operations of the underworld by which gangsters levied tribute upon labor unions, employers' organizations, and business of various types. Failure to respond to the demands brought destruction of property and sometimes bodily injury; tribute secured immunity and protection. One writer, thoroughly acquainted with Chicago in those lush days for the criminal, estimated that 50 major and 150 minor rackets flourished in the city. The loot from bootlegging, gambling, prostitution and rackets in that city was estimated at more than $100,000,000 a year. An Illinois Crime Survey, reporting in 1929, asserted that in 1926 and 1927 there were 130 gang murders in Cook County (in which Chicago is located), and not one man was punished. Not one of the murderers was apprehended!

Although gang rule and political corruption were probably no worse in New York, the situation in the nation's largest city received the greatest publicity. It may serve here as the typical example.

Just as in the days of Boss Tweed and later of Boss Croker, New York symbolized the political corruption of the sixties and the eighties, so in the 1920's the city played again the same representative role. The reasons were threefold. In the first place, its very size allowed the underworld to operate on a large scale. In the second, repeated investigations made perfectly clear the tie-up between gang rule and city government. Finally, the slimy trail of graft seemed to lead directly to the Mayor himself.

The investigations of political corruption in New York City were not inspired, as in Philadelphia, by gang murders, or by the suspected relations between political leaders and illegal liquor operators, but rather by corruption in the Magistrates' Courts. The Magistrates' Court in New York was composed of fifty-five judges who were appointed by the Mayor for ten-year terms at salaries of $10,000 a year and were distributed throughout the city. These judges presided over courts of original criminal jurisdiction. It has been part of American folklore, although the belief is not entirely based upon actual experience, that substantial justice is achieved in our courts and that members of the judiciary somehow divorce themselves from politics and business and thus carry on their duties in a quite objective manner.

When rumors reached the man in the street that

certain New York judges had bought their jobs from Tammany politicians, he was profoundly shocked. He was even more shocked when other rumors suggested that some judges in their leisure time engaged in shady business practices, and during their hours on the bench were at the beck of corrupt politicians and gangsters. Among numerous episodes that centered attention upon the Magistrates' Courts was a famous dinner given by a political club in December, 1929, to Judge Albert H. Vitale, which was rudely interrupted by seven gunmen who stripped the diners of their valuables. It appeared that among the guests honoring Vitale were seven men with police records, one of them a leading racketeer in the artichoke business. All seven had been saved at one time or another from further prosecution by being discharged in Magistrates' Courts. Another magistrate, George E. Ewald, was caught as an income tax evader and also indicted for use of the mails to defraud. The jury disagreed on the charge that he had paid a politician $10,000 for his judgeship. The disappearance in 1930 of Justice Joseph F. Crater of the Supreme Court tended to raise interest to white heat. In a grand jury inquiry an effort was made to discover whether he, too, had bought his job, and whether this might have had something to do with his disappearance.

Under public pressure the Appellate Division of

the State Supreme Court appointed Samuel Seabury as referee to conduct an investigation. In March of the following year, Governor Roosevelt named Seabury a commissioner to inquire into charges brought by the City Club of New York against District Attorney Thomas C. T. Crain. Finally in April, 1931, Seabury was appointed as the counsel to a joint committee of the state senate and assembly (the Hofstadter Committee) which had been created to investigate the various departments of government of the city of New York.

The central figure in these investigations represented the best traditions of New York culture, education, and public service. Seabury sprang from a family prominent in Colonial days. An independent Democrat in politics, he had held various elective and appointive judicial posts. A methodical, patient, and unruffled investigator, he was perfectly fair in his handling of witnesses but quite relentless in his search for the facts. After he and his able staff of younger men had finished their work, the country possessed a clear-cut picture of the interrelations of crime and politics in the great metropolis. This was accomplished, it should be added, despite every barrier that the Tammany administration under Mayor James J. Walker could erect, and against the constant opposition of minority members of the Hofstadter Committee. Moreover, at the beginning the investigations were given but slight aid by Governor Roosevelt, who had been elected with the aid of the Tammany machine.

When the report on the Magistrates' Courts was finally submitted, it revealed what Seabury accurately termed a "ludicrous caricature which parades as justice." Judgeships were found to be "plums to be distributed as rewards for services rendered by faithful party members." The same was true of the court clerks and of minor attendants. The one woman magistrate, whose conduct of the Women's Court was a parody on judicial procedure and who was later removed from office, was herself a co-district leader of the Tammany machine. It was, indeed, in her court that conditions were perhaps worst. It took little investigation to discover that respectable and innocent women were continually "framed" by policemen of the vice squad. If they allowed themselves to be fleeced by bondsmen and shyster lawyers, the case was usually quashed; otherwise, they were likely to land in jail. A certain Assistant District Attorney assigned to the Women's Court for seven years admitted that he had accepted bribes to allow some 600 cases to be thrown out. "Any time one of my cases goes out I will see that you get $25," was the bargain which this man admitted that twenty-one different lawyers had made with him.

Although helpless women were thus arrested

upon false charges and then robbed, powerful gangsters with political affiliations were able to operate with virtual immunity, while their smaller employees were often freed in the Magistrates' Courts before the case could go further. One of the simplest methods was to get the court clerks, either through political pressure or bribery, to employ Form O-14 in making out the complaint. This form was used whenever there was doubt whether the facts warranted holding the defendant; when it was presented to the magistrate, he almost invariably dismissed the case. But the magistrates themselves often cooperated in freeing such people. This role Seabury summed up in one pregnant sentence: "The selection of magistrates upon the recommendation of district leaders results in a debt from the magistrate to the political party responsible for his appointment, which he spends the rest of his term of office in repaying."

The investigation of District Attorney Crain, initiated at the request of the New York City Club, was founded on the charge that he was incompetent and inefficient, and that his office allowed crime to operate almost unchecked. Testimony showed that the District Attorney and his office had signally failed to attack in any real way the problem of the Magistrates' Courts, the racketeering so prevalent in New York at the time, certain stock-fraud causes, and individual cases of political corruption then pending in the courts. In the opinion of most unbiased observers, the inquiry fully sustained the charges of the City Club. Nevertheless, Mr. Seabury did not feel that ineffectiveness or incompetency had "been so general in scope and so gross in character that it requires the removal of the incumbent." He did, however, with stinging words, throw the blame for inefficient law enforcement back upon the electorate. "The fact that the people of the county," said he, "do not elect the best man to the position, or one who acts in the most efficient manner, is not ground for his removal. In such cases the people must suffer the consequences of their conduct. . . . Popular government can be no better than public opinion and the public conscience insist upon."

Along with the city-wide investigation, Seabury's scrutiny of the District Attorney's record helped complete the picture sketched by the investigation of the Magistrates' Courts. It was discovered that more than a hundred district leaders (both Democratic and Republican) were on the city payroll, many of them enjoying incomes far greater than their salaries—incomes which, presumably, could be accounted for only by graft. It was discovered that the law firm of which George W. Olvany, leader of Tammany Hall, was a member, practiced before the Board of Standards and Appeals (zoning), hiding its activities by having some other lawyer act as attorney of record. It was learned that political appointees dominated not only the Board of Standards and Appeals, but other municipal boards and commissions, which used their power to grant special favors and promote the private interests of favored politicians. It was found that the North German Lloyd had paid $50,000 in "lawyers' fees" to obtain the lease of a city pier, a process which should not have cost them a cent. An intimate connection was demonstrated between crooked politicians and the illegal manufacture of liquor, and between politicians and gambling.

The investigation disclosed that Tammany, as in bygone years, still engaged in election frauds. Its vote was padded by "floaters," "repeaters," and fraudulent counting. Its strength was also maintained by channeling unemployment relief only to those who were loyal supporters. Its political clubs were in many instances simply gambling joints protected by political influence. The corruption revealed in Tammany-dominated New York, unfortunately, was by no means peculiar to that city or that decade. Moreover, it was found to have been practiced with equal readiness in New York by Democratic and Republican politicians. Nothing could illustrate this fact better than the deal put through in 1931 by the bosses of the Second Judicial District, under which seven Democratic and five Republican Supreme Court judgeships "were bargained for over the counter like so many sacks of wheat."

It was the discovery that the popular Mayor Walker was implicated in the scandals, however, that drove home the seriousness of the situation and the need for drastic correctives. After fifteen years in the state legislature, where he had gained reputation as an efficient minority leader and a man who could always be trusted to follow the dictates of the machine, Walker was promoted by Tammany in 1925 to the mayoralty. He soon enjoyed a reputation as a "man about town," more interested in night clubs than meetings of the Board of Estimate or any other city business. During his tenure the city was "wide open"; political corruption and racketeering flourishing as never before. The "Tweed Ring" of a half century earlier had built parks and made some contribution to the city along with their loot; the Tammany machine under Walker contented itself with unadorned graft.

As the Seabury investigators pushed their search, they discovered facts which seemed to implicate the Mayor. Among them were circumstances surrounding the award of a franchise to the Equitable Coach Company to operate buses in certain parts of New York. This concern had been formed by a group of bus and tire manufacturers of Ohio, who hoped for enormous profits as New York turned

from streetcars to buses. They succeeded in inducing Walker himself to press their franchise upon
the Board of Estimate, despite the fact that the
Equitable Coach Company had no adequate financial backing. Although the State Transit Commission later refused to validate the franchise, the
Mayor had meanwhile received a letter of credit
for $10,000 from an agent of the company to finance
a trip to Europe. Seabury also showed that for no
apparent reason the Mayor had received $26,000
in bonds from J. A. Sisto, head of a brokerage concern interested in taxicab companies, just before a
Board of Taxicab Control was to be appointed by
the Mayor—a board whose power would be considerable. It was discovered that another brokerage
firm interested in a taxicab company had bought
from the Mayor's financial agent, Russell T. Sherwood, stocks for which they had paid $22,000 more
than the market price.

Sinister as all this seemed, what really drove
Walker from office was his readiness to accept gifts
from friends—whose generosity suddenly developed
after he took office. The largest donation brought
to light was a present of $246,000 from Paul Block,
a newspaper publisher. The Mayor, of course, had
explanations, but they hardly satisfied even the
most tolerant listeners. It was the unexplained millions which evidently passed through the hands of
Russell T. Sherwood, a man with a $10,000 salary,

that ended Walker's political career. Although Sherwood and the Mayor had a joint safe-deposit box and Sherwood took care of the Mayor's personal finances, Walker asserted that the bank accounts were Sherwood's money and not his own. When Sherwood was subpoenaed to appear before the legislative committee, he fled to Mexico. As presumably he had nothing to conceal except his relations with the Mayor, his disappearance could bear but one interpretation.

All these facts and more were presented in the form of charges to Governor Roosevelt on June 8, 1932. The Governor submitted the specifications to Mayor Walker and requested an answer. After thirty-five days, the mayor replied, denying the charges and questioning the jurisdiction of the Governor over matters which occurred during the Mayor's first term. Roosevelt allowed Seabury to reply, and then opened hearings to determine whether the facts warranted removal of the Mayor. Walker appeared but applied for an injunction to restrain the Governor from going on with the removal proceedings. Failing in this, he abruptly resigned (September 1, 1932); and Tammany significantly refused to renominate him.

Although the reforms emanating from the Seabury exposures were by no means as far-reaching as many New Yorkers desired, they were not without value. Some of the worst magistrates either resigned or, like the Sheriff of New York County, were ousted. So discredited was Tammany that it lost control of the city when a coalition candidate, Fiorella LaGuardia, was elected mayor in 1933. One recommendation of the Hofstadter Committee, that the charter be revised to provide for a single legislative chamber elected by proportional representation, was accepted by the voters in 1936. A year earlier Governor Lehman appointed Thomas E. Dewey as special prosecutor to investigate crime, and some of the worst of the gang rackets in New York were broken up.

While political corruption has been common in American cities, it has rarely penetrated into high Federal offices. During the twenties, however, even the Federal Government did not escape. President Harding himself was honest. Although Senate investigations combed far and wide, not the faintest stain of financial corruption ever touched him. Nevertheless, he was in part responsible for the scandals of his Administration; for a better choice of assistants and a more vigilant supervision would have gone far to safeguard the public interest. To Harding, an intensely human man, the chief satisfaction of his Presidency was the opportunity to do favors to old friends and political helpers. Although he realized that the responsibility for efficient and honest government rested in his hands, he believed his appointments were good, and expected his followers to render loyal and honest service to the nation. In this he was wrong.

When Harding's Cabinet was first announced, criticism was directed mainly toward Hays and Daugherty, the first a political, and the second essentially a personal, choice. Hays, however, turned out to be an excellent public official. Despite the fact that Harding had issued an order shifting 13,000 postmasterships from the protection of civil service regulations, Hays refused to allow his department to fall into the hands of spoilsmen. When he resigned after twelve months and was succeeded by Dr. Hubert Work, the Post Office Department deteriorated rapidly. But with Daugherty the story is different. When this Ohio lawyer became Attorney-General he was a poor man, heavily in debt; when he resigned four years later, he was affluent. Federal prosecutors failed to convict him, but there were few Americans who did not believe that he had used his position to enrich himself. Secretary of the Interior Fall, as highly regarded by the Senate as by Harding, accepted bribes for leasing rich Government oil lands to private companies.

Many of Harding's lesser appointments were as bad as those of Daugherty and Fall. In some instances he merely placed little men in big jobs; in others, he gave office to outright thieves. One group of officeholders, most of them personal and political cronies, the nation soon dubbed the "Ohio

Gang." At its head was the Attorney-General. Others included Daniel R. Crissenger, a small-town Marion banker, first given the post of Controller of the Treasury and then promoted to be Governor of the Federal Reserve; Edward F. Scoby, a former county sheriff who became Director of the Mint; and the Reverend Heber H. Votaw, brother-in-law of the President and former Seventh Day Adventist missionary to Burma, who became Superintendent of Federal Prisons (after that office had been removed from the civil service list by executive order). Doctor Charles E. Sawyer, a Marion physician brought to Washington as the White House physician with the rank of Brigadier-General, proved a man of integrity. Among other outstanding members of the "Ohio Gang" were E. Mont Riley, whose governorship of Puerto Rico was largely a series of scandals; Albert J. Lasker, an advertising agent who was made Chairman of the United States Shipping Board; and Elmer Dover, Assistant Secretary of the Treasury, whose wholesale introduction of the spoils system shocked even hardened politicians. Among the most disreputable of the gang were Colonel Charles R. Forbes, whose monumental corruption in the Veterans Bureau shook the Administration to its depths; Jesse Smith, personal handy man of Harry Daugherty; and William J. Burns, who in the words of Samuel Hopkins Adams, was "to turn the Federal Bureau of Investigation into a medium of political blackmail and oppression."

The "hang-out" of the Ohio Gang was the "little Green House on K Street" (1625 K Street), rented by a couple of the more shady members. "It was," says Adams, "a port of call for big liquor operators, office-buyers, jobbers in bribery, and all the sorry, furtive drift of the political underworld." It was also a place where Senators, Congressmen, and Cabinet members could drop in for a poker game or a drink from stock confiscated by the Government. And it was the place where certain of the Ohio Gang "traded in liquor withdrawal permits, protection to bootleggers, appointments to office, illegal concessions, immunity from prosecution, pardons, paroles, privileges, and general graft." *

Although Daugherty insisted that he never visited the "Little Green House," it is obvious that connections between that rendezvous and the Department of Justice must have been close. The type of business which went on there necessitated it. The go-between was Jesse Smith, who lived with Daugherty and maintained an office in the Department of Justice, but spent much of his time on K Street. All indications pointed to questionable practices in the Department. The affluence of the inside men at K Street, the sudden prosperity of

* Samuel Hopkins Adams, *Incredible Era* (Boston, Houghton Mifflin Company, 1939), p. 235.

Daugherty's former law firm, the type of cases prosecuted and those that were not, the problem of illegal withdrawals of alcohol, and the whole pardon situation gave cause for suspicion.

One of the most disgraceful activities of the Department of Justice during Daugherty's regime was furnished by the Federal Bureau of Investigation under Burns. Officially an agency for the detection of crime, it became also a medium for blackmail and a weapon against law and order. Its most widely publicized member was Gaston B. Means, a professional criminal. Any official who became dangerous to the Attorney-General or the Administration was promptly investigated. The senior LaFollette, whose motion initiated the investigation of the oil scandals, had his office looted by Government operatives under the direction of Burns. Senator Walsh had no sooner opened the investigation than Government detectives were combing Montana to dig up something that would injure him. When Senator Wheeler was beginning an investigation of the Department of Justice, Burns's agents were again in Montana trying to work up a flimsy case. That the Department of Justice sank to its lowest depths under Daugherty is a judgment that few would question.

The Attorney-General ran his most serious risk of jail in the prosecution resulting from the case of the American Metal Company. This corporation, taken over during the war by the Alien Property Custodian as German property, was sold for $6,000,000, which accrued interest brought in 1921 to about $7,000,000. Late that year there appeared in New York a German by the name of Richard Merton, claiming that ownership had passed before the war from the Germans to a neutral Swiss corporation which he represented. The transfer, he said, was oral, so that little evidence existed to substantiate it. Merton was able to make contacts with Jesse Smith and with Thomas W. Miller, the Alien Property Custodian. Although the claim was too flimsy for serious consideration, Miller in record-breaking time recommended transfer of the property to the alleged Swiss owners and Daugherty approved it. When Merton departed for Europe with more than $6,000,000, he left $441,000 with John T. King (a leader high in Republican politics), mostly in Liberty Bonds. Of these, $49,000 were traced to Miller, who in 1927 was sent to jail for eighteen months and fined $5,000. Another block of bonds amounting to $40,000 or more was traced to a bank at Washington Court House, Ohio, headed by Daugherty's brother. Here they had been deposited in a political account directed by the Attorney-General, but were used by his henchman, Smith, and labeled "Jesse Smith Extra No. 3." When Daugherty was tried for conspiracy to defraud the Government, the jury disagreed.

By that time (1927) the bank records had been destroyed, King and Smith were dead, and an assistant to the Attorney-General took full responsibility for the transfer of the property. Skillfully clouding the issue by intimating that his friendship for Harding silenced him, Daugherty refused to testify.

Of all the crooks who found their way to Washington during these years none was more flamboyant in his robberies than Charles R. Forbes, Director of the Veterans Bureau. Harding had met him while on a Senatorial junket to Hawaii and had been easily taken in by his glib tongue and genial personality. After turning down several Government positions, Forbes accepted the appointment to the Veterans Bureau. No sooner was he established than he persuaded Harding to transfer to his jurisdiction the building of Veterans' Hospitals. By padding construction and supply contracts, Forbes diverted considerable amounts to himself. He obtained further graft by selling, without bids, army surpluses at values far below their true worth. The swath of high living cut by the Director should have made even the most naïve observer suspicious, but it was almost two years before Sawyer and Daugherty were certain enough of Forbes's peculations to tell the President. It was hard to convince Harding of his friend's dishonesty, but evidence piled up, and Forbes resigned in February,

1923. The legal adviser of the Bureau, Charles F. Cramer, himself probably innocent of wrongdoing, committed suicide. A Senate investigation revealed much of the sorry mess, and a Federal Court in 1925 found Forbes guilty of conspiracy to defraud, sentencing him to two years in Leavenworth and a $10,000 fine. Those who followed the investigation closely believed that Forbes had stolen or squandered approximately a quarter of a billion dollars.

Most damaging of the scandals involving the Harding Administration were those in the lease of naval oil reserves. It took Senator Walsh many months of arduous labor to dig out the facts, but when finally revealed they were simple and clear. To safeguard the Navy in any future emergency, President Taft by executive orders in 1912 had set aside 38,000 acres in the Elk Hills district of California (Naval Oil Reserve No. 1) and 29,000 acres in the Buena Vista Hills. In similar manner President Wilson in 1915 had set aside 9,500 acres to create Naval Reserve No. 3 at Teapot Dome, Wyoming. In 1920 a General Leasing Act was passed by Congress to permit the Secretary of the Navy to grant leases within the reserves if they were needed to protect the interests of the Government. The Harding Administration was hardly in the saddle before Secretary Fall had drafted an executive order transferring the oil reserves from the Navy Department to the Interior, had obtained the approval of Secretary of the Navy Denby, and in May, 1921, gained the signature of Harding. Stupid but honest, Denby accompanied his approval with a letter to the President stating the opposition of some of the Navy's officers. These documents were coolly suppressed by Fall and were never seen by the President. Harding's executive order modified the General Leasing Act, and it is more than doubtful if he had a Constitutional right to issue it. Said Senator Walsh: "I have repeatedly asserted before the committee that, in my opinion, the leases are utterly void for want of power or by reason of the exercise of undelegated power on the part of officers of the government who purported to execute the leases."

Albert Bacon Fall, the central figure in the oil tragedy, had come to Washington in 1913 as Senator from New Mexico. With his broad-brimmed hat, flowing tie, bronzed skin and alert blue eyes, he gave the impression of a forthright son of the open West. People associated him with ranching and mining, although his main occupation for years had been office-holding. He had been a member of the New Mexico legislature, attorney-general of that territory, and a justice of its Supreme Court. With the general run of Senators he was popular as a good fellow, loyal to his own group and party machine. When nominated for the Cabinet he was given the rare honor of a *viva voce* confirmation.

With the oil reserves in the hands of the Department of the Interior, Fall leased the Teapot Dome reserve secretly and without other bids to Harry F. Sinclair on April 7, 1922. In like manner, by two leases dated April 7 and December 11, 1922, Fall turned over to his friend, Edward M. Doheny (dominant figure in the Pan-American Petroleum and Transport Company), the entire Elk Hills Reserve. Three months later, March 4, 1923, he resigned as Secretary of the Interior.

The secrecy with which these valuable oil properties were surrendered to private exploitation aroused the suspicion of the elder LaFollette. He obtained from the Senate (April 26, 1922) authority for an investigation, which was directed by Senator Thomas J. Walsh. Walsh, says Mark Sullivan, "had an emotion of affection for integrity." He also had persistence, and was finally able to prove that before the leases were signed Fall had received an unsecured cash loan of $100,000 from Doheny; two loans from Sinclair to the amount of $71,000; and Liberty Bonds from the same source amounting to $230,000. Fall's sudden prosperity proved his undoing. On the stand everybody concerned had plausible explanations. Fall leased the reserves, he said, because the oil was being drained off to adjoining lands (this was contradicted by experts). The $100,000 delivered in cash in a little black satchel, said Doheny, was simply a loan to an old friend; while the lavish payments by Sinclair were merely to purchase a third interest in the Fall ranch.

The explanations could not obscure the bitter fact that a Cabinet officer had been guilty of corruption. "Therefore," said Senator Caraway, "we are faced with this humiliating situation that for the first time in the history of America, as far as I know—and I hope it will be the last time—a Cabinet officer betrayed the high trust imposed in him, and for a corrupt consideration sold the very means by which our national existence is to be protected."

As a result of these investigations the Senate demanded prosecution by the Government, but refused to allow it to be conducted by the distrusted Department of Justice. President Coolidge eventually appointed two able lawyers, Owen J. Roberts and Atlee Pomerene, who pushed the cases vigorously. The rest of the story is interesting chiefly as a commentary on the courts. Fall and Sinclair were indicted for conspiracy, as were Fall and Doheny. Doheny was also indicted for bribery. In a series of trials Fall and Doheny were acquitted of the conspiracy charge, and so were Fall and Sinclair. Doheny was likewise acquitted of bribery, but Fall was found guilty of receiving a bribe from him, and sentenced to a year in prison with a fine of $100,000. Although nobody was adjudged guilty of conspiracy, the Supreme Court held that the leases were the product of fraud and corruption, canceled them, and returned what was left of the property to the Government. Neither of the two major actors, Sinclair and Doheny, was found guilty of the alleged crimes. Sinclair, however, spent three months in jail for contempt in refusing to answer certain questions asked by the committee, and later another six months for contempt for employing the William J. Burns detective agency to shadow the jurors when he was called to trial with Fall. During the investigation Denby resigned to save embarrassment to the Coolidge Administration.

Before the Senate Committee finished its work, oil had spattered far and wide. Irritated at one point in his testimony, Doheny had truculently boasted that he employed for their influence many ex-Government officials, including three of Wilson's Cabinet officers. These employees, the most prominent of whom was William G. McAdoo, retained at $25,000 a year, had severed all connections with the Government, but their situation was nevertheless embarrassing. One of the most interesting bits of information brought out by the investigation had to do with the operations of the Continental Trading Company, Ltd., of Canada. This was organized by Sinclair and three other prominent oil men to buy oil and then sell it to their own companies at a profit. The profits, amounting to about $3,000,000, were divided among the four in the form of Liberty Bonds. Whether this fund was originally established for political purposes is not clear. It was from Sinclair's share of the booty, nevertheless, that the bonds came which reached Fall. It was also from Sinclair's share that $185,000 in Liberty Bonds was "loaned" (later some $100,-000 of it was returned) to help make up the deficit of the Republican National Committee. The situation of the party was not improved by the mess which Will H. Hays, former Chairman of the committee, made in trying to explain the "loans."

Even to the most superficial student of American history, the likeness between the tone of the Grant Administration and that of Harding is striking. In the Grant regime the great crusade for political and humanitarian reforms degenerated into a Republican effort to capture Southern votes and offices; in the Harding Administration the quest for social justice was blocked by the defeat of the steel strike, the Palmer raids, and the decisions of a reactionary Supreme Court. As, in the time of Grant, Americans turned from war ideals to devote themselves to a more intensive conquest of the West and the exploitation of raw materials, so in the Harding period Americans turned to reap the economic rewards of a great boom era. In both

Administrations the country had an honest President, but one who was too loyal to dubious friends and incapable of picking honest and efficient public officers. Under both Presidents we find the same inefficiency, the same corruption, and the same scandals.

Which Administration represented the more deplorable descent in public morals it is difficult to say. On the whole, it was probably Harding's. But what is far more significant and important is the fact that public resentment and protest were much less vigorous under Harding than under Grant. Few important Republican leaders and few of the great Republican newspapers rose in horror in the twenties to denounce the venality of their own party and the bribers who had corrupted it. Democrats, of course, attempted to make the most of the scandals, but they failed to arouse any large part of the electorate during the campaign of 1924. The Republicans soon sank back into a smug complacency, thankful that nothing worse had happened. In combination, the post-war disillusionment and the great prosperity had apparently done something to dull the moral sensibility of the nation.

CHAPTER VII

FROM HARDING TO COOLIDGE

In the late spring of 1923 Harding determined to
seek a much-needed vacation by a trip to Alaska.
Republican reversals in the mid-term election of
1922, which had lost the party 69 seats in the
House and 7 in the Senate, seemed a reflection on
his Administration. The last session of the Sixty-
seventh Congress, which had closed on March 3,
had been particularly unproductive. It had passed
the Capper Agricultural Credits Act, and, at the
President's request, an act to refund the British
debt. On the other hand, Harding had felt bound
to veto the bonus bill, and Congress had rejected
his plea that the United States join the World
Court. The session had been distinctly disappoint-
ing. Beyond mere political reversals, however, lay
other worries which weighed heavily upon the President. He was shaken by the treachery and corruption of Forbes, and by the suicide of two other
friends, Cramer and Smith. By this time he had
begun to realize that both Fall, who had recently

resigned, and Daugherty, along with others of the "Ohio Gang," had compromised his Administration in a way that might prove disastrous. Early in the trip he made the revealing remark to William Allen White that his enemies gave him little trouble; his chief worry was his friends. The President was despondent and his health breaking.

The trip to Alaska was also to be a "voyage of understanding." It was to provide Harding with an opportunity to feel out the mood of the nation by personal contact and to present his ideas in preparation for a campaign for reelection. Speeches were prepared on various subjects and delivered as the party traveled across the continent—speeches always urbane and serious, but usually inconsequential. Many, nevertheless, saw in them a groping for new social concepts and an attitude that transcended mere party politics. Instead of furnishing rest, as the President had hoped, the trip made new demands on his waning strength. Between June 2 and July 31 he made eighty-five speeches, an average of more than two a day. By the time the party left Alaska and reached Seattle, he was obviously a very ill man. Despite the advice of physicians and friends, however, he insisted on completing the scheduled program.

An attack at Seattle of what appeared to be indigestion, but was probably a symptom of heart disease, was followed by pneumonia at San Francisco. From this the President rallied successfully, only to succumb to a heart ailment which for months had undermined his strength. On the evening of August 2, Mrs. Harding was reading the President an article in the *Saturday Evening Post* by Samuel G. Blythe, "A Calm Review of a Calm Man." It was an appreciative appraisal of Harding, and he listened with interest. Mrs. Harding paused to assure herself that he was not getting overtired. "That's good," said the President, "go on. Read some more." As he spoke, a sudden change came over his face and he slumped into the pillows. Death was instantaneous. Physicians ascribed it to cerebral embolism and there is no evidence to countenance the subsequent rumors of suicide or poisoning. Those best able to know the facts have discarded them as fantastic. The death certificate was signed by five physicians of the highest personal and professional integrity.*

Sincere sorrow followed the news of Harding's death. By the man in the street he was understood, and to some extent beloved. The public recognized in him an ordinary man, without particular ability, but well meaning and anxious to serve the

* Dr. Ray Lyman Wilbur, President of Stanford University and one-time President of the American Medical Association; Dr. Charles M. Cooper, an eminent heart specialist; Dr. Charles E. Sawyer, the President's personal physician; Dr. Joel T. Boone, a distinguished Navy physician, and Dr. Hubert Work, then Secretary of the Interior.

nation. Much more than most Presidents, he had been a man of the people. Except for the dereliction of Forbes, the political corruption that was later to blacken the memory of his Administration was not yet generally known. Little evidence exists to show that Republican leaders were greatly dissatisfied with their choice. He was the type of President they had intentionally picked. National leaders in many walks of life had commended the first two years of his Administration, and journalists of experience and ability had praised his efforts.

It was only as one revelation of corruption after another came to light that the popular estimate of Harding and his Administration declined. For the low level of political morality during these years, however, the blame must be distributed. Some of it belongs to Harding himself. A man of many fine personal qualifications, including honesty, loyalty, sincerity, and kindliness, he had little political or executive ability. He possessed neither the background nor education to understand the world in which he lived; he lacked the capacity for hard mental effort necessary to master important domestic and foreign problems. Deficient in the ability to accumulate data upon which wise decisions might be made, he was also without moral courage to make up his mind and stick to it. Irresolute and overanxious to please, he was pushed about almost at will by friends and associates with stronger minds. In brief, he was a small man in a big job and he knew it.

It was Daugherty who had persuaded Harding to be a candidate for the nomination, and it was the Senate cabal which had secured the nomination. This was a mistake, but the Senators were tired of being ruled by a strong-minded President who believed that the chief executive should play the role of a prime minister. To the people who elected him by a majority of almost seven million Harding evidently personified some idea that they liked; probably a relief from eight years of crusading and a return to quiet and normalcy. What Senators and voters apparently asked for, Harding tried to give them. If the Senate wanted a follower rather than a leader, that is what Harding believed they should have. He abdicated the position of prime minister which Roosevelt and Wilson had assumed, and let Congress, in general, run itself. Only by placing strong men in the State, Treasury, and Commerce Departments did he notably challenge the supremacy of the legislative branch. Certainly, the State Department under Hughes was not dominated by the Senate, nor were the Departments of Commerce and Treasury under the thumb of Congress.

The trouble with Harding's conception of government was that it failed to meet the nation's needs. Without leadership Congress never accomplishes much, and it is seldom able to supply its own leadership. In the early twenties this legislative incapacity was accentuated. Former leaders were passing away. Penrose and Knox died in 1921. Others were old and losing their grip. What aggressiveness and leadership the Senate had was largely exhibited by LaFollette and the farm bloc; but since this bloc was in the minority, the leadership accomplished little. No one could logically complain of the situation. The desire of the nation as reflected in the 1920 election appeared to be a return to normalcy. This meant no bold or far-sighted policies; it meant getting rid of as much of the Wilson legislation as seemed desirable. Harding may have been quite incapable of leading a difficult program of reconstruction legislation, but such a program apparently was not wanted.

But though Congress under Harding was concerned chiefly with a return to old conditions, the Administration did not stand still. It made a number of important decisions which set a pattern for the decade. The Fordney-McCumber Tariff set the nation back on the road to high protection, where it had been before the Wilson interlude. Reduction of taxation was to be expected, but under Mellon and Harding a decision was made in favor of a special type of reduction—favoring chiefly the higher income brackets. Economy in government was a constant Administration demand. With respect to Allied debts, a firm policy was established. As for the veterans, Congress adopted a liberal program of care for the disabled, although the President consistently opposed a bonus. Price-fixing of agricultural commodities was relinquished, but other aids to the farmer were favored, the most important legislation passed under Harding being the Capper Agricultural Credits Act. The long fight for adequate immigration restriction culminated in the quota system. Restoration of the merchant marine under private ownership was attempted. Federal aid to interstate road-building was continued, and for the first time grants were made to the states for maternity and infancy care. In foreign affairs the Washington Conference, with its reduction of naval armaments and its Far Eastern treaties, blocked out new policies.

Such in brief is the record of the Harding Administration. Whatever may be the verdict of history as to its success or failure, there can be no doubt that it formulated the policies of the decade. The initiative for these policies undoubtedly came chiefly from Hughes, Mellon, and Hoover, but the President gave them the prestige of his high office. When Coolidge entered the White House, he announced that he would follow the policies of his predecessor and he meant it. Little or no change took place. Any final judgment of Harding and his Administration must in the end rest essentially upon the validity of the domestic and foreign policies established during his two years in office and closely followed by Coolidge and Hoover.

At the time of Harding's death, Coolidge was spending his vacation at his father's farmhouse in the tiny village of Plymouth, Vermont. Newspapermen in near-by towns, picking up the news by telephone shortly after midnight, raced to Plymouth to inform the new President. Aroused by his father, Coolidge dressed and descended to the living room to meet the waiting reporters. Satisfied that the report was correct, he called his secretary into an adjoining room and dictated to the nation the following message:

Reports have reached me, which I fear are correct, that President Harding is gone. The world has lost a great and good man. I mourn his loss. He was my Chief and friend.

It will be my purpose to carry out the policies which he has begun for the service of the American people and for meeting their responsibilities wherever they may arise.

For the purpose I shall seek the cooperation of all those who have been associated with the President during his term of office. Those who have given their efforts to assist him I wish to remain in office that they may assist me. I have faith that God will direct the destinies of our nation.

While reporters hurried to the nearest towns to file their stories, the telephone company set up a temporary wire to connect Plymouth with the outside world. After talking to Secretary Hughes in Washington, Coolidge found a copy of the Constitution, turned to his father, a notary public, and asked him to administer the oath. There in the farmhouse living room, lighted by oil lamps, and with the family Bible resting on a marble-topped table beside him, Calvin Coolidge took the oath of office. Witnesses of this simple ceremony were his wife, secretary, chauffeur, and four others who had just arrived. Later in the morning, he left for Washington.

What kind of man the new President was, few people knew. Although Coolidge had won some fame at the time of the Boston police strike and during the campaign of 1920, soon after arriving in Washington he had sunk into the customary obscurity of a Vice-President. His official duties as presiding officer of the Senate he had performed efficiently, and his unofficial social duties he had endured punctiliously and unhappily. Most Washingtonians thought of him as a taciturn, tight-fisted Yankee, a shy man devoid of personal charm and without influence. A survival from an earlier social era, he was interesting chiefly as a "museum piece," transported to Washington by some curious quirk of fate. He made some speeches, to be sure, while Vice-President, but few read them and they revealed little. More closely integrated than the florid addresses of Harding, they were even more platitudinous, if possible, in their exposition of the obvious.

Even after six years in the White House the masses found it difficult to appraise Coolidge. To some he seemed to represent the fundamental greatness of a Lincoln, to others he was merely a dull, cold, and reactionary politician. His virtues were of a negative rather than positive type—thrift, honesty, caution, simple morality; virtues which a spendthrift and confused age preferred to honor rather than practice. The newspapers quickly played up the idiosyncrasies of the Vermont farm lad who found himself in the White House. Devoid of the usual arts of the politician and reserved in speech and writing, he was incapable of stirring utterance or inspired leadership. He had none of the attributes of popularity, yet he was one of the most popular Presidents the nation has had. This popularity, it is true, was to a considerable extent due to the current prosperity, and to the excellent press relations which Coolidge was able to maintain. But some of it was attributable to his political capacity. A shrewd, clever, ambitious, and not always scrupulous politician, Coolidge had the consummate art of keeping out of trouble. If by mischance he got into it, he usually emerged the gainer.

He succeeded in persuading the voters that he was conscientious, sound, and trustworthy.

No better evidence of the political acumen of Coolidge is needed than a brief recital of his career. Born at Plymouth, Vermont, in 1872, he graduated from Amherst in 1895 and read law for two years in the neighboring town of Northampton. Whether Coolidge would have developed into either an office or trial lawyer we shall never know; before he had built up a sizable practice, he turned to politics. Far more a professional politician than Harding, Coolidge began as a Northampton councilman, and then moved up the ladder as city solicitor, representative in the legislature, Mayor, state Senator, Lieutenant-Governor, and Governor. Quiet, close-lipped, and tightly allied to the Republican state machine, headed by W. Murray Crane, he won the confidence of both voters and Republican bosses.

It was the Boston police strike that made Coolidge a national figure. Except for that he would have bloomed for a day like hundreds of governors, and then in all probability faded into provincial obscurity. In protest against low wages and unfavorable working conditions, the policemen's organization of Boston joined the American Federation of Labor on August 15, 1919. This action was taken in defiance of Edwin U. Curtis, the Police Commissioner. Curtis immediately put nineteen leaders of the union on trial for violation of his orders; the union responded by threatening a strike if their leaders were discharged. The Boston Police Commissioner is appointed by the Governor, and the Mayor has no control over the Department. Nevertheless, Mayor Andrew J. Peters, who understood the situation better than any of the other government officials involved, appointed a citizens' committee under James J. Storrow to investigate and report. The Storrow Committee recommended a compromise; the policemen were to continue their long-established independent organization, withdraw from the A. F. of L. without prejudice, and arbitrate their differences with the city. Curtis refused to accept these recommendations or subsequent pleas of the Committee. The union officers were placed on trial, found guilty, and suspended. On Tuesday, September 9, by a vote of 1,134 to 2, the policemen walked out.

Few preparations for the strike had been made and during the night there was some violence, looting, and destruction of property. On Wednesday the Mayor, informed of a statute which empowered him to call out the state militia in the city, took charge of the situation. The militia were called out and a request made to the Governor for three additional regiments. Coolidge immediately complied. The situation, however, was so well in hand by Thursday morning that thereafter there was little danger. That afternoon, nevertheless, the Governor suddenly took control of the affairs away from the Mayor, called out the National Guard, and telegraphed the Secretary of War for aid in case of a general strike. A protest from Gompers received Saturday elicited the famous answer: "There is no right to strike against the public safety by anybody, any time, anywhere."

Although Coolidge emerged from the police strike a national hero, his conduct during the affair was by no means heroic. All kinds of personal, economic, and political cross-currents, it is true, were at play, and they make a fair appraisal difficult. Certain facts, nevertheless, seem clear. In the first place, a forthright statement at any moment up to the time the strike was called, either approving of arbitration or definitely upholding the position of Curtis, might have prevented the strike and loss of property. At no time during the days of heated controversy did Coolidge give the slightest aid in solving the situation. Not only did he remain away from Boston on his vacation during the days when trouble was brewing, but he deliberately absented himself from the city during the hectic hours from Saturday to Monday. Despite the certainty of a strike on Tuesday and the fact that the Police Commissioner was his own appointee, Coolidge preferred to dodge the responsibility of calling out the troops, and to throw it

upon the Democratic Mayor. The Mayor, likewise, uncertain of his power and not anxious to
assume the responsibility evaded by the Governor,
delayed until Wednesday. As a matter of fact, a
call from either Governor or Mayor for the National Guard on Tuesday night would have quickly
ended the violence.

When the violence was over and the situation
under control, Coolidge jumped in on Thursday
afternoon with his high-sounding proclamation to
take the glory. The nation acclaimed him for
breaking the strike and restoring order. Actually,
he did neither. His own explanation in his *Autobiography* was that he "did not see how it was
possible to arbitrate the question of the authority
of the law, or of the necessity of obedience to the
rules of the Department and the orders of the Commissioner." * Many interpretations of the Boston
police strike have been offered. Of them all the
most fantastic was the one suggested by Coolidge
himself in his *Autobiography*. "Just what lay behind the event," he wrote, "I was never able to
learn. Sometimes I have mistrusted that it was a
design to injure me politically; if so it was only
to recoil upon the perpetrators for it increased my
political power many fold." †

* *The Autobiography of Calvin Coolidge*, p. 128. Copyright 1929
by Calvin Coolidge and reprinted by permission of Rinehart and
Company, Inc., Publishers.

† *Ibid.*, p. 141.

Coolidge's refusal to take any action in the Boston police strike until the crisis had virtually passed illustrates the outstanding feature of his political character. Congenitally, he hated to be rushed and disliked to take any action or commit himself until absolutely necessary. Walter Lippmann, one of the ablest political commentators of the period, recognized this. "Mr. Coolidge's genius for inactivity," he wrote, "is developed to a very high point. It is far from being an indolent inactivity. It is a grim, determined, alert inactivity which keeps Mr. Coolidge occupied constantly. . . . Inactivity is a political philosophy and a party program with Mr. Coolidge." This statement is somewhat exaggerated, but it does point to a trait which goes far to explain the lack of important action during the six years of Coolidge's Administration. His philosophy was not only to let well enough alone, but also to let ill enough alone.

Another factor which explains the legislative aridity of these years was the essential politico-economic conservatism of the new President. His political faith, insists Gamaliel Bradford, "grew to be that of the mid-nineteenth century, the optimistic ideal of Democracy as the final solution of all problems and cure of all evils." His economic faith seemed to be derived with few modifications from Alexander Hamilton. "It can hardly be said," adds Bradford, "that Calvin Coolidge had much to

do with the twentieth century." Coolidge's faith in
the essential soundness of the economic and political system was as profound as that of Hoover or
Mellon. The corruption rapidly coming to light
was in his mind only the evil work of dishonest
men, not in any way the product of the system.
When Coolidge became President (writes William
Allen White),

he pitchforked the muck of oil and petty graft from
the Augean stables of the White House, but he let in,
all smartly frock-coated . . . another crew which was
to devastate the country more terribly than Harding's
greasy playfellows. All the day the friends and emis-
saries of Krueger, the match king, Wiggin, the Wizard,
Mitchell, the manipulator, Doherty, the monarch of
gas, the Morgans, the Rockefellers, and Mellon in
person, the bad and the good, unchecked and unidenti-
fied, sat at his council table.*

To the liberals, the accession of Coolidge seemed
as great a catastrophe as that of Harding. In an
editorial on Harding's death the *Nation* sharply
expressed their point of view:

And now the Presidency sinks low, indeed. We doubt
if ever before it has fallen into the hands of a man so
cold, so narrow, so reactionary, so uninspiring, and so
unenlightened, or one who has done less to earn it,

* William Allen White, *A Puritan in Babylon* (New York, Macmillan Co., 1939), p. 294.

than Calvin Coolidge. . . . Every reactionary may today rejoice; in Calvin Coolidge he realizes his ideal, and every liberal may be correspondingly downcast.

If liberalism was dejected, not so with finance and business. When the scepter passed from Harding to Coolidge, there was hardly a ripple in Wall Street. The new President was recognized at once as the "high priest of stability." Under Coolidge there would be no rocking of the boat.

For the moment there was no change in the official family at Washington. Harding's Cabinet continued, and Coolidge made no effort at the time to get rid of Denby or Daugherty, who were bound to embarrass his Administration. He insisted that dismissal of these men would be a reflection on the previous Administration. He was more than half-convinced, as was Chief Justice Taft, that the oil investigation was a Democratic conspiracy to blacken the Republicans. Never did the new President denounce the culprits or give comfort to those trying to convict them. On the contrary, he sometimes appeared to be shielding them. A Senate resolution in February, 1924, urging the dismissal of Denby, was rejected as an interference with the Constitutional responsibilities of the President. Denby, however, soon resigned. Late in March, Coolidge finally asked for the resignation of Daugherty, not because he had been remiss in office but because he had refused to open certain files to a Congressional Committee. To the Navy Department the President appointed Chief Justice Curtis D. Wilbur of the California Supreme Court and, to the Department of Justice, Harlan F. Stone, Dean of the Columbia Law School. Stone, who was later (1925) named to the Supreme Court upon the resignation of Joseph McKenna, was perhaps the best appointment made by Coolidge during his six years as President.

So far as policies were concerned, his first annual message, sent to the Sixty-eighth Congress in December, might as well have been written by Harding, favoring as it did economy in Governmental expenditures, the World Court, Mellon's tax reduction plan, prohibition enforcement, the transfer of shipping to private ownership, consolidation of railroads, and abolition of tax-exempt securities. Like his predecessor, Coolidge opposed cancellation of war debts, the soldiers' bonus, and any effort to reach the root of the agricultural malady. Congress received his message, carrying thirty-three items of suggested legislation, with a coldness never displayed toward Harding. Four months later not a single executive proposal had been acted on favorably, while measures which Coolidge opposed were passed. Opposition to the World Court, led by Lodge, prevented American membership in that body. Coolidge's pet policy of economy was flouted by two pension measures. He vetoed both, but the Bonus Bill, involving an estimated cost of $3,500,-000,000, was passed over his veto. The Japanese exclusion clause was kept in the Immigration Act despite his pronounced opposition. Here Coolidge took a far more statesmanlike position than Congress. Finally, the "Mellon Plan" for taxation, recommended by the President, was rejected by Congress in favor of a compromise plan.

This Mellon Plan had called for reducing surtaxes from 50 to 25 per cent, abolishing the excess profits tax, and eliminating tax-exempt securities through a Constitutional amendment. Remembering his difficulties in 1921 and the fact that an election was in the offing, Mellon, backed by the President, also suggested a reduction on moderate incomes. He argued that the existing taxes were not suitable for peacetimes, and that too high a levy would prevent the growth of capital and its use in industry. Congress also was awake to the impending election, and the "radical Republicans" were no less suspicious of Mellon than in 1921. The two houses finally reduced rates all along the line and abolished the excess profits tax, but kept the maximum surtax as high as 40 per cent and actually increased certain of the estate taxes. As a final jab at Coolidge and Mellon, a provision was inserted for publicity of tax returns. Coolidge signed the bill (June 2, 1924) but protested that many of its provisions "were not only unsatisfactory, but harmful to the future of the country."

The President's inability to work effectively with this and later Congresses was not due to any repugnance to the ordinary party machinery. Three causes mainly explain his failure with the Sixty-eighth Congress. One was the Democratic resurgence in the election of 1922, which made it possible for a combination of Democrats, liberal Republicans, and Independents to block legislation. The strength of the left-wing Republicans was demonstrated by the bitter fight which they put up in the House against the return of Frederick H. Gillette, candidate of the regular Republicans, to the speakership. His election was secured only after he had promised a revision of rules limiting the arbitrary control of the Speaker, the majority leader, and the Chairman of the Rules Committee. In the second place, the progressive Senators of the West and the agricultural block distrusted Coolidge's conservatism. Finally, the President was by no means on close terms with many Old-Guard Senators of his own party. Lodge, from his own state, consistently opposed his measures.

Although Congress snubbed the new President, the country watched him closely. Congress adjourned to face a widespread feeling that it had been delinquent and inefficient. The President, on the other hand, had grown in popularity—and also

in power. Coolidge may have had a "genius for
inactivity," but this was not evident where his own
political ambitions were concerned. Quietly but
cleverly, his boom for the Presidency was launched
early in the autumn and under the right auspices.
The Republican National Committee was taken out
of the control of the Old Guard who had nominated
Taft, Hughes, and Harding, and put in the hands
of a new group friendly to Coolidge. An olive
branch was held out to the Progressives, and in a
thousand places the seed was sown for an easy
nomination.

When the Republican Convention met at Cleveland, the fortunes of Coolidge were in the hands
of William B. Butler, a Massachusetts textile manufacturer; Frank W. Stearns, Boston merchant and
close friend of the President; and C. Bascom Slemp,
the President's secretary. What was even more
important, the convention was also under their control. Lodge, who had thrice been permanent chairman of a National Republican Convention, was not
even given a committee assignment. It was Coolidge and his representatives who picked Theodore
E. Burton to be temporary chairman and deliver
the keynote speech, Frank W. Mondell of Wyoming to be permanent chairman, Charles B. Warren
of Michigan to head the committee on resolutions
and President Marion L. Burton of the University
of Michigan to make the nominating speech. Care-

fully staged also was a brief appearance of Andrew W. Mellon, who went to the platform to offer a routine resolution. So impressively had Mellon's reputation been built up as the "brains" of the Administration that his fleeting appearance brought more applause than Coolidge's nomination.

With the precision of a well-oiled machine, the convention named Coolidge on the first ballot. He received 1,065 votes, Senator LaFollette 34 votes (28 from Wisconsin and 6 from North Dakota), and Senator Hiram Johnson 10 from South Dakota. The motion to make the nomination unanimous was greeted by a chorus of "No's" from LaFollette men, and the chairman announced: "With the exception of a very few voices, the nomination of Calvin Coolidge for President of the United States is made unanimous." The cheering lasted less than five minutes.

The nomination for a Vice-President was not cut and dried. Coolidge wanted Borah and, despite the Idahoan's clear and unequivocal refusal, Butler was prepared almost to the moment the voting started to have him nominated. With Borah out, the delegates turned to Lowden and nominated him on the second ballot. But Lowden refused to be considered and the convention was hastily adjourned until he could again be consulted. When he stood adamant, the delegates turned to Charles G. Dawes, and the nonplused Coolidge machine allowed the convention to make this choice. Actually it was the Old Guard leaders who were responsible for the nomination, but this made no difference, for Dawes was acceptable to the Coolidge machine. The Vice-Presidential candidate, a Chicago banker and politician, had become famous as chairman of the Reparations Committee which had suggested the "Dawes Plan."

In their platform, the Republicans largely contented themselves with extolling the policies followed during the previous four years. Rigid economy, tax reduction, extension of the civil service system, endorsement of the World Court, maintenance of high protection, and measures to place agriculture on a basis of economic equality with other interests were recommended. The party expressed opposition to cancelation of war debts, demanded a strong and permanent merchant marine, endorsed a restrictive immigration policy and called for a liberal attitude toward veterans. Though gestures were made toward labor and social legislation, the platform was essentially conservative. LaFollette's followers offered a substitute more in line with progressive sentiments, but it received no support. The day after the convention adjourned, Senator LaFollette issued a statement declaring that the party had turned its back on the farmer.

Whatever chances the Democrats might have had for victory were thrown away at their national convention in New York. When the platform was brought in, two minority reports were offered, one endorsing the League and the other condemning by name the Ku Klux Klan. After long and bitter debates, the League resolution was overwhelmingly defeated (742½ to 353½), while the other was rejected by fewer than five votes. So bitter were the animosities aroused by the Klan resolution that the delegates took 103 ballots to nominate a Presidential candidate. The aspirants with the greatest strength were William G. McAdoo, former Secretary of the Treasury, supported by the "drys," the Protestants, and the rural democracy of the South and West; Governor Alfred E. Smith of New York, Catholic, wet, and leader of the urban Democrats; and Senator Oscar W. Underwood, representative of the best traditions of Southern politics. To Smith's supporters, McAdoo was the embodiment of religious and racial bigotry, while McAdoo's followers considered Smith the candidate of Tammany Hall and the Catholic immigrants.

The first ballot was taken on the evening of June 30; and it was not until July 8 that Franklin D. Roosevelt, representing Smith, announced that his candidate would withdraw if McAdoo would also retire. When the latter freed his followers to do as they felt best, the nomination went to a compromise candidate, John W. Davis, a native of West Virginia but a Wall Street lawyer, who favored joining the League and enforcing the Eighteenth Amendment. The Vice-Presidential nomination was given to a liberal Westerner, Governor Charles Bryan of Nebraska, who was expected to attract the rural Democracy so long attached to his more famous brother.

As was natural, both the keynote address and the platform of the Democrats bore heavily upon the corruption and scandals of the Harding Administration. Stressing a scientific tariff and tax reduction, the platform also promised improvement in the condition of the farmers, condemned monopolies, urged a readjustment of railroad rates on heavy commodities, endorsed immediate operation of Muscle Shoals at capacity, and called for the construction of deep waterways from the Great Lakes to the Gulf and to the Atlantic. As for labor, the platform asserted that it "is not a commodity" and favored collective bargaining. On the League the party renewed "its declarations of confidence," but suggested that the question of entrance be submitted to referendum. The stormiest nominating convention in the annals of American political parties finally adjourned on July 10. Its chief result was to split the party over the worst of issues, religion and race, and to set the rural Democracy against the urban. For the first time the radio gave the American people in 1924 an opportunity to listen to the proceedings of their national conventions, and it took the Democratic Party years to recover from the bad impression it made.

From the Civil War to 1932 the Democratic Party was usually the minority party. It had been successful only by splitting the Republicans and attracting to itself the liberal and independent vote. The opportunity of winning the liberals was ruined in 1924 by the emergence of a Progressive Party under Robert LaFollette. Rapid development of the railroad unions during the World War had revived in the minds of many of their leaders the idea of organized political action. With this in mind, some chieftains of the railroad unions sent out a call for a Conference for Progressive Political Action to meet in February, 1922. It was attended by representatives of other progressive unions (particularly the needle trades), of the Socialist Party, and of the disintegrating Farmer-Labor Party. Subsequent meetings perfected the organization of liberals and reached a decision to enter the campaign of 1924. At its fourth national conference at Cleveland in July, 1924, the party offered its nomination to LaFollette with the power of picking his running mate and writing his own platform.

This opportunity of running on an independent progressive ticket supported by powerful labor unions appealed to the veteran liberal. As leader of the progressive Congressional bloc, he had opposed and sometimes defeated reactionary Republican proposals. He believed that perhaps organized labor, discontented farmers, middle-class liberals, and Socialists might really unite in a revolt which would create a permanent and powerful third party. Perhaps this party might win enough votes to throw the election into the House of Representatives, and thus gain the balance of power. LaFollette accepted, chose Senator Burton K. Wheeler to run with him, and offered his platform. It was a typical liberal document of the Roosevelt-LaFollette era, dominated by fear of monopoly and filled with promises of excellent reforms. "The great issue before the American people today," it said, "is the control of government and industry by private monopoly." Essentially, it was an agrarian, not a Socialist, platform. Most interesting of the changes which it advocated were public ownership of railroads, a referendum on threatened wars, and the abolition of power in the Supreme Court to nullify acts of Congress.

What little fire the campaign offered came from the pugnacious and eloquent little Senator from Wisconsin, now approaching his seventieth year. To Americans of the first quarter of the century the name of "Fighting Bob" LaFollette was synonomous with the movement for progressive legislation. Born in a log cabin, he had battled his way against the corrupt and reactionary Spooner-Sawyer machine to three terms as Governor. Railroad regulation, an inheritance tax, a graduated income tax, a direct primary law, and free use of expert administrative commissions were among his contributions which made Wisconsin the leader in progressive state legislation. When he came to the Senate in 1906 LaFollette carried his program with him. In the Taft Administration he rallied the insurgent Republicans against the Payne-Aldrich Tariff and the first unsatisfactory draft of the Mann-Elkins railroad regulation bill. A convinced isolationist, he became the target of much opprobrium when he opposed Wilson's bill to arm ships and was one of the six Senators who voted against war with Germany. Later he violently opposed the League. It was LaFollette who introduced the resolution which started the Teapot Dome investigation. An industrious student of economics who never debated without preparation, an inspired orator and a grim fighter, LaFollette remained in the twenties, as in earlier years, the undisputed leader of left-wing liberalism.

Coolidge's biographer, Claude M. Fuess, characterizes the campaign as "unimportant, uninteresting, and unexciting." Certainly it was not exciting. Coolidge largely avoided meetings and political speeches, contenting himself in his few public appearances with platitudinous remarks. The Republican strategy was to emphasize the prosperity of the previous two years, the stability of their candidate, and the dangers of change. They also undertook to paint LaFollette as a dangerous radical. "Keep cool with Coolidge" was their motto. Certainly Coolidge kept cool during the campaign, even if his party worked itself into a highly nervous state.

For the Democrats, John W. Davis, a finished orator of much quieter type than LaFollette, charged the Republicans "with corruption in administration . . . with favoritism to privileged classes in legislation . . . with division in council and impotence in action." He described Coolidge as "an Executive who cannot or will not lead a Congress that cannot and will not follow." This might all be true, but the nation refused to get excited. The chief handicap of the Democrats was the fact that the political and economic philosophy of Davis differed from that of Coolidge only as Cleveland's had differed from McKinley's. Davis gloried in his specialized practice for Big Business and seemed to identify America with the great industrialists and bankers. "I have a fine list of clients," he said early in 1924:

What lawyer wouldn't want them? I have J. P. Morgan and Company, the Erie Railroad, the Guaranty Trust Company, the Standard Oil Company, and other foremost American concerns on my list. I am proud of them. They are big institutions, and so long as they ask for my services for honest work I am pleased to work for them. Big Business has made this country what it is. We want Big Business. But it must be honest.

This was honest talk but it hardly pleased the Progressives, particularly in the Middle West, and without their vote victory was hopeless. His running mate, Bryan, hardly took the curse off such a viewpoint. One journalist suggested that Coolidge was "an arid conservative who makes conservatism repellent" while Davis was "an engaging conservative who makes it attractive." Davis stood for international cooperation and lower tariffs, but the difference between the two was not enough to shift many votes. LaFollette swung around the country with something of his old-time fire, castigating the old parties and calling the liberals to arms. Those who still survived responded.

Many ingredients were assembled for a thrilling campaign, but somehow it did not crystallize. Only 51.1 per cent of the voters went to the polls. Coolidge won by an electoral vote of 382 to 136 for Davis and 13 for LaFollette. The popular vote gave Coolidge 15,725,000, Davis 8,385,600, and LaFollette 4,822,900. It was the largest plurality in Republican history. Davis carried only the eleven states of the solid South and Oklahoma. LaFollette carried only Wisconsin, but ran second in eleven other states, all west of the Mississippi.

Coolidge's victory assured a comfortable Republican majority in the Sixty-ninth Congress. The Senate would have 55 Republicans, 40 Democrats, and 1 Farmer-Laborite; the House, 264 Republicans, 148 Democrats, and 1 Socialist.

Considering all its difficulties, the Progressive Party made a splendid showing. It was supported by the Railroad Brotherhoods and by the Socialist Party. The Executive Committee of the American Federation of Labor, for the first time in its history, endorsed a Presidential candidate. LaFollette also had the aid of the Scripps-Howard newspaper chain. In the cities he received strong support from Irish voters, who resented the treatment of Smith at the Democratic convention and who knew that La-Follette favored a free Ireland. Many Germans, who applauded his anti-war record, voted for him, as did others who knew him as the nation's outstanding liberal. But all these elements were not enough. Conservatives, as in the Bryan election of 1896, not only pictured the veteran liberal as a dangerous radical, but threatened dire woe if he were elected. Many labor leaders attached to the old parties opposed the new movement, and it is doubtful if labor as a whole sympathized with the idea of a third party. Above all, the rising prosperity beyond question placed sharp limitations upon the Progressive vote. Even agricultural prices showed a slight swing upwards in 1924.

Neither the Republican record nor its candidate were such as to arouse much enthusiasm, yet the party polled almost 16,000,000 votes. Evidently the nation was in no heroic mood. Still inertly relaxed after the tension of the war years, it was little disturbed by the revelations of corruption among high Government officials. Instead of being aroused to drive out the rascals, the nation wanted only peace, quiet, and continued enjoyment of prosperity. Though there was nothing exciting about Coolidge, though he was just an ordinary, everyday person, though he might never do anything spectacular, he was safe and honest. He fitted the mood of the nation. It was a "desire for something solid, safe and familiar," suggested the *Review of Reviews,* that worked "day and night for the success of the Coolidge Administration."

The campaign of 1924 may have been unexciting and unedifying, but it was not unimportant. As a result, the Democratic Party was battered beyond easy repair. Its revival eight years later was due much less to internal strength or to mistakes by the opposite party than to an economic depression for which neither party was responsible. To Progressives, who believed that the two old parties were essentially the same, and that American politics needed the realism which a Progressive Party would give, the campaign was a disappointment. It was not the failure to poll more than five million votes that was discouraging; the figures were in many ways remarkable. It was the revelation that organized labor was not yet ideologically prepared for party action.

As for the nation as a whole, the most immediate result was definitely to place the Government in the hands of the business interests. Indeed, it was in the hands of the most conservative element of business, men of the type of Andrew W. Mellon. Coolidge had encouraged the process; the election sanctioned it. Up to 1924 the Republican Party had assumed the position of arbitrator between Government and capital, but it no longer bothered to do this. "Coolidge," writes William Allen White, "gave his leadership frankly, openly, proudly, to American business by direct rather than indirect control." There was no longer the slightest camouflage. Government and big business were now synonymous. The change, however, was no improvement. For four years high-handed speculation, reckless financing, and ruthless economic exploitation ran unchecked. Then came the deluge.

CHAPTER VIII

GOVERNMENT AND BUSINESS

THAT the Republican Party under Coolidge had become essentially the agent of big business was increasingly evident as the years passed. Nothing, perhaps, emphasized this more strongly than the rapid and unrestrained consolidation of industry. There have been three great periods of consolidation in American history—the eighties, followed by the Sherman Anti-trust Act of 1890; the years from about 1897 to 1904, followed by the Clayton Act and the Federal Trade Commission Act; and, finally, the 1920's. In none of these periods was the movement more widespread than in the decade of Harding and Coolidge. In none did it reach higher proportions.

It was particularly noticeable in the new industries which had developed since the previous era of consolidation—those manufacturing automobiles, chemicals, aluminum, moving pictures, radios and electric power. The movement was specially striking in the field of electric power. Between 1919 and 1927 more than 3,700 utility companies, including many municipally operated concerns, disappeared. While thousands vanished, the larger ones were being welded into huge holding corporations. "In 1915," according to the Federal Trade Commission, "the 16 largest groups controlled about 22.8 per cent [generating capacity of the country], while in 1925 the 16 largest interests, consisting of 11 holding-company groups and five independent operating interests, controlled approximately 53 per cent of the country's total." After 1925 this consolidation, chiefly through holding companies, proceeded even more rapidly. By 1930 one half of the electric power generated by the great utility companies was in the hands of three holding-company groups, the United Corporation, the Electric Bond and Share, and the Insull interests; two thirds of the electrical energy was controlled by six groups, and over 90 per cent by fifteen groups.

Although consolidation was more spectacular in the new industries largely developed since 1904, it was by no means limited to them. Between 1919 and 1928 more than 7,000 mergers took place in industry and mining, the movement being most pronounced in companies producing iron, steel, and machinery. Important consolidations also appeared in old industries which had previously largely escaped the tendency. Examples may be readily found in the manufacture of packaged food and in banking. During 1928 and 1929 occurred, for example, the merger of the Fleischmann-Royal Baking interests, the merger of the Gold Dust Corporation and the American Linseed Company, and the acquisition of various brands by the Postum Company under the name of General Food Products.

Of great significance also was the amazing consolidation which characterized banking. In 1921 the number of banks in the nation reached a peak of 30,812. Although population, wealth, and resources greatly increased, the number ten years later had dropped to about 22,000. Some of the banks had failed, others had merged with neighboring institutions. In large cities, particularly, the consolidation of banks spurred a mad race for supremacy. The lead was taken during 1928–1930 by the three titans in New York when the National City Bank joined with the Farmers' Loan and Trust Company; the Guaranty Trust Company with the Bank of Commerce; and finally, the Chase National Bank with the Equitable Trust Company. The new Chase became the largest bank in the world.

While large-scale mergers were taking place among city banks, a similar concentration of resources was carried into rural areas by the development of chain banking. In California, where chain banking flowered most magnificently during this decade, a huge holding company, called the Transamerica Corporation, controlled the Bancitaly Company of America, the Bank of America of

California, and other large banks which, in turn, had scattered 500 chain banks across the state. This tremendous financial empire had been developed from a small one-man bank in San Francisco by Amadeo Peter Giannini, a son of Italian immigrants who had started work at the age of twelve in a commission house. While some of Giannini's methods were questionable, his success rose in part from his theory that a banker should charge for his product only what was absolutely necessary, a principle rapidly becoming old-fashioned in the expansive twenties. The merging of urban banks and growth of chain banking carried banking consolidation to an alarming point by the end of the decade. When the Pujo Committee reported in 1913 that a "money trust" existed, financial consolidation was actually in its infancy.

The marketing of capital through chain banks, however, was far less widespread and imposing than the marketing of merchandise through chain stores. The development of chain-store retailing, in fact, was one of the striking aspects of consolidation during the twenties. Chains became most powerful in the sale of drugs, tobacco, groceries, variety goods, and oil and gasoline, but they also made impressive strides in many other fields. In all parts of the country the small merchant winced under the same sort of competition which the little manufacturer had been facing for decades. F. W. Woolworth's, largest of the five-and-ten-cent chains, had but 600 stores in 1911; by 1930 the number had tripled. More rapid still was the advance in the grocery field. The Great Atlantic and Pacific Tea Company, which had 5,000 stores in 1922, six years later counted 17,500 with an annual business of $750,000,000. Little merchants faced even fiercer competition in the late twenties when the two largest mail-order houses, Sears, Roebuck and Montgomery Ward, set up retail outlets in most of the cities. To what extent the chains had taken business away from local individual proprietors is not entirely clear. A Department of Commerce study in eleven cities in 1926, however, showed that gasoline and oil chains obtained 73.5 per cent of total sales; variety chains, 70.7; dairy and poultry products, 44.0; grocery and delicatessen, 41.3; millinery, 36.9, and tobacco, 35.5.

Merrily the consolidation rolled along in manufacturing, banking, and marketing. Affecting every phase of economic life, it increased in speed toward the end of the decade. In mining and manufacturing the number of mergers recorded in 1921 was 89 and in 1928 was 221; while the number of concerns which disappeared in 1921 was 487 and in 1928 was 1,038. The great banking mergers, as we have seen, came in the last two years of the decade. As the whole movement reached its climax it was evident that economic integration had advanced beyond any point previously reached, and that the concentration of economic power had also increased. In 1930 it appeared that 250 of the 24,000 banks held resources of $33,400,000,000, nearly half of the nation's total of $72,000,000,000. To be exact, slightly more than one per cent of the banks controlled 46 per cent of the total banking resources. Not only was this so, but 24 New York banks, one tenth of one per cent of the total number, held combined resources in 1930 of about $10,800,000,000, or 15 per cent of the total banking resources of the nation. Their capitalization of almost $700,000,000 was comparable to that of the 20,000 country banks situated in cities of 10,000 or less.

Outside of banking, the picture was much the same. By 1930 the 200 largest corporations controlled nearly half of all non-banking corporate wealth (or nearly two fifths of all business wealth), received 43.2 per cent of the income of all non-banking corporations, and were controlled by approximately 2,000 individuals. Of these great companies the largest was the American Telephone & Telegraph Company, a holding company the assets of which had grown by 1930 to more than four and one-quarter billions of dollars. It then represented more wealth than was contained within the borders of the twenty-one poorest states in the Union. At least four others in that year had esti-

mated assets of over two billion: the Pennsylvania
Railroad Company ($2,600,000,000); United States
Steel Corporation ($2,286,100,000); the New York
Central Railroad Company ($2,257,000,000) and
the Southern Pacific Company ($2,156,700,000).
Other giants included the Standard Oil Company
of New Jersey ($1,767,300,000) and General Mo-
tors Corporation ($1,400,000,000). These were all
huge holding corporations, leaders in their respec-
tive field, which had grown to gigantic size both by
consolidation and by keeping pace with the economic expansion of the nation.

For this remarkable revival of the consolidation
movement some causes were old and some new.
When the Industrial Commission in 1899 had made
its preliminary report, it asserted that excessive
competition—"so vigorous that profits of nearly
all competing establishments had been destroyed"
—was the chief motivating force for business consolidation. This factor still operated in the 1920's,
but probably with lessened force. Artificial stimulation during the war years had undoubtedly left
American business overbuilt and overexpanded,
compelling many concerns to seek salvation by
mergers. More important, undoubtedly, were the
widespread confidence in a continuance of industrial prosperity, the ease with which security issues
could be floated, and the opportunities for promotional profits.

It seemed possible in the golden twenties to sell almost any kind of stock. So hungry were investors that banking houses experienced no difficulty in financing mergers by selling bonds, preferred stock, and non-voting Class A common stock at large profits, while they kept in the hands of the promoters control of the Class B voting stock and thus domination of the new merger. This type of promotion was particularly frequent in the utilities, where one holding company was piled on another until a few owners of common stock in the top company were able to control vast empires of electric power. Hundreds of thousands of unhappy investors grasped this fact when the vast holding companies built up by Samuel Insull collapsed like a house of cards in 1932, wiping out $700,000,000 of investors' money. After the Associated Gas and Electric Company went into bankruptcy in 1939 the 250,000 security holders in the two top holding companies discovered that this huge combination of 150 corporations, with paper assets of a billion dollars, was actually controlled by a voting trust of five persons.

How far business morality had deteriorated was later repeatedly demonstrated by Congressional investigating committees. While the most reputable bond houses, including J. P. Morgan and Company, admitted rigging the market to dispose of their commodities and then "pulling the plug" to let them decline, the greatest banks of America confessed to operating syndicates or pools which encouraged speculators through high-pressure sales campaigns. In the words of that "prince of speculators," Mathew C. Brush, "the Wall Street racket made Al Capone look like a piker." Both the Chase National Bank and the National City Bank of New York, the two largest in the country, maintained security affiliates to sell stocks and bonds which later sometimes proved of little or no value. The business of banking seemed to have shifted largely from providing credit for legitimate business to selling securities, playing the stock market, and encouraging others to do likewise. As one observer remarked, "the banks provided everything for their customers but a roulette wheel."

Even after the depression came, high bank officials, including Albert H. Wiggins, chairman of the Chase board, and President Charles F. Mitchell of the National City, were receiving inordinate salaries and bonuses. Income taxes they escaped by "personal" or "family" corporations to which they sold securities at a loss. Mitchell's income in 1929 was more than $4,000,000, but he paid no income taxes. Criminal proceedings against him failed, but civil suits going as high as the Supreme Court eventually collected $700,000 in back taxes. During the investigation of the Senate Banking Committee in the spring of 1933, Mitchell testified that directors of the National City Bank had lent funds aggregating $2,400,000 to officers of the bank to protect their stock holdings in the market crash of 1929. Such loans had been made without interest and in most cases without security. Only about 5 per cent had been paid back. At the same time, underlings in the bank had been forced to meet full installment payments for stock in the National City Bank which they had bought at $200 or over, but which was then selling at $40.

Such facts were not generally suspected by the public, who cared little what was going on behind the scenes as long as the nation seemed prosperous and speculation produced easy gains. A few students who watched the decline into bankruptcy of the great Chicago, Milwaukee and St. Paul Railroad system during a period of relative prosperity realized the deterioration of business leadership. Many more were appalled by the widespread monopolies developing in public utilities. But the masses little appreciated the dangers inherent in a heavy concentration of wealth and power or the reckless use of this power.

This decline of the critical temper may have risen from a belief in the inevitability of concentration in a capitalistic system; it certainly was encouraged by the incessant propaganda of big business. Probably the old-time fears of monopoly were quieted by prosperity and the rising standard of living. If the people seemed to care little, it was hardly to be expected that the Government would show alarm, particularly under the direction of Coolidge, Mellon, and Hoover, who believed it the mission of Government to help and not "hinder" business.

That many of the consolidations and many of the activities of business during the twenties were in violation of the anti-trust acts seems quite apparent. There was no lack of laws, or of agencies to enforce them. The Sherman and Clayton Acts covered monopoly and monopoly practices with reasonable completeness. The Federal Trade Commission had been set up to watch monopoly and prosecute it; the Department of Justice and the Supreme Court were supposedly ready to support the laws. Except for a small minority of old-fashioned liberals, however, few seemed to care whether the laws were applied or not. The Supreme Court itself went far to make enforcement of the anti-trust acts impossible. In the case of the United Shoe Machinery Company (1918), a concern controlling more than 90 per cent of the shoe machinery, Justice McKenna had said: "The company indeed has magnitude, but it is at once the result and cause of efficiency, and the charge that it has been oppressively used is not sustained." This same point of view was emphasized when two years later, in the United States Steel case, the Court refused to dissolve that corporation, holding that neither size (short of complete monopoly) nor the possession of potential power to restrain trade was necessarily a violation of the Sherman Act. "The power obtained was much greater," said the Court, "than that possessed by any one competitor—it was not greater than that possessed by all of them. Monopoly, therefore, was not achieved." This statement was made in the face of common knowledge that the United States Steel Corporation had virtually dictated prices in the industry for fifteen years.

Figuratively speaking, all fetters on big business were struck off by the steel decision. No consolidation thereafter seemed too large to be legal. But in many other ways the Court also hampered enforcement of the anti-trust acts. Trade associations, earlier frowned on by the Government but now tenderly encouraged by the Secretary of Commerce, were approved by the Court. This approval gave industry an opportunity of performing many acts whose legality had once been questioned. Regulation of public utilities, long recognized as vitally important, was badly weakened in a number of ways, but particularly by introducing into valuation cases the theory of "reproduction costs." This made the whole problem of determining equitable rates more difficult and put the consumer at a disadvantage. Likewise, the old theory that regulation of business might be achieved by extending the principle of public interest over a wider field of activities was squelched by three decisions within two years, the Court holding that gasoline dealers in Tennessee, employment agencies in New Jersey, and ticket brokers in New York did not fall into the category of "public interest" enterprises. "It is highly significant," remarked one student in 1928, "that in recent years not a single adverse decision has been rendered requiring the dissolution of an actually functioning merger."

Since the establishment of the Federal Trade Commission in 1914, the chief responsibility for enforcing the anti-trust acts had rested upon its shoulders. Despite Supreme Court decisions which had somewhat curtailed its activities, the Commission, dominated by old-fashioned liberals, had attempted during its earlier years to fulfill the purpose for which it was established. These activities aroused conservatives to demand that the Commission be abolished. Although it continued to exist, its effectiveness was greatly crippled.

Harding began the attack by appointing Vernon W. Van Fleet, a former Indiana judge and candidate of the reactionary Senator Watson, to the Commission; in 1924 Van Fleet became chairman. The Commission still had enough vitality to prepare a report (part of an investigation on house furnishings ordered by the Senate in 1921) on the monopoly allegedly exercised by the Aluminum Company of America, completely controlled by the Mellon family. This report, tactlessly issued during the campaign of 1924 with a recommendation for prosecution, hardly improved the standing of the Commission with the Administration. Coolidge in his annual message of 1923 had already recommended "reform" of its rules of procedure, and he repeated this proposal in 1925. In January, 1925, he appointed to a vacancy on the Commission William E. Humphrey, a lame-duck Congressman from Washington, who had been one of his campaign managers in the West. This gave the conservative Republicans a majority, and they immediately revised the rules of procedure in a way highly favorable to business. One new rule was that information given by a firm under investigation for violation of the anti-trust acts could not be turned over to the Department of Justice without the firm's consent. Minority Commissioners Huston Thompson and John F. Nugent loudly protested, but after 1925 violators of the anti-trust acts had little to fear from the Federal Trade Commission.

Senators like Borah, Norris, and LaFollette were naturally indignant over the "packing" of the Federal Trade Commission and gave much publicity to complaints of the minority Commissioners. They also raised enough disturbance about the aluminum reports to compel some action by the Department of Justice. As Attorney-General Stone prepared to prosecute, Associate Justice McKenna resigned from the Supreme Court and Stone was promoted to succeed him. Stone's successor, John G. Sargeant, admitted before the Senate Judiciary Committee that he had never heard of the Aluminum Company before he came to Washington and seemed confused about the whole matter. The testimony of his assistant, William J. Donovan, was equally unproductive of information. After the hearings the Judiciary Committee recommended an investigation, but the proposal lost in the Senate by two votes. Upon the loud insistence of the two minority members of the Federal Trade Commission, however, and after the filing of complaint, the Commission in 1925 again began to investigate charges of monopoly, this time on aluminum sand castings widely used in the automobile industry. The Commission's counsel reaffirmed the old charges. In 1928 it added six new ones, but these were eliminated by the Commission majority as tending to protract the hearings. Finally, in 1930 the Commission dismissed the complaint without explanation. Thus collapsed the prosecution of the Mellon company, which controlled almost the entire bauxite deposits and aluminum manufacture of the nation.

Both the Harding and Coolidge Administrations

were equally intent upon making the Federal Tariff Commission subservient to its will. Harding began by appointing two well-known Republican high-tariff lobbyists to the Commission and a high-protectionist Democrat. Not only did Coolidge ignore its recommendations, but he soon reorganized the Board to put it under complete high-tariff domination. When the term of Daniel S. Lewis, a low-tariff Democrat, ran out in 1924, he was replaced by Alfred P. Dennis, a strong protectionist. Although this gave the high protectionists a majority, the Commission still contained two advocates of moderate tariffs, William S. Culbertson and Edward P. Costigan. When these men protested vigorously against the practice of members of the Commission sitting upon cases in which they were personally interested, they met no sympathy on the part of the President. They did, however, bring about a Congressional resolution to end the practice. Culbertson was soon kicked upstairs by appointment as Minister to Rumania, while Costigan resigned in disgust in 1928.

Said Costigan in closing a blistering letter to Senator Robinson in which he reviewed the history of the Tariff Commission and announced his resignation:

I fully realize that the manipulation of the Tariff Commission since 1922 is but part of the total picture of present-day Washington. In an era in which history may yet summarize as the age of Daugherty, Fall and Sinclair—in which another government body, the Federal Trade Commission, is widely looked upon as the legitimate prey of those who deal in the unfair practices that Commission was created to destroy—in which even the national Senate is not immune against the trespass and dictates of powerful lobbies —the fate and fortunes of the Tariff Commission may be thought unimportant. Yet no part of the public edifice can be undermined without danger to the whole structure. Public service still demands public fidelity.

In the meantime, Senator Robinson in 1926 secured a Congressional inquiry into the Commission. When the investigating committee reported two years later, the majority recommended that the flexible provision of the tariff law be repealed, and that the Commission report its findings to Congress instead of to the President. The packing of the Commission and the investigation did much to discredit it.

For the right of a popularly elected President to appoint subordinates sympathetic with his own point of view, something can be said. But still more is to be said for appointing men who are keenly interested in enforcing laws, particularly on boards which are theoretically independent and non-partisan. This was the view taken by liberal and progressive Senators; and for this reason they resented the packing of both the Federal Trade Commission and the Tariff Commission. They were similarly indignant over an *ad interim* appointment of Thomas F. Woodlock to the Interstate Commerce Commission after the Senate had twice refused to confirm him. The resentment of this group, working, of course, with opposition Democrats, prevented the confirmation in March, 1925, of Charles B. Warren as Attorney-General.

Warren was an able lawyer with a long and distinguished career, but he was anathema to the farm bloc and to progressive Senators because of his affiliation with the "sugar trust." In particular, they resented his connections with operations in 1910 which had given the American Sugar Refining Company virtual control of the beet-sugar industry. Coolidge was warned by Chief Justice Taft and by Republican Senate leaders that confirmation was doubtful, but he stubbornly persisted. To make the President's discomfiture more galling he lost his battle on a fluke under circumstances not without a touch of humor. The vote on confirmation (March 10) was 40 to 40, as Vice-President Dawes was taking his noonday nap at the Willard Hotel. Aroused by frantic telephone messages, Dawes charged down Pennsylvania Avenue in a taxi expecting to break the tie and cast the deciding vote in favor of Warren, only to arrive too

late. During the spectacular ride Senator Reed of
Pennsylvania changed his vote so that he might
move a reconsideration of the roll call. No sooner
had he moved to reconsider than Walsh of Montana jumped to his feet and moved to table Reed's
motion. The Walsh motion was a 40–40 tie. At
this point Senator Overman of North Carolina, the
only Democrat who had originally voted for Warren's confirmation, changed his vote, leaving the
final count 41 to 39 in favor of the Walsh motion.
A few days later the President tried again, but this
time the Senate refused confirmation by the more
decisive vote of 46 to 39. It was the first time the
Senate had rejected a Cabinet appointment since
the days of Andrew Johnson.

Western Progressives considered the nomination
of Warren a deliberate prostitution of the Department of Justice. Their point of view was well expressed by Senator Norris in an article in the
Nation:

I do not charge that any of the men appointed to
the various positions are dishonest or incompetent,
but without exception as far as I know every appointee
has been some one who has no sympathy with the
various acts of Congress passed for the purpose of regulating different activities but on the other hand be-
lieves that there should be practically no restraining
hand placed upon trusts and monopolies. . . . It is an
indirect but positive repeal of Congressional enact-

ments, which no Administration, however powerful, would dare to bring about by direct means. It is the nullification of federal law by a process of boring from within.

While the Administration was thus fettering the great regulatory agencies of the Government, it was preparing to confer the richest of all its favors upon business. The Revenue Act of 1924 had fallen far short of Secretary Mellon's original proposals. Coolidge, after signing it, vigorously criticized its provisions as "tax reduction, not tax reform." To Mellon and Coolidge "tax reform" meant the elimination of high surtaxes, abolition of inheritance and gift taxes, reduction of income taxes, particularly in the higher brackets, and repeal of the publicity clause. It was frankly and unblushingly a program of relief for the higher income-tax payers. Progress had been made in 1921 and 1924, but much remained to be done. While the overwhelming victory of Coolidge in 1924 appeared to be an endorsement of his Administration, Mellon had no intention of entrusting his program to a lame-duck Congress. He waited until the fall of 1925, when the Ways and Means Committee prepared a new measure which closely followed his recommendations, and which was approved by Coolidge in his annual message of December 8.

This time the Mellon Plan went through practically unopposed. With both houses overwhelmingly Republican, with Mellon at the height of his prestige, Congressmen climbed hastily on the band wagon. The only difficulty was to restrain them from going beyond the Secretary's recommendations and creating a deficit. The "Progressive bloc" gave up the fight; the vote for the Revenue Act of 1926 was 354 to 28 in the House and 61 to 10 in the Senate. The inheritance tax in the highest brackets was slashed from 40 per cent to 20; income taxes were cut in all brackets and surtaxes greatly reduced. Exemptions were raised, and occupational and gift taxes repealed. Publicity of returns went out the window. Only the corporation tax, which was $12\frac{1}{2}$ per cent in 1924, was raised $\frac{1}{2}$ per cent for one year and 1 per cent thereafter. Two years later, however, it was reduced to 12 per cent. Mellon's chief argument for the wholesale reductions of 1926 was the familiar assertion that they would release capital for productive industry. Whether that is where the money saved by high-bracket taxpayers went, no one, of course, can tell. On the basis of returns for 1924–1926, however, such taxpayers were saved $2,000,000 a day.

While Republican Administrations from Harding to Hoover aided business by reducing taxation and nullifying the anti-trust acts, they made it clear that they took no interest in extending Government controls. The problem was dramatized in the struggle over Muscle Shoals, but its ramifications reached far beyond power dams or nitrogen plants on the Tennessee River. Since the turn of the century the production of electric power had grown enormously, from 4,768 million kilowatt-hours in 1902 to 95,925 million kilowatt-hours in 1929. In terms of everyday life, electricity had largely taken the place of oil for lighting purposes and steam power for factory production. Its use in transportation and for many other purposes was widening. Particularly important was its entrance into the American factory. "Practically all of the increase in factory power equipment since 1914," said a Government report in 1930, "has been in electric power motors operated by current from central stations." By that year three fourths of the power used in American factories was electric.

It was evident by 1920 that a new and mighty force had been unleashed, and was rapidly changing methods of production and ways of living. Presumably the Government would be concerned with an influence which was revolutionizing the life of its people. Moreover, there were at least three direct reasons which necessitated Federal action of some kind. Although electricity could be manufactured from coal, oil, and gas, it came increasingly to be produced from water power. To provide this power, dams were built, often on Government reservations or on navigable streams involving interstate commerce and other Federal interests. In the second place, electric power was to an increasing extent being transported across state lines. Engineers were inventing methods of transmitting it over longer and longer distances at the same time that they were demonstrating that it could be most cheaply produced by water power. As the years went on, therefore, more and more electricity was manufactured from water power and carried by high-voltage transmission lines to areas where water power did not exist. By 1930 almost one seventh of this power crossed state lines.

More important, however, was the fact that electric power, for all practical purposes, was a monopoly. A few regions found two privately owned companies competing for business, or a municipally owned and a private company in competition. In general, however, the distribution and sale of electricity was a monopoly conferred by local governments upon some power company. As monopolies, these power companies were subject to Government control both under common and statute law. As in the early days of railroad regulation, many states had established public utility commissions to supervise the power monopolies; but in actual practice their control was feeble. Lack of authority, difficulty in obtaining data, the political influence of the power companies, and other factors prevented effective control. Even in the few states, such as

California, Wisconsin, New York, and Massachusetts, where some effort was made to protect the public, it was often a question whether the commission represented the utility interests or the people. The whole problem of regulation was complicated by other important factors. When legislatures began to exercise control over power companies, they made the same mistake they had made forty years earlier with railroads in attempting to regulate charges rather than capital structure.

This antiquated approach to the problem of utility control was particularly unfortunate during the boom days of the twenties, when utility companies resorted to every method of questionable finance. Reorganizations and expansions piled up promotional profits in the hands of outsiders, while the issuance of non-voting and management stock and the pyramiding of holding companies kept control in the hands of a few promoters. Stock was continually watered, but so complicated became the capital structure that earnings were easily hidden. It became difficult for investors to determine the true value of securities, and practically impossible for a utility commission to determine a fair charge for electricity. Service, it is true, improved while rates declined, but profits also increased. When objections were raised to unusually high profits on this necessity of life, the power companies, like the railroads in earlier years, corrupted legislatures, fought commission decisions in the courts, and conducted a propaganda which for extent and unscrupulous methods has rarely been equaled. Their influence was so great that they were able to control the discussion of utilities in the textbooks of one of the leading schoolbook publishers.

Clearly, local regulation was inadequate. The strength of the power companies was so enormous, their interstate ramification so widespread, and the inadequacy of existing laws so obvious, that only a further extension of Federal control could meet the situation. Long reports of the Federal Trade Commission, popularized by numerous writers, made the situation clear, while a group of Senators led by Couzens of Michigan and Norris of Nebraska urged more effective national action. Coolidge nevertheless believed that state control was adequate, and consistently opposed a further extension of Federal supervision. What national control was exercised during the twenties was largely under the Water Power Act of 1920, approved by Wilson. The Power Commission set up by this act, composed of the Secretaries of War, Agriculture, and the Interior, exercised administrative control over all power sites on public lands of the United States and navigable rivers. It had authority to license for fifty years concerns erecting such plants, and to require uniform accounting systems. It was given jurisdiction over security issues, and over the rates for electricity when its licensees sold power across interstate boundaries or when there was no effective local regulation.

Although the Act of 1920 appeared adequate, it contained many loopholes. Administration by three Cabinet officers was too clumsy. A full-time regulating body, with a status like that of the Interstate Commerce Commission, was needed. The Act of 1920 applied only to public lands, Indian reservations, and navigable rivers. It conferred no power over rates and security issues of Federal licensees in those states which had created utility commissions. A decade of agitation and a major depression were required to bring a change. Hoover urged "effective regulation of interstate electric power" that would "preserve the independence and responsibility of the states." But Congress was satisfied with merely an administrative reorganization. In 1930 a full-time Federal Power Commission of five men, appointed by the President with consent of the Senate, was set up to administer the Act of 1920. Extension of the Commission's power waited upon the Roosevelt Administration.

It was over the question of Muscle Shoals that conflicting philosophies came to a showdown. Under authority of the National Defense Act of 1916, the Government in 1918 began constructing two plants on the Tennessee River in Alabama. They

were to produce nitrates for use in munitions and
agriculture. To provide the electric energy needed,
a series of dams was also authorized, the most important being the Wilson Dam at Muscle Shoals,
completed in 1925. The total cost was between
$130,000,000 and $140,000,000. Nitrate production
at the close of the war was discontinued, and the
power created by the Wilson Dam was leased to the
Alabama Power Company.

Led by Coolidge and Hoover, the groups opposed
to Government manufacture of nitrogen and Government production of hydroelectric power urged
the sale of these plants to private interests. Coolidge
recommended this in each annual message. Opposing groups demanded operation under a Government-owned corporation. Various plans for private
purchase, in particular one offered by Henry Ford
and another by the Associated Power Companies of
the South, were proposed. The House actually
voted for the Ford plan, but such projects were
blocked in the Senate. Sentiment favoring Government operation gradually increased. Finally, in
1928 the Norris-Morin Resolution, calling for com-
pletion of the project and operation by a government-owned corporation, was passed by both
Houses. Coolidge pocket-vetoed it. The issue was
prominent in the campaign of 1928, Smith endorsing Government operation, and Hoover opposing it.
Another joint resolution was passed in 1931, only to

be excoriated by Hoover in a veto message describing Government operation as not "liberalism" but "degeneration." Like rigid extension of Federal control over interstate power, the Government operation of Muscle Shoals waited upon the next Administration. When it came it brought a program far wider than even Norris had hoped for during the twenties.

Coolidge might hold high the banner of *laissez-faire* and Hoover extol the glory of "rugged individualism," but in the actual operation of government it was impossible to follow any narrow philosophy. It was doubtful whether some industries could exist, much less prosper, without Government help. This was particularly true of transoceanic shipping. A decade after the World War so much of the vast merchant fleet built during the conflict was still afloat that the United States held second place on the high seas. On paper this looked encouraging. As a matter of fact, however, the situation of the merchant marine was yearly becoming worse. Tonnage engaged in foreign trade had declined from 11,077,000 in 1921 to 6,906,000 in 1929, and the proportion of imports and exports carried in American bottoms from 42.7 per cent in 1920 to 33.4 in 1929. While foreign nations were building modern liners and Diesel-engined tramps, our shipyards were empty and our fleet was rapidly becoming antiquated.

Under the Merchant Marine Act of 1920 the Shipping Board and the Merchant Fleet Corporation had been ordered to keep an American merchant marine on the seas—by Government operation, if necessary, but preferably by persuading private interests to take over the Government vessels on liberal terms. A merchant marine, such as it was, continued on the sea, but the Board found it difficult to induce private corporations to take over Government ships on almost any terms. Of the seagoing merchant ships (1,000 gross tons and over) the Government still owned 4,337,000 tons in 1928 as against 6,078,000 owned by private corporations. For the lack of interest among private shippers there were two chief reasons: the high cost of building, maintenance and operation of American ships, and the bitter competition arising from overexpansion in the world supply of shipping. Only by indirect subsidies were private companies kept alive, and only by the loss of millions annually were Government boats maintained in service.

Obviously, the situation was difficult. A merchant fleet, either Government or private, could not be maintained without large subsidies, and this violated both the economic principles of Coolidge and his belief in thrift. Insisting that Government ownership and operation had proved a failure, Coolidge criticized the Shipping Board for not selling the ships rapidly enough, and repeatedly urged a reorganization of that body. As a majority disliked to sell Government ships at the ridiculous prices offered, a deadlock ensued between the President and the Board. It was finally broken when in 1926 Coolidge forced the resignation of B. E. Haney, a Democrat, obtained a majority, and reorganized the shipping administration. After that the sale of ships proceeded rapidly. On the Pacific the disposal of Government ships was completed in 1928; on the Atlantic the Government retired completely from the passenger business in 1929, when it got rid of the United States Lines and the American Merchant Lines. Between 1925 and 1930 the Shipping Board sold 104 vessels which had cost $258,-000,000 for $23,000,000.

Meanwhile, Congress tried a second time to save the merchant fleet by the Merchant Marine Act of 1928 (Jones-White Act). Briefly, this legislation reaffirmed the general policy laid down in the 1920 Act and proposed to aid the industry by loaning money for shipbuilding at low rates of interest, and by paying for the transportation of mails at many times the cost. The loans were to be made from a revolving fund of $250,000,000 for twenty years, and up to three fourths of the cost of construction or reconditioning. In other words, the indirect subsidies were extended. Thus after 1928 the Government was subsidizing the merchant marine, now largely privately owned, by selling ships at a fraction of their cost, by loaning money at low rates, and by paying far more for service than it was worth.

Since European nations could carry American passengers and freight on the high seas at less cost than our own merchant marine, the only reason for subsidies lay in the promotion of national defense. This was also the main reason for subsidizing air transportation, a policy followed by all the great nations of the world. Here again the subsidization was mainly indirect. Although such forms of assistance as the provision of airports and weather information were given by various branches of the Government, the aid was mainly by mail contracts. Until 1925 the Government carried its own mail, but in the conservative reaction following the election of 1924 this was abandoned, and the Postmaster-General was instructed to turn the business over to private concerns. During the fiscal years 1926–1932 the Government obtained from postal revenues roughly $27,008,000 while it paid air carriers $68,165,000. The Army and Navy were meanwhile doing much to promote the manufacture of airplanes by purchasing about one third of those built. Despite subsidization, the American Merchant Marine failed during the twenties to prosper. Air transportation, on the other hand, jumped ahead rapidly in the years after 1927 and Government aid was undoubtedly a factor. In 1927 the number of passengers carried was only 8,679; by 1932 it had skyrocketed to 540,681.

No argument of national defense could be adduced to justify the large amounts spent on inland waterway transportation. Nor was there any crying need on commercial grounds for enlargement of the nation's transportation facilities. Big business was generally indifferent to the waterways, while the railroads vigorously opposed the subsidization of rival facilities. As in other decades, however, a demand for better water routes came from various groups, chiefly farmers living in the eighteen states bordering on the Ohio, Missouri, and Mississippi. The problem of flood control, particularly with respect to the Ohio and the Mississippi, added to the demand for Federal subsidies.

During the twenties and early thirties the intracoastal waterway first envisaged by Gallatin more than a century earlier, and now mapped from Boston to Corpus Christi, Texas, was developed. The Ohio River canalization, under way for many years, was completed (1929), and the Lakes to the Gulf Deep Waterway, linking Lake Michigan and the Mississippi, was finally opened in 1933. No project was more discussed during these years than the St. Lawrence Ship Canal. Middle Western farmers suffering from depressed agricultural prices saw in it an opportunity to save on transportation costs to Europe. Opposition, on the other hand,

came from railroads, citizens of New York State
who had just completed a costly new barge canal,
and those who believed that the great expense could
hardly be justified on economic grounds. The difficulties of agriculture, it was argued, were so fundamental that a small reduction in transportation
costs would not lessen them. Although both
Coolidge and Hoover endorsed the St. Lawrence
Waterway, Congress failed to act.

Criticism cannot be fairly directed against the
Coolidge-Mellon-Hoover regime because it aided
big business. That, in general, has been the Government policy since the days of the Industrial
Revolution. It can, however, be justly charged that
these men allowed big business to dictate the rules
of the game and manage the economic life of the
nation with virtually no restraint. No sensible
critic, of course, would assert that the great depression following the crash of 1929 was the work of
these men. Economic cycles have been far more
powerful than the actions of any individual or the
policies of any government. But the Coolidge-
Mellon-Hoover policies can be blamed for their encouragement of many unsound business activities.
The nation was driving headlong toward an economic catastrophe. Washington did not seem to
perceive this, and certainly did little or nothing to
prevent it.

One of the most dangerous aspects of economic

life was the expansion of credit far beyond the legitimate needs of the nation; so far, in fact, that it got completely out of control of the Federal Reserve System. In the end it was mainly responsible for the unprecedented stock-market speculation that characterized the boom. Many factors played a part in this expansion of credit. The most important, perhaps, were the heavy flotations of Government bonds during the war and the heavy importation of foreign gold. The Federal Government began the decade with a debt of approximately $33,000,000,000, much of it in bonds available for credit expansion. Between 1915 and 1929 the gold coin and bullion in the country increased from $1,986,000,000 to $4,284,000,000. In the five years from 1922 to 1927 alone approximately $900,000,-000 in gold flowed into the United States. Credit was also built up by large surpluses earned by industry and by the savings of well-paid workers. Savings and other time deposits in United States banks grew from $15,314,000,000 in 1920 to $28,485,000,000 in 1930.

With this as a reservoir, ample means were available for credit expansion. High profits in industry encouraged borrowing for investment and speculation in stocks and bonds. The desire for such new products as automobiles, radios, and iceless refrigerators encouraged borrowing, and one student has estimated that while only one tenth of retail sales were made on credit in 1910, one half were so made by 1929. At the same time competition between banks and a deterioration in bank inspection helped to promote unwise credit expansion. The larger banks assisted the movement by opening security affiliates to promote the selling of stocks and bonds, both domestic and foreign.

Under this pressure, credit expansion advanced rapidly, with only minor setbacks in 1924 and 1927. As usual, it was most dramatically displayed in stock-market speculation. Prices of industrial stocks multiplied more than five times between 1921 and 1929, activity on the stock market tripled, and the price of seats on the New York Stock Exchange jumped from a low of $76,000 in 1923 to the astounding figure of $625,000 in January, 1929. Most of this expansion occurred after 1924 and was popularly known as the "Coolidge market." How much the Government could have done to halt the runaway expansion in credit and speculation is uncertain. The Federal Reserve banks made some effort toward control by easing rediscount rates during setbacks and increasing them when speculation was too rampant. Nevertheless, its policies in 1922, 1924, and 1927 were undoubtedly such as to encourage credit expansion; particularly in 1927, when it reduced its discount rates from 4 to $3\frac{1}{2}$ per cent. The Federal Reserve had lost control of the nation's credit, a fact which it admitted. Business, nevertheless, is extremely sensitive, and clearly enunciated words of warning might have done something to check inordinate speculation. The mere fact that Professor Ripley of Harvard, who had done much to expose the evils of certain types of high financing then current, dined at the White House was once enough to give the stock market a healthy setback.

Unfortunately, however, the national Government appeared continually to give its benediction to current business tendencies. At the height of the stock-market boom one prominent financier after another was the honored guest of the President. An occasional note of warning sounded by some apprehensive businessman was promptly answered by words of reassurance from Washington. When Mellon in March, 1927, left for a trip to Europe with the statement that "the stock market seems to be going along in an orderly fashion, and I see no evidence of overspeculation," the signal was given for full steam ahead.

CHAPTER IX

FOR industry the decade seemed a golden age. For agriculture, it was a period of decline and discouragement. While industry expanded and prospered, agriculture retreated in the face of difficulties greater than it had yet experienced. While cities grew rapidly in population and urban real estate boomed, farm population declined and the value of tillable land fell. It was a collapse so complete and overwhelming that the whole future of American agriculture seemed hanging in the balance.

It is not difficult to sketch the background of agrarian distress. Despite the romance which has surrounded the expanding frontier and the settlement of a continent by independent homesteaders, the lot of the American farmer has generally not been happy. For his surplus products, if he could find means of transportation, there was usually a market. The population of Europe and the seaboard states, expanding under the impetus of the Industrial Revolution, needed American crops.

Furthermore, these agricultural exports provided the principal means by which the young nation could obtain capital from abroad. But prices were often all too low—sometimes sickeningly low. Grain and cotton-growing areas expanded too rapidly for the maintenance of high agricultural rewards. Rural prosperity, when it actually appeared, was generally the result of rising land values rather than lucrative prices for crops.

During the twenty years after 1900 the American farmer had enjoyed one of his few long periods of prosperity. The almost intolerable pressure under which he had labored between 1880 and 1898, primarily as a result of overproduction, high credit costs, and monetary deflation, was lifted. With the end of the advancing frontier, the expansion of agriculture had slowed down. At the same time a new immigration was flowing from Southern and Eastern Europe at the rate of almost a million people a year. These millions, absorbed by an expanding industry able to pay living wages, increased the domestic market. Agriculture, furthermore, was not disturbed by any great revolution in technique which suddenly increased production. In short, demand had caught up with supply.

Such were the facts which explained the sunny period of agrarian prosperity. To these influences was added after 1914 the artificial stimulation of the World War. Europe, with her energies and man power engaged in destruction, was unable to maintain peacetime production and came to depend more and more upon the American surplus. After the United States entered the war the farmer was under even greater pressure to increase production. With rising demand came higher prices. Spring wheat which had sold for 93 cents a bushel at Chicago in 1913 had jumped to $2.76 in 1919 and corn had advanced from 70 cents to $1.59. Cotton which had sold in New York at 13 cents a pound in 1913 brought 38 cents in 1919. Only Government control kept prices even within these limits. Under such circumstances it is not surprising that farmers pushed onto marginal and submarginal land, invested in new machinery, and even borrowed to modernize their homes. Nor is it astonishing that rural areas demanded improved roads and better schools. Between 1900 and 1920 total agricultural production increased less than 50 per cent, but the value of farm lands and crops advanced more than fourfold and prices of farm products nearly threefold.

For almost two years after the armistice the artificial prosperity continued. Then came the sudden and inevitable collapse. Prices paid to farmers for corn in 1921 dropped to a third of the 1919 level; cotton, wheat, and hogs fell to half the 1919 figure, and cattle to almost half. While the prices of most agricultural commodities recovered somewhat during 1923–1926, they relapsed again in the late twenties and plunged down still further after the crash of 1929. In view of the heavy borrowings in boom years, tragedy was inevitable. The bankruptcy rate for each thousand farms jumped from 0.21 in 1920 to slightly more than 1.20 for the years 1924–1926, while farm-mortgage indebtedness increased almost $2,000,000,000 between 1920 and 1929. Agricultural land values became utterly demoralized. Government experts estimated that they dropped from $79,000,000,000 in 1920 to $58,000,000,000 in 1927, and to $44,000,000,000 in 1932. Put in another way, the average price of land fell from $108 per acre in 1920 to $76 in 1926 and continued downwards. The total farm income of $12,000,000,000 in 1919 declined to $5,200,000,000 in 1932.

Other effects of the depression were quite as significant. One was the increase in the number of farms operated by tenants. For the nation as a whole the proportion rose from 38 per cent in 1920 to 42 in 1930. The tenancy, moreover, appeared to be of a new type. Instead of a rung on the ladder upwards to independent ownership, it was a descent toward the status of agricultural laborer, a class rapidly growing during the decade. Tenant occupation of land generally resulted in deterioration both of soil and equipment. Sometimes when the title lapsed to a bank or insurance company, small farms

were united into larger holdings, supervised more
scientifically by agents of the new owners. But even
so, the tendency was away from the old-time farm
independence. Looking at this rise in tenancy and
the increased mortgage debt, many students won-
dered whether the American farmer was destined to
sink to the status of the European peasant.

Multitudes of impoverished farm workers turned
toward mill, shop, and counter. Industrial advance
and agricultural decline, along with the introduction of improved farm machinery, brought a decrease in population on farms from 31,614,000 in
1920 to 30,169,000 in 1930. We have mentioned
that the decade saw an average net movement from
the farms of about 600,000 each year, this taking
place while the population for the nation as a whole
increased by over 17,000,000.

A complete picture of the farmer's difficulties requires other dark strokes. Prices of everything he
sold might collapse, but there was no comparable
deflation in the prices of commodities which he
must buy. Industry, well protected by tariffs and
bulwarked by consolidations, was in a strong position to stabilize prices at monopoly levels. Similarly, wages paid to agricultural labor did not decline comparably with prices. Nor did taxes; indeed,
the proportion of farm income going into taxes increased during the decade. Freight rates rose, and
the costs of handling and selling crops increased. As

many times before, the farmer was caught between deflated prices on the one hand and relatively fixed charges on the other.

Many causes contributed to this agricultural collapse. First and most important was the sudden contraction of the market. As Europe returned to a peace basis, she curtailed her purchases. This was not only because European nations could supply a greater proportion of their own needs, but because they were deeply in debt. These debts might have been paid in part by exchanging manufactures for agricultural commodities, but high American tariffs hindered this. And the effort of the American farmer to recapture his European markets became increasingly difficult under the competition of other young countries. While the United States was growing more grain and meats, so also were Canada, Australia, the Argentine, and many other lands. Since these nations were less industrialized and less hedged about by high tariffs, Europe found it easier to buy from them.

Although population in the United States was increasing, the domestic market for certain kinds of agricultural products also declined. A slim figure was now considered both fashionable and healthy. Americans not only shifted from cereals and meats to fruits and vegetables, but also ate less food. It is true that this shift gave an impetus to fruit raising and to truck and dairy farming, but it was not long before these industries were also overexpanded. Meanwhile, there were fewer farm animals to feed. Mechanization of farms, particularly the introduction of trucks and tractors, had eliminated since 1916 about 6,000,000 horses and mules and released from 15,000,000 to 18,000,000 acres formerly used in production of feed. This mechanization, it should be added, had increased the farmer's debts while diminishing his market for hay and other commodities. It helped make the adjustment to peacetime conditions and to a narrowing market more difficult.

While markets declined, agricultural production actually increased by 20 per cent. Unlike many manufacturers, the farmer is unable to curtail production quickly or reduce his overhead easily. Having once put land under cultivation, he continues to use it. Since the Civil War, Federal and state governments had spent millions for agricultural investigation and education; as a result, farming technique and hence farm production were constantly improving. At the same time, the farmer during his boom days had invested heavily in machinery which made it possible to produce more with the same amount of labor. Moreover, the development of the gasoline-powered tractor in the war years and thereafter forced him to continue buying new machinery when he could ill afford it.

When the prosperity of the war years crashed in

1921, neither the agricultural experts nor the farmers themselves had any appreciation of the severity of the blow. Few expected that the depression would continue indefinitely. Wilson's two great contributions to rural betterment had been improved credit facilities, and a reduction of the tariff to encourage foreign trade. When the Republican Congress passed an Emergency Tariff Bill in 1921, Wilson vetoed it with a message in which he pointed out that a return to high protection would blight the foreign market for American crops. This sound argument made no impression upon Republican leaders. Immediately after his inauguration, as we have seen, Harding called a special session which rushed through an emergency tariff (May 27, 1921). This emergency tariff, along with the Fordney-McCumber Tariff of the following year and the Hawley-Smoot Tariff of 1930, raised duties on both agricultural and industrial commodities to unprecedented levels.

It was expected that the duties would raise the price of agricultural commodities, and in a few instances this really occurred. Economists, however, are generally agreed that the rates had little or no effect upon the prices of high-protein wheat, corn, barley, cotton, and other important exportable commodities. The price of these staples, of which a large surplus was exported, was fixed by the world market rather than by American tariff walls. It is likewise the almost universal opinion of economists that one effect of the high tariffs was, as Wilson had predicted, a curtailment of agricultural exports.

By the late spring of 1921 deflation was in full swing. Members of both Houses from the predominantly agricultural states organized early in May to promote legislation for farm relief. This group, led first by Senator William S. Kenyon of Iowa and later by Senator Arthur Capper of Kansas, was termed the "farm bloc." A breakdown of political lines over economic issues was by no means new in American history, but the "farm bloc" was nevertheless eyed distrustfully in the industrial states. Months before it was formally organized, representatives from agricultural states had helped to pass over Wilson's veto (January, 1921) a bill to revive the War Finance Corporation. This agency, whose powers were extended later in the year, was expected to finance the exportation of agricultural products and extend emergency agricultural credits. It was a forerunner of later agricultural legislation. Late in the spring the "bloc" succeeded in establishing a Joint Congressional Commission of Agricultural Inquiry, which during the following six months made a rather thorough investigation of the situation. As conditions showed no signs of improving, President Harding in January, 1922, called together a National Agricultural Congress to advise him.

Some legislation was inevitable. Among the important bills approved by Harding was the Packers and Stockyards Act (August, 1921), which made it unlawful for packers to engage in unfair practices, to combine to control prices, to apportion markets, or to create a monopoly. Charges must be reasonable and non-discriminatory. Those engaged in packing or marketing were to register with the Secretary of Agriculture, whose business it was to supervise the packing and marketing of live stock in much the same way that the Federal Trade Commission was expected to supervise business in general. In February, 1922, the President signed the Capper-Volstead Act, which exempted farmers' associations and cooperatives from attack under the anti-trust laws. A year later he approved the Agricultural Credits Act (March, 1923), which set up a Federal Intermediate Credit Bank in each Federal land-bank district, with a capitalization of $5,000,-000 and the power to issue debentures to ten times that amount. The security was to be notes, drafts, and bills of exchange already discounted by national banks, trust companies, and agricultural credit associations. These banks might also loan to agricultural cooperatives on warehouse receipts and bills of lading. The purpose of the Intermediate Credit Banks was at least twofold: first, to extend agricultural credit by establishing a new group of banks which would facilitate the discount of agricultural paper; and second, to extend credit for periods intermediate between the usual short-term commercial loan and the long-term obligations secured on land. Through these banks credit could be granted for from six months to three years.

There can be no doubt that Congress under the Harding Administration was alive to the maladies of agriculture. The acts above-mentioned and many others passed between 1921 to 1926 were, nevertheless, chiefly an extension of earlier facilities. They contributed somewhat to alleviate the symptoms, but they were unable to cure the disease. By the middle twenties this became clearly evident. Republican farmers began to realize that an industry with exportable surpluses could not be helped by high protection. Many also came to understand that it was impossible to borrow themselves out of debt. Since the Federal Farm Loan Act of 1916 a considerable mass of farm legislation had been passed. Almost every known method of aiding the farmer except price-fixing had been tried. As a last resort, agricultural leaders now turned to this. With the argument that agriculture had the same right to protection and aid as any other industry, they proposed various schemes by which the Government could artificially maintain prices.

Unfortunately for advocates of price-fixing, the Administration after the election of 1924 was even more conservative than before. Coolidge, whose agricultural experience was limited, seemed to take little interest in the problem. To the Chairman of the Farm Loan Board he once remarked that the life of the farmer had always been one of hardship. "Well, farmers never have made money," he observed. "I don't believe we can do much about it. But of course we shall have to seem to be doing something; do the best we can without much hope." Fortunately no such defeatist attitude was taken by the Department of Agriculture. Henry C. Wallace, appointed by Harding, actively supported remedial legislation. Upon his death in October, 1924, he was succeeded for a few months by Howard M. Gore and after March 4, 1925, by William M. Jardine. Jardine, who had been President of the Kansas State Agricultural College, was thoroughly acquainted with farmers' problems, but he had as little sympathy as the President with schemes for price-fixing.

If not disturbed by the plight of the farmers, Coolidge was at least consistent. He promised during the campaign of 1924 another agricultural conference, which he called late in November. In his annual message he appeared willing to go with Congress to any length short of price-fixing. In 1926 he reviewed at length the recent farm legislation and suggested further progress along the lines of freight rate readjustment, consolidation of railroads, continual development of waterways, production of cheap fertilizers, strengthening of cooperatives, and elimination of farm and plant diseases. A year later he even went so far as to endorse the creation of a farm board to aid farmers' cooperatives in orderly marketing and control of production. An administration bill to promote these objectives was introduced in 1926, but by this time the "farm bloc" was interested in more radical measures.

The demands of the farm group for artificial price maintenance were incorporated in various proposals known as the McNary-Haugen bills. Although differing in details, the purpose of all was to raise the domestic price, by various methods, to a level which would yield a fair profit. Under the first McNary-Haugen bill passed in 1927, the surplus not needed at home was to be sold abroad at what it would bring, the loss on the foreign sales to be assessed in the form of an equalization fee against every unit of the product sold by the producer. The net price to the producer, therefore, was to be the fixed domestic price minus the equalization fee. The law, it was expected, would discourage a surplus, because the larger the surplus, the larger the equalization fee and the smaller the return to the farmer. The bill as originally passed provided for only five commodities: cotton, wheat, corn, rice, and hogs. Later tobacco and other commodities were added in an effort to gain wider support. As the producers of tobacco and cotton sold too great a proportion of their crop abroad to be much interested in the scheme, and as many other products were sold abroad only in small quantities, the bill was essentially a Middle Western measure designed primarily to help the producers of wheat and hogs.

As the years passed, the McNary-Haugen proposals commanded increasing support. Introduced as early as 1924, a bill looking toward price maintenance and including an equalization fee finally went through both Houses in February, 1927. Coolidge promptly vetoed it on the ground that it was unconstitutional, unworkable, sectionally discriminatory, and certain to impose additional burdens upon the generality of farmers while giving doubtful help to the minority. In his opinion it would encourage overproduction and raise prices of farm products at home, while the nation sold the same products more cheaply abroad. He also argued that it would develop a huge bureaucracy. With his veto the President submitted an opinion of the Attorney-General that certain parts of the bill were unconstitutional. Farmers asserted that they were merely asking for the same aid that domestic manufacturers were obtaining and that the President's arguments against this plan applied quite as forcibly to a protective tariff.

Although unable to pass the bill over the President's veto, the "farm bloc" was undaunted. The proponents of the equalization fee again pushed through a McNary-Haugen bill in May, 1928. Again Coolidge vetoed it (May, 1928), declaring it unconstitutional. He minced no words in denouncing the measure as a "fantastic promise of unworkable governmental price regulation," as certain to encourage "bureaucratic tyranny of unprecedented proportions," and as tending to foster profiteering, wasteful distribution, and overproduction. An effort to override the veto failed narrowly in the Senate by a vote of 50 to 31 in which party lines were completely lost.

The idea of price-fixing and subsidization, however, could not be killed. In 1929 the Senate added a "debenture plan" to both the Smoot Tariff bill and the Administration's agricultural bill. Under this scheme the Government would pay export bounties on the chief agricultural commodities up to one half of the current tariff duties. The bounties were to be paid in debentures, negotiable instruments which could be used to defray import duties. A board was to be created to control the domestic surplus, if possible, by reducing the debenture payments whenever the surplus increased. Only the bitter opposition of the Administration, effective in the House, defeated this measure.

In the meantime the agricultural problem was injected prominently into the Presidential campaign of 1928. The best efforts of the farm leaders failed to extort from the Republicans more than an endorsement of the Administration program and a promise from Hoover to call a special session of Congress, if necessary, to pass a farm-board bill. The Democrats evaded a specific endorsement of the McNary-Haugen bill, but they did give platform promises of Federal intervention "in order that the price of the surplus may not determine the price of the whole crop" and of steps necessary "to plan and maintain the purchasing power of farm products and the complete economic equality of agriculture." Although this was a virtual promise of an equalization fee, or something similar, most farm leaders endorsed Hoover. His election brought a special session of Congress and the enactment of the program long advocated by himself and Coolidge.

Rejecting price-fixing and subsidies, the Agricultural Marketing Act of 1929 sought to solve the problem by encouraging the voluntary combination of farmers under Government supervision. A Federal Farm Board of eight members was established and was given a revolving fund of $500,-000,000 to encourage the organization and development of cooperatives. If necessary, the Board might set up subordinate stabilization corporations to maintain prices. Whether the Agricultural Marketing Act offered the basis of a solution of the farm problem is highly doubtful. Within six months a major depression started agriculture on a new period of deflation which no Government machinery could stop. During its first year the Federal Farm Board loaned more than $165,000,000 to 132 cooperatives, and set up a Grain Stabilization Corporation and a Cotton Stabilization Corporation to purchase surpluses of these commodities. The Wheat Stabilization Corporation bought 330,000,-000 bushels and managed to peg the price of wheat at satisfactory levels for a half year. In the end the price slumped again, and when the Government finally got rid of its holdings it had lost most of its investment. With cotton the experience was about the same. To maintain prices the Cotton Stabilization Corporation bought both the 1929–1930 carry-over and that of 1930–1931. In the end prices slumped anyway, and the corporation was left in 1932 with 3,250,000 bales in its warehouses. The loss to the taxpayers was about $150,000,000.

Despite the predominant influence of financial and industrial interests on the Government during the Harding-Coolidge era, agriculture had not been neglected. The united political strength of the farmers had seen to that. A mass of agricultural legislation had been passed, only the most important parts of which we have described. With the exception of the tariff, most of it had been helpful. As time passed, the Government had shifted its emphasis from encouragement of production to control of marketing. It aimed at a stabilized agriculture. For Administrations which glorified "rugged individualism," the promotion of cooperatives, of course, seems a little inconsistent. After all, however, they were attempting to lead farmers out of the wilderness of destructive competition along much the same path that business had used to save itself in earlier decades. Both Coolidge and Hoover gagged at actual price-fixing, but the thirties were to see even this remedy finally attempted.

While the farmer had many friends in Washington, labor as a whole was largely neglected. Foremost among the reasons for this was the conservative reaction following the war. Second in importance was the decline and demoralization of organized labor itself, weakening its prestige and political influence. Another factor was the widespread belief that labor had profited during the World War, and was generally in a prosperous condition. This belief actually had no foundation. It was in the post-war years beginning in 1920 that real wages advanced. On the other hand, the work week had been shortened roughly five hours since 1914. For labor as a whole the average in 1920 was still 54.4 hours, but in the skilled trades, particularly those well organized, it had dropped 10 per cent.

On the face of the evidence, labor appeared to be moving ahead rapidly. A closer examination, however, reveals a less encouraging picture. Since 1900 the production per capita had increased 60 per cent and the output per worker engaged directly in production had increased 80 per cent. Nevertheless, the share of the wage earners in the total national income rose but slightly, if at all, during the prosperous twenties. This was despite the fact that real wages after 1919 were actually increasing. It should be added that industry failed to take care of available labor. Even in the boom years the average number of unemployed, as we have noted, ran well above a million and a half, while in the recession years of 1921, 1922, 1924, and 1927 the estimates were from two to four millions.

In some important respects the standard of living for labor undoubtedly improved steadily up to 1929. New inventions had made work easier and life more comfortable; social legislation had done much to protect the health, well-being, and working conditions of the wage earner and his family. Whether from a purely economic angle labor had gained ground was an open question. But there could be no doubt that it had declined in morale, independence, and prestige. The best measure of this decline was the falling status of the unions.

The outstanding labor organization of the nation, the American Federation of Labor, stood at a new height of its power in 1920. In that year it boasted a membership of 4,078,740, more than double its strength in 1914. Except for the few unions which had become stationary before the war or were harassed by internal dissensions, every one of its 110 national organizations showed gains. In the trades affected by the war, such as munitions, ship-building, car repairs, railroads, textiles, and clothing, these gains had been spectacular. Income from the affiliated unions had similarly increased. With this new power and strength, unions had been able to introduce in many industries the eight-hour day and the forty-four-hour week. Nine years later what was the situation? Annual average membership had sunk to 2,933,545. Of the 105 international unions then existing 36 had lost in membership while 25 had remained about stationary. Income had decreased and many activities were curtailed. Judicial decisions had cut deeply into labor's hard-won legal rights, and the wide middle-class sympathy enjoyed in the pre-war years had been largely lost.

This decline was attributable to many causes both within and without the unions. Over some labor had no control; with others it failed to cope intelligently. The wave of conservatism which swept the nation in the twenties was obviously detrimental to the labor movement. Although organized labor might have met the reaction more effectively, it could not prevent it. Nor was organized labor responsible for the depression of 1921–1922, which

hurt it severely. It could hardly prevent membership losses in unions of cigarmakers, molders, metal
polishers, journeymen tailors, brewery workers,
and garment workers, where new machinery or
other technological changes were eliminating workers. Furthermore, it could not prevent a decline in
membership in such "sick industries" as hard and
soft coal mining. There were, however, certain
unions, such as those among foundry workers, railway carmen, seamen, and textile operatives, which
had grown rapidly during the war and with better
leadership might have been kept strong. The traditional opposition of organized labor to Government
price-fixing and control of labor conditions hastened
the dismantling of the Government war boards,
and accelerated the disintegration of the new
unions. Failure adequately to support the coal
strike of 1919 and other strikes during the next
three years proved costly. Meanwhile, no aggressive unionization work was attempted in the new
mass industries—among them rubber, electric appliances, automobile manufacturing, and radios.

Organized labor was also weakened by internal
conflicts. The democratic and socialist revolution
in Europe resulting from the war had stirred liberals
and radicals in the American labor movement to
new hopes and greater demands. There was widespread dissatisfaction with the existing leadership
and its "old line unionism," and a demand for more

socialistic policies. It was this dissatisfaction which thrust forward John L. Lewis for president of the American Federation of Labor in 1921 against the aging Samuel Gompers. While that effort failed, the opposition to the conservative leadership was so strong that concessions had to be made. The Federation in 1920 endorsed Government ownership of railroads and in 1924 the candidacy of LaFollette. In 1919 it even laid down a "reconstruction program" of decidedly progressive type, calling for democracy in industry, abolition of unemployment, prohibition of child labor, equal pay to women, right of public employees to bargain collectively, restriction of the judicial power, Government ownership of public and semi-public utilities, better Federal and state regulation of corporations, absolute freedom of expression and association, extension of workmen's compensation, establishment of Government employment agencies, and Government construction of model homes to be sold on credit to the workers.

The trend toward more progressive policies was in the end hindered rather than promoted by the aggressive technique of the more radical labor groups. Under the leadership of William Z. Foster and the Trade Union Educational League, American Communists attempted aggressively to "bore from within." They worked chiefly among the immigrant garment workers of New York, whose

natural sympathy for the Russian experiment provided a promising field. Their activities, as in the
Passaic woolen strike of 1926, showed a sincere desire to improve the lot of underpaid and exploited
operatives. The result, however, was generally
destructive. For a time the Communists obtained
control of most New York locals in the Fur Workers
Union and some in the International Ladies' Garment Workers' Union and all but destroyed them.
Efforts to capture the Amalgamated Clothing
Workers were foiled by skillful union leadership.
By 1928 the "boring from within" program of the
Trade Union Educational League had collapsed,
and the fourth Congress of the Red International
of Labor Unions ordered it to give up its old tactics
and try to organize the workers into separate
unions. No hope, the Congress declared, could be
placed in the so-called progressives of the old
unions. In line with these instructions the Communists, renaming their organization the Trade
Union Unity League, attempted to organize separate unions, particularly among the miners and the
textile and needle workers. But these unions failed
to develop into strong organizations and the strikes
in which they engaged were usually unsuccessful.

Failure of the Communists led various Socialists
and "progressives" to organize in 1929 the Conference for Progressive Labor Action in the hope of
swinging organized labor to a more radical policy.

This effort also proved futile, for the Federation press denounced the Conference as Communist-inspired and it made little progress. In the end the chief result of the Communist tactics was to stiffen the conservative leanings of old-line union leaders. Fighting to retain their offices, they prevented a normal replacement by younger men, many of whom finally had to come to the older leaders to seek aid against the undermining tactics of their Communist foes. Instead of yielding to progressive views, Woll and other leaders set their faces against change. The death of Gompers in 1924 and his replacement by William Green brought no new policy. In resisting radicalism, the leaders of the American Federation curtailed the liberal labor press, outlawed the Brookwood labor school, and consumed their energies in internal conflict. At a time when international labor was seeking new roads, American labor turned its face backward.

While organized labor was weakened by internal dissensions, it was being ruthlessly hammered at from without. First of all, it had lost Government support. The interest in the welfare of labor so warmly manifested by the first Wilson Administration had subsided by 1919. The increasing chilliness of both Federal and state governments was shown in three ways: first, increased use of Government agencies to break strikes; second, passage of anti-labor legislation; and third, the hostility of the judiciary. The attitude of the Federal Government was made dramatically evident by its before-mentioned disruption of the bituminous coal strike in 1919 by a sweeping injunction under the Lever Act (see Chapter III). That same year the railroad shopmen's strike met Government opposition, as did the steel strike. In Indiana both state and national troops were called out to keep the peace in Gary, where General Leonard Wood declared martial law. In Pennsylvania, Governor Sproul refused state protection to strikers and turned them over to local authorities and private police, both controlled by the steel companies. As a result, civil liberties and constitutional rights, as far as strikers were concerned, virtually lapsed during the conflict.

Fearful of post-war social upheavals, twenty-one states and two territories passed anti-syndicalist laws between 1917 and 1920. These laws were generally ignored by the American Federation and by the "respectable" elements of organized labor because they were aimed at the Industrial Workers of the World and Communists. Nevertheless, various states did not hesitate to use them against "well-behaved" labor organizations if an industrial conflict became too hot. In 1921–1922 a number of anti-strike bills were actually introduced to take away labor's most important weapon. Only one passed, a Kansas law of 1920 forbidding strikes in basic industries and creating a Court of Industrial

Relations to investigate and settle disputes. If work was unlawfully suspended in any industry designated as vital, the state was empowered to take it over. The Kansas Act was widely discussed and its author, Governor Henry J. Allen, rose to considerable political influence. The law was declared unconstitutional (1923) in several important sections, however, and dropped into oblivion.

Of all departments of the Government the most hostile in the long run to labor was the judiciary. The liberal point of view taken by the courts just before the war was largely reversed thereafter. In 1918 (Hammer *v*. Dagenhart) and again in 1922 (Bailey *v*. Drexel Furniture Company), the Supreme Court killed two Congressional efforts to end child labor. The movement for social legislation was likewise imperiled by a Supreme Court decision in 1923 (Adkins *v*. Children's Hospital), which declared a minimum wage law in the District of Columbia unconstitutional.

More serious than the antipathy of the Supreme Court toward social legislation was its apparent opposition to unions. In 1915 it upheld the "yellow-dog contract" (Coppage *v*. Kansas); that is, a contract forced by some companies on their employees preventing membership in a union. Two years later it confirmed a decision declaring it illegal to attempt to organize workers who had signed such contracts (Hitchman Coal and Coke Co. *v*. Mitchell). Two

decisions in 1921 (Traux *v.* Corrigan, and American
Steel Foundries *v.* Tri-City Trades and Labor
Council) greatly restricted the use of picketing.
In the latter case the Supreme Court actually de-
clared all forms of picketing unlawful, but in prac-
tice mitigated the severity of the decision.

Two other legal trends were disturbing to labor:
the growing use of the injunction in labor disputes,
and the undermining of rights granted in the Clayton Act of 1914. Articles 6 and 20 of the Clayton
Act had specifically exempted labor from prosecution under the Anti-trust Act and greatly limited
the use of the injunction. This apparent protection,
however, was soon cut away by the Court. By the
early twenties the Clayton Act, which labor had
hailed as its Magna Charta, was a broken reed. In
Duplex Printing Press Co. *v.* Deering, 1921, the
Court declared a secondary boycott illegal, and in
United Mine Workers *v.* Coronado Coal Company,
1922, it allowed suit against an unincorporated
union for damages under the anti-trust laws.
Labor's rights were further demolished in the Bed-
ford Cut Stone Case in 1927, when the Supreme
Court issued an injunction forbidding the stone-
cutters' union to refuse to handle products of
quarrying companies where non-union labor was
used. So low had the legal position of the workers
fallen that Morris Hillquit, one of the ablest labor
lawyers of the period, commented bitterly that in

theory labor might still have the right to organize, strike, picket, and boycott, but "in practice the rules have been hedged in by so many modifications and departures that they have been reduced to the status of an abstract social philosophy rather than a statement of positive law."

The record of the Supreme Court on labor issues gives clear indication of a persistent division on the basis of conflicting economic and social philosophies. Only three Justices who were in office at the beginning of the Harding Administration (Willis Van Deventer, James C. McReynolds and Louis D. Brandeis) were still on the Court at the beginning of the Roosevelt Administration. The general viewpoint of the Court, nevertheless, had changed but little. The year after ex-President Taft succeeded Chief Justice White in 1921, Sutherland succeeded Clarke and Butler took the place of Day. Both the new Justices were conservative in their economic and social views. The resignation of Justice Mahlon Pitney shortly brought in Edward T. Sanford, whose conservatism was but slightly less rigid than that of Sutherland and Butler. Upon the retirement of Joseph McKenna in 1925 Coolidge appointed Harlan F. Stone to the vacant seat. Stone, who had defended the Supreme Court against the rising criticism of Progressives, was undoubtedly considered by the President a stanch conservative. It was not long, however, before he took his place with Brandeis and Holmes among the "liberal minority."

Indication of the opposition to the conservatism of the Supreme Court was furnished by the Progressive Party in the campaign platform of 1924. It demanded a Constitutional amendment which would protect from judicial veto a law reenacted by Congress after it had been nullified by the Supreme Court. The opposition was also evident in 1930 when Hoover nominated Charles E. Hughes to succeed Taft as Chief Justice. Hughes was confirmed by a vote of 52 to 26, but only after Senators had questioned his fitness on grounds of politics and social philosophy. Resigning from the Supreme Court in 1916 to run for the Presidency, Hughes had spent the next fourteen years as a highly paid counsel of great corporations. Opponents insisted that the appointment seemed like an award for political services and that his long connection with Wall Street unfitted him for the objectivity necessary in the exalted position of Chief Justice.

Progressive Senators were unable to prevent the ratification of Hughes, but later in the same year they turned down the nomination of John J. Parker of North Carolina by 41 to 39. Parker had disqualified himself in the minds of many Senators because of his opposition to the participation of Negroes in politics and because of a decision in which he had upheld an injunction forbidding the

United Mine Workers of America from attempting to unionize workers who had signed "yellow-dog contracts." Although the Senate turned down Parker, they accepted with little opposition the nomination of Owen J. Roberts, whose career had shown no particular evidence of liberalism.

When Oliver Wendell Holmes retired in 1932 at the age of ninety, Hoover nominated in his place Benjamin N. Cardozo. It was the only nomination to the Supreme Court between 1921 and 1932 intentionally given to a liberal. Any other kind of nomination at the time could hardly be justified on any grounds, and Hoover was thoroughly aware of it. For over a quarter of a century Holmes had been the leader in the tiny group of liberal opposition in the Supreme Court where his brief but penetratingly clear dissenting decisions had more than once pointed the way to positions later accepted by the majority. In the later twenties the alignment of the Court on economic and social problems was clear and the decisions predictable. On the one side were four conservatives; on the other were three liberals. The phrase, "Holmes, Brandeis, and Stone dissenting," became a commonplace to those who followed Supreme Court decisions. In between were Chief Justice Hughes and Justice Roberts, who movd back and forth between the two extremes and were often in a position to determine some of the most important issues argued before the Court.

Not alone in labor cases was the conservative attitude of the Supreme Court evident. There seemed also to be a definite and persistent effort on the part of the majority to prevent the extension of state and Federal regulatory power over economic enterprise. Time and again the Court restricted the police power of the states and prevented an expansion of the public interest theory over various types of business which the states were attempting to control (Chapter VIII). And, as suggested in an earlier chapter, it confused and made more difficult the determination of public utility rates by the Government. On the other hand, the Court took a reasonably liberal position on civil liberties. Although it upheld anti-syndicalist laws in the Gitlow case in New York and the Whitney case in California, it did declare unconstitutional state laws which appeared to infringe the First Amendment. Examples of such legislation declared unconstitutional include a Pennsylvania law which forbade the conducting of schools in other languages than English, the Oregon law which would have destroyed parochial and other private schools, a California law forbidding the display of a red flag, and a Wisconsin law which provided that a newspaper or magazine publishing malicious and defamatory material might be abated as a nuisance. It should be noted that the Court proved a stanch defender of the procedural rights of Negroes in the courts.

Injurious as were the anti-labor decisions of the Supreme Court, organized labor was faced, particularly in the early twenties, with a more immediate danger. This was the open-shop drive, euphemistically known as the "American plan," which employers pushed vigorously in the post-war years. In the belief that wartime wages should be deflated and union gains eliminated, the National Association of Manufacturers, the National Metal Trades Association, and their numerous subsidiaries, backed in many cities by Chambers of Commerce, set out to break the power of the unions. Wilson made some effort to discourage this campaign by calling an Industrial Conference in October, 1919, but it failed miserably. By the end of 1920 the nation was covered with a network of open-shop organizations; one labor student asserted that there were at least three hundred in the eight states of New York, Illinois, Ohio, Pennsylvania, Michigan, California, Texas and Iowa. With American business and finance behind it, the drive made great gains. Scores of cities became open shop. Even San Francisco, noted as a strong union town, saw important labor defeats. The war gains in the seamen's, the packers' and the textile unions were largely wiped out and the union organizations were smashed for a decade. On the other hand, attacks on the printing crafts and the needle trades unions failed.

In the open-shop drive employers developed a technique involving a wide variety of methods. Some were designed to intimidate workers, others to win their cooperation. The use of the labor spy, the hired strikebreaker, and the *agent provocateur* probably date back to the first unions, but it is doubtful if they were ever employed more widely than in the 1920's. Their prevalence was not revealed until the LaFollette Committee, a decade later, dug into the business of the private detective agencies. When the facts came to light it appeared that numerous agencies provided annually a small army of spies at an approximate annual cost of $80,000,000. One labor leader of many years' experience stated that he never "knew of a gathering large enough to be called a meeting and small enough to exclude a labor spy."

To counteract the influence of *bona fide* unions or to push the open-shop movement many employers organized their own unions. Prior to 1917 not more than a dozen plants of importance had introduced the company union; a decade later between four and five hundred existed, with a membership of more than 1,400,000. The greatest development of the company union was in the railroads, where, beginning with the Baltimore and Ohio, they made rapid progress after the collapse of the shopmen's strike of 1922. They were also pushed in public utilities, in iron and steel, in electric supplies, and in street railroads. The most elaborate scheme, however, was in the rubber industry, where the Goodyear Tire and Rubber Company introduced an employee representation plan patterned after the United States Government and including a House of Representatives, a Senate and other features of our national administration. Interesting as was the development of company unions in the twenties, they also expanded in the early thirties, when they were used to stem the tide of unionism after the passage of Section 7a of the National Industrial Recovery Act.

No student of the economic history of the period can fail to be impressed by the development of what labor writers have called "welfare capitalism." In certain instances and to some extent this may have been motivated by a desire to paralyze unionization as well as to develop a more loyal, stable, and efficient working force. In general, however, it was a humanitarian effort to improve the lot of the worker. In its best form, "welfare capitalism" looked toward not only a loyal and efficient working force but a guarantee on the part of capital of decent wages and job security. It was also concerned with the health and safety of the worker and his family. In some instances managers promoted the introduction of "industrial democracy," with workers helping to shape the labor policy of the company. Some companies carried on elaborate educational programs, encouraged workers in various ways to purchase their own homes, provided low-cost cafeterias under the charge of trained dieticians, offered free medical service, introduced profit-sharing, vacations with pay, and insurance policies paid in whole or in part by the company. These services, as unions often asserted, may have encouraged workers to look toward the employers rather than the union for many of the better things of life. Nevertheless they were often of great immediate value and had far-reaching importance in raising the living standard of workers to a higher level.

Among the efforts used during these years to encourage stability and cooperation was the promotion of employee stock ownership. In some companies, ownership was virtually compulsory; wherever it was tried the company made it possible to purchase on the installment plan. Leadership in the promotion of stock ownership was taken in the industrial field by United States Steel, Bethlehem Steel, and the Eastman Kodak Company; in the utilities by the American Telephone and Telegraph Company; among railroads by the Pennsylvania and the New York Central, and in oil by the Standard Oil Company. Just what progress was made it is difficult to determine accurately, but by the end of the decade, certainly a million or more American workmen owned stock, representing a current value of more than a billion dollars, in the concerns in which they worked.

So rapidly had the movement for employee stock ownership progressed that certain followers of "Pollyanna economics" hailed it as proof of an "economic revolution" in which the ownership of the country's wealth was passing from the hands of the employer to those of the wage earner. In comparison with the total wealth represented by industrial stocks, the part owned by labor was in reality small. A Federal Trade Commission study revealed that in 1922 "employees comprised 7.5 per cent of the common stockholders reported, and 3.5 per cent of the preferred stockholders, but they had only 1.5 per cent of the common stock and 2 per cent of the preferred." Another study made by private individuals some years later revealed that in twenty important companies which had vigorously pushed employee stock ownership, only 4.26 per cent of the stock was owned by employees. When it is realized that a part of this was owned by executives, superintendents, and salaried men, and that at the same time the technique whereby a small group could control an industry was being rapidly perfected, the hope of democratizing industry through employee stock ownership was slender. That ownership of stock by workers may have improved morale and diminished labor troubles and turnover during the twenties is readily conceded.

But when labor awoke after the crash of 1929 to find the current value of its stock but a fraction of what it had cost, much of the former good will dissolved into resentment.

Far more useful from almost every point of view was the development of various forms of group insurance covering disability and death. This was in addition to workmen's compensation, which by 1920 was compulsory in most of the industrial states. Estimates in 1926 show 4,700,000 workers covered by group insurance schemes of a total value of more than $5,500,000,000, a figure which increased to $10,000,000,000 by 1931. Pension schemes also had made rapid progress. A survey by the Pennsylvania Old Age Pension Commission in 1926 revealed that more than four hundred firms, with four million employees, had pension plans.

Almost every trend during the twenties tended to weaken organized labor and put it on the defensive. Failure of strikes in the post-war years undermined morale and diminished the number of labor conflicts. The annual average number of strikes between 1916 and 1921 was 3,503, involving 1,798,809 workers; during the years 1926 to 1930 the annual average was 791 and the number of workers 244,947. The rise in real wages and the stock-ownership plans were developing both in organized and unorganized workers a middle-class psychology. "Welfare capitalism" was weakening the ability of labor to stand on its own feet and achieve its own destiny. The traditional attitude of labor had been to demand high wages, or at least "a fair day's wage for a fair day's work," and then look after its own welfare. Finally, labor had lost much of the sympathy which the middle class had given it in the pre-war years. For this, a reactionary propaganda was in part responsible, with its continued reiteration that organized labor was in the control of racketeers and that high wages were responsible for the high prices of commodities.

It was a difficult situation, and old-line leaders, distrustful of new methods, showed insufficient ability in meeting the problems of a new age. Some efforts were made to clean out racketeering, particularly in the building trades, and progress was made. Certainly the building trades continued during the twenties to be the backbone of organized labor. Efforts were also made to organize textile mills in the South and in the rapidly growing automobile industry, but they failed. A campaign to push the use of union label goods among organized workers aroused little interest. To win over public opinion, labor offered to cooperate in raising production and reducing costs. Although this idea was successfully applied by the Amalgamated Clothing Workers (men's clothing), it was generally ignored by employers. For organized labor, as a whole, the twenties were years of decline and discouragement.

CHAPTER X

END OF AN ERA

"WHAT the country requires," said Coolidge in his annual message of 1926, "is not so much new policies as a steady continuity of those which are already being crowned with such abundant success." No one ever expressed the Coolidge policy better than the President himself did in these words. They strike the keynote of his Administration, and in part explain the lack of legislation during his six years in office. It should be added, of course, that he laid an unceasing emphasis upon economy, a balanced budget, and the payment of the national debt. Coolidge believed sincerely that "the government can do more to remedy the economic ills of the people by a system of rigid economy in public expenditures than can be accomplished through any other action."

It was not alone the inactivity of Coolidge that accounts for the dearth of legislative action; the indifference of Congress also played a part. After his amazing victory in 1924, Coolidge proposed in his annual message (December 3) a mild and conservative program. He called for economy, river improvements, sale or lease of Muscle Shoals, railroad consolidation, penal and judicial reforms, a humanizing of the administration of the immigration acts, full Constitutional rights for Negroes, extension of the civil service, reorganization of Governmental departments, reduction of taxation and adherence to the World Court. Except for reduction of taxation along the lines advocated by Secretary Mellon, the Sixty-ninth Congress, elected with him in 1924, paid no attention to the President's wishes.

A number of reasons account for the President's lack of any strong influence over Congress. The Senators who picked Harding had deliberately intended to transfer the balance of power from the executive to the legislative branch, and did not propose to return it under Coolidge. Old Senate leaders, it is true, were passing from the scene, but their emerging rivals had not sufficient prestige to deliver votes to the Administration. The Progressives, it should also be remembered, held almost a balance of power in the Sixty-eighth and the Seventieth Congresses. They distrusted Coolidge, and with reason, for he neither understood nor was interested in their problems. Even conservative Senators disliked the President's efforts to bend to his own will such theoretically independent bodies as the Ship-

ping Board, the Federal Trade Commission, the
Tariff Commission, and the Interstate Commerce
Commission. They may also have felt a twinge of
jealousy over the popularity which the President
enjoyed throughout the country, while they must
have resented the critical attitude of the press
toward Congress. Congress never took Coolidge as
seriously as did the nation, and the Senate showed
little hesitation in turning down Presidential nominations. We have mentioned Charles B. Warren's
fate; the appointment of Cyrus E. Woods and the
reappointment of John J. Esch to the Interstate
Commerce Commission were also rejected.

Industrial prosperity, of course, had much to do
with the failure to enact outstanding legislation
during the Coolidge years. But in addition, Progressives were opposed to the Coolidge program and
many Democrats were mainly interested in expos-
ing the scandals of the Harding period. Combinations of Democrats and Progressive Republicans
harassed the Administration by investigations of
the oil leases, the Bureau of Internal Revenue, the
Treasury Department, the Attorney-General's office, the Federal Trade Commission, and the Tariff
Commission. As a matter of fact, the two major
parties showed few basic differences, and the votes
in Congress tended to be dominated by geographic
and economic influences rather than by party
policy. This breakdown of old party lines was most

strikingly demonstrated in the Presidential election of 1928 by the swing of part of the "solid South" to Hoover. Regular Senate Republicans attempted to restore discipline in that body after the election of 1924 by reading out of the party the insurgents —LaFollette, Ladd, Frazier, and Brookhart—but this made little difference. When the results of the elections of 1926 were known, the insurgents were hurriedly welcomed back.

Altogether, Coolidge found it easy to stand by and allow the Governmental machine to proceed under its own momentum. The Republicans stood pat on immigration restriction, tax reduction, a mild enforcement of prohibition, and a refusal to join the World Court, all policies which the party had accepted in the days of Harding. In his last annual message Coolidge was still calling for the same program as in 1924: railroad consolidation, continued enforcement of prohibition, private operation of Muscle Shoals, and maintenance of a merchant marine. By then, however, he had also made up his mind upon the type of agricultural relief he was willing to accept, and upon the Colorado River flood control.

The six-year record of Coolidge may seem sterile, but to the retiring President the fruits of legislative inactivity appeared good. For the majority of the people and for many sections of the country the years 1925–1928 had been prosperous. Why, asked

Coolidge, should the nation be disturbed by legislative experiments? Indeed, the President could be pardoned for turning his final message of 1928 into a paean of praise. "The requirements of existence," he said, "have passed beyond the standard of necessity into the region of luxury. . . . The country can regard the present with satisfaction and anticipate the future with optimism." Not a few observers believed that Coolidge had made to the American people a gift of continuous prosperity, a "new economic era."

Whatever may be the final estimate of Coolidge, he made at least one important contribution in the reduction of the national debt. It is true the policy was begun under Harding, and that industrial prosperity made it possible. Nevertheless, as Coolidge once said, "Nothing is easier than the expenditure of public money," and he had the strength to resist the constant temptation. "Four times," said he in his message of 1928,

we have made a drastic revision of our internal revenue system, abolishing many taxes and substantially reducing all others. Each time the resulting stimulation to business has so increased taxable incomes and profits that a surplus has been produced. One-third of the national debt has been paid, while much of the other two-thirds has been refunded at lower rates, and these savings of interest and constant economies have enabled us to repeat the satisfactory process of more tax reductions.

Coolidge may have overestimated the effect of tax reduction on business, but otherwise his summary was correct.

Despite his generally unimpressive record and the fact that he had served six years, Coolidge in all probability could have obtained the nomination and won the election in 1928. His popularity was unshaken. Nevertheless, he had determined not to seek another term. The summer of 1927 he spent in the Black Hills of South Dakota. On August 2, the fourth anniversary of his entrance into the Presidency, he drove to his office at Rapid City, held his regular nine o'clock conference with newspapermen, and at the end remarked casually, "If you will return at twelve o'clock, there will be an additional statement." Shortly before twelve the President wrote on a memorandum pad the words, "I do not choose to run for President in nineteen twenty-eight," and handed the sheet to his secretary with directions to have enough copies made to supply the newspapermen. "I am going to hand these out myself," he informed Sanders. "I am going to give them to the newspapermen, without comment, from this side of the desk. I want you to stand at the door and not permit anyone to leave until each has a slip, so that they may have an even chance." As the reporters came in the President told them that the line would form on the left and then handed to each a slip of paper. When Sanders opened the door there was a wild scramble for long-distance telephones to make known the political sensation of the year.

In the light of subsequent knowledge, the President's statement seems clear enough, but to the politically minded of 1927 it was the height of ambiguity. Did the President mean that he *would* not run, or that he just did not prefer to run? Recalling his statement four months later (December 6) to members of the Republican National Committee, Coolidge amplified it by stating, "My decision will be respected." But there still remained the question: What *was* his decision?

There is little reason to believe that Coolidge meant to be ambiguous. Nor is there much reason to believe that he was later influenced by the LaFollette resolution carried in the Senate (February 10, 1928), which stated that non-observance of the third-term tradition would constitute a precedent "unwise, unpatriotic, and fraught with peril to our free institutions." Actually, Coolidge was worn out with the responsibility of the Presidency, doubtful if he could survive the strain of another term, and convinced that his retirement would be beneficial to the nation.

His statement opened the way for various Republican candidates. These included numerous favorite sons and receptive politicians. From the beginning, however, the leading candidate was Secretary of Commerce Hoover. Because of Hoover's record of party irregularity some interest was whipped up among Old-Guard leaders in Charles Curtis of Kansas, floor leader of the Senate. Ex-Governor Lowden, who had endorsed the McNary-Haugen bill, found some agricultural support. Although Coolidge evinced no enthusiasm for Hoover, the Californian was in a favorable strategical position. He met defeat from favorite sons in the primaries of Nebraska, Illinois, Indiana, and West Virginia, but he nevertheless came to the national convention with at least 673 votes in his pocket, including the solid South.

In the pre-convention campaign the Democrats faced the same serious dilemma that had confronted them in 1924. Again the leading candidates were Governor Alfred E. Smith of New York, representing the liberal, wet, and Catholic element of the great cities of the North and East, and William G. McAdoo, leader of the conservative, dry, and Protestant South and West. Fortunately, the party was saved from the factional battle which had destroyed its effectiveness in 1924. McAdoo announced in September, 1927, that he would not be a candidate, and of the remaining field Smith was far in the lead. Opponents attempted a boom for Senator Thomas Walsh of Montana, a dry and a Catholic, but it failed. There was but little interest in such candidates as Governor Albert Ritchie of

Maryland, champion of state rights; Governor
Harry Byrd of Virginia, a spokesman for the
younger element of the Democracy; Senator James
Reed of Missouri; and Cordell Hull of Tennessee.
Smith, backed by the powerful New York *Times*
and New York *World*, came to the convention with
713 out of the 1,000 delegates.*

When the Republican convention met on June 12
at Kansas City it was evidently under the control
of the Hoover contingent and the industrial interests of the Northeast. Simeon D. Fess of Ohio,
arch-reactionary of the Senate, eulogized his party
in the keynote speech, while Senator George H.
Moses of New Hampshire was made permanent
chairman. A third representative of the Old-Guard
Senators, Reed Smoot of Utah, was chairman of
the Resolutions Committee. A typical Republican
platform of the twenties, consisting of thirty planks
and 7,000 words, was produced. Only two planks,
those on prohibition and agriculture, aroused much
interest. On prohibition the party pledged "itself
and its nominees to the observance and vigorous
enforcement of this prohibition of the Constitution."
Dr. Nicholas Murray Butler spoke for an amendment calling for the repeal of the Eighteenth

* Neither Smith nor Hoover had made any personal bid for votes.
A Senate committee investigating campaign expenditures put the
pre-convention campaign costs of the major parties at between
$800,000 and $900,000. Of this amount the Hoover followers spent
approximately $395,000 and Smith's backers $152,600.

Amendment and the recognition of the principle of state rights in the regulation of the liquor traffic. It was voted down by a practically unanimous vote.

More time was spent debating the plank on agriculture. The majority plank had promised almost everything but the equalization fee. A minority plank incorporating this was offered but finally defeated by 807 to 277. When the full majority platform was first read, Robert LaFollette, Jr., moved to substitute a more progressive platform which he presented. At the same time he reminded the delegates that of the 35 planks offered by his father in similar fashion in 1908, only to be spurned, 32 had since become law. He was given an ovation, but his platform received few votes.

When the convention refused to follow the agricultural program endorsed by Lowden, that leader declined to allow his name to be presented. This removed one of the few strong opponents which Hoover might have had. The names of Senators Watson, Curtis, Norris, and Goff were put in nomination; but they had no strength, and Hoover was selected on the first ballot by 837 votes. Other nominees received votes as follows: Lowden, 72; Curtis, 64; Watson, 45; Norris, 18; Coolidge, 17; Dawes, 4; and Hughes, 1. Although Curtis had attacked Hoover and had insisted that he never would accept the Vice-Presidential nomination, he was chosen on the first ballot and accepted. It was the first time in the history of national political parties that both candidates had been taken from states west of the Mississippi.

The Democratic Party had learned well their lesson from the Madison Square fiasco of 1924. Their harmonious convention at Houston, Texas, might almost be described as a political miracle. Animosities engendered by the 1924 convention had subsided, while the reputation of Smith had grown. Far in the lead among the candidates, his control of the Houston convention was as obvious as Hoover's at Kansas City, and the result as much a foregone conclusion. As temporary chairman, Claude G. Bowers, well-known historian and an editor of the New York *Evening World,* blasted the Republican Party in rhetorical phrases. The Democratic Party, he declared, had gone forth to "battle for the honor of the nation, besmirched and bedraggled by the most brazen and shameless carnival of corruption that ever blackened the reputation of decent and self-respecting people." Describing Alfred E. Smith as the "happy warrior," Franklin D. Roosevelt for the third time in eight years placed him in nomination. Most of the rural drys of the South and West had made up their minds to swallow him. When it was discovered on the first roll call that he was within ten votes of victory, Ohio shifted to him and on the revised count the New York Governor received 849⅔. The three men standing next highest were Senators George and Reed and Representative Cordell Hull, each of whom received around 50 votes. The next day Senator Joseph T. Robinson, Protestant and dry, was nominated for the Vice-Presidency on the first ballot.

Those who had expected that the convention would come to blows over the platform again discovered that the Democrats had learned much since 1924. The agricultural plank did not use the term "equalization fee," but it seemed to countenance price-fixing. That was as much as anyone could hope for, and it went through. The prohibition plank castigated the Republicans for "failure to enforce laws enacted by the Congress" and pledged the "party and its nominees to an honest effort to enforce the eighteenth amendment." This was not nearly strong enough for the ardent drys, but they were prevailed upon to keep quiet and the whole platform was accepted by a practically unanimous vote.

At the very end of the convention, with a third of the delegates gone, a telegram of acceptance arrived from Governor Smith.

It is well known [said he] that I believe there should be fundamental changes in the present provisions for national prohibition, based, as I stated in my Jackson

Day letter, on the fearless application of the principles of Jeffersonian democracy. While I fully appreciate that these changes can only be made by the people themselves, through their elected representatives, I feel it to be the duty of the chosen leader of the people to point the way which, in his opinion, leads to a sane, sensible solution of a condition which, I am convinced, is entirely unsatisfactory to the great mass of our people.

That this message was unsatisfactory to the great mass of the convention there can be little doubt, but no one felt called upon at the moment to protest.

With the death of LaFollette and the desertion of organized labor, the Progressive Party of 1924 had fallen to pieces. Since that time the Socialists had thrown their resources into the uphill fight to rebuild their organization. Considering the Coolidge prosperity and the factional conflicts among the left wing, the results had not been entirely hopeless. The party had sent Victor Berger back to Congress in 1926, had captured the city of Reading, Pennsylvania, in 1927, and regularly reelected Daniel Hoan to the mayoralty of Milwaukee. In 1928 the party nominated Norman Thomas, a former Presbyterian minister and a brilliant journalist and orator, and as his running mate, James H. Maurer, long president of the Pennsylvania State Federation of Labor. Their chief plank was the public ownership of natural resources and public utilities. The Workers Party (Communist), having reconciled their internal differences sufficiently to exhibit a united front, nominated William Z. Foster, leader of the steel strike of 1919, and Benjamin Gitlow. Its primary objective was overthrow of capitalism and the establishment of a workers' and farmers' government. Two other left-wing groups—the Socialist Labor and the Farmer Labor parties—nominated candidates; and the Prohibition Party, denouncing "the present unsatisfactory enforcement of prohibition, amounting to nullification over wide areas in great centers of population," also presented its slate.

As for the platforms of the major parties, the "ins" lauded their record and the "outs" criticized it. Otherwise the documents showed few differences. On prohibition the Democrats promised "an honest effort to enforce" and the Republicans "vigorous enforcement." The agricultural programs did not seem far apart. With respect to the tariff, a traditional battleground, the Democrats were in retreat. Democratic tariff legislation, they asserted, should be shaped toward "the maintenance of legitimate business and a high standard of wages," and toward "safeguarding the public against monopoly." Whether this meant high, low, or moderate rates, the reader would have to guess. Except for the utterly different personalities of the two major candidates, there seemed to be little reason for the campaign.

In harmony with the general American tradition of success, both candidates had risen from humble surroundings. Hoover had been born on an Iowa farm and Smith in the slums of New York. But there the similarity ended. Orphaned in childhood, Hoover was befriended by relatives, graduated in engineering from Leland Stanford, and rapidly accumulated a fortune as a mining engineer and financial promoter. He won fame during the war as head of the Belgian Relief Commission, as United States Food Administrator, and as chairman of various war bodies. Then followed eight years as a capable and efficient Secretary of Commerce. His experience had been almost entirely in executive and administrative posts. He had never stood for election, his knowledge of politics was slim, and his cold and precise personality had little popular appeal. His economic philosophy was that of the Manchester Liberals of a century earlier, modified to meet the needs of industrial and financial imperialism.

In striking contrast was Alfred E. Smith. His career had been almost entirely political, a rise from the "Sidewalks of New York" to four terms as Governor of his state. This rise had been achieved through the help of Tammany Hall, but Smith was no pliant tool of that organization. His formal education was slight and his experience provincial, but he was unsurpassed in his knowledge of the machinery of American government. Warm and personal in his approach, he was surpassed by no living politician in his ability to handle political friends and foes. His economics were those of a mild liberal.

At least eight issues received some discussion during the campaign: prosperity, prohibition, corruption, religion, water power, agricultural relief, Government economy through reorganization, and foreign affairs. Only prosperity, prohibition, and religion, however, seemed to catch the interest of many people. Smith waged an aggressive campaign, and tried to smoke out his opponent. Virtually repudiating the Democratic platform on prohibition, he advocated turning the liquor problem back to the states. He denounced the "power trust," urging public ownership of power sites and plants. He attempted to "call the bluff" of Coolidge economy, and in discussing agriculture finally announced his adherence to the "equalization fee." On the other hand, he soft-pedaled the tariff. As a whole, Smith had no well-rounded economic program. The great issues of Muscle Shoals, conservation, and social legislation—soon to be in the forefront—received little of his attention.

Smith's blistering attacks failed to disturb the Republicans. Except that Hoover was finally forced to pronounce definitely against the equalization fee, they refused to be "smoked out." Wisely they rested their campaign on the prosperity issue, and deluged the nation with statistics of economic progress. "We in America today," proclaimed Hoover, "are nearer to the final triumph over poverty than ever before in the history of any land." In similar vein he insisted that "the slogan of progress is changing from the full dinner pail to the full garage." "Hoover and Happiness or Smith and Soup Houses" was the cheering alternative offered by the Republicans. The Democrats, of course, did what they could to counteract this propaganda. For chairman of the Democratic National Committee, Smith chose John J. Raskob, vice-president of General Motors and a director of numerous great corporations. No one could more perfectly symbolize the easy wealth of the Coolidge boom than Raskob. It was clear, at least, that the Democrats had no intention of injuring business.

While the Republicans rested their main strategy on prosperity, Smith had to face the problems of prohibition and religion. Hoover had accepted prohibition as "a great social and economic experiment, noble in motive and far-reaching in purpose." This may have been an accurate description, but it hardly solved the problem. While Republicans dodged the issue, many drys of the rural South and West turned against the Democratic candidate, who urged change. There can also be no doubt that Smith's Catholicism greatly weakened his candidacy. Tolerant people tried to keep the issue in the background, but it provided a strong undercurrent against him throughout the campaign. Smith's affiliation with Tammany also hurt him. The Democratic candidate may not have had the stigma of Wall Street, but to many a farmer he was a clever city politician who could not be trusted.

Smith's aggressive campaign helped bring out the largest vote cast up to that time in American history. It also brought the Democratic Party its most humiliating defeat. Hoover received approximately 21,392,000 votes; Smith, 15,016,000; Thomas, 267,000, and Foster, 48,000. The electoral vote was 444 to 87. Smith carried only eight states: Arkansas, Louisiana, Mississippi, Alabama, Georgia, and South Carolina in the South and the Catholic states of Massachusetts and Rhode Island in the North. For the first time since 1876 the Republicans really smashed the solid South. Industrial penetration and prosperity had an influence, but it was probably the prohibition issue and Catholicism which accounted fundamentally for the Republican victory in Virginia, North Carolina, Tennessee, Florida, and Texas. Hoover carried along with him an overwhelming Republican majority in the Seventy-first Congress. It seems hardly necessary to add that in the golden glow of the "Coolidge prosperity," the left-wing parties attracted little attention.

Cynics might well have entitled the campaign of 1928, "Much ado about nothing." Although there was little fundamental difference in the economic philosophy of major candidates or platforms, many years had passed since any national election had developed the bitterness and resentment of 1928. Campaign expenditures as well as rancor reached a high point. For once the Democrats were in a position to spend about as much as the Republicans. According to a report submitted by a Senate committee, the Republican National Committee spent approximately $9,434,000 and the Democrats $7,153,000. The total amount raised and spent locally no one knows.

Despite the large vote and heavy expenditures, the campaign represented as well as any other the political futility of the decade. Surveying national politics in 1927 Walter Lippmann insisted, "There are no parties, there are no leaders, there are no issues. There are parties only in the states, there are leaders only of sections, there are issues, but they are either evaded by national public men or carefully confined to the localities." Great national leaders of the type of Roosevelt and Wilson had passed away; the masterful inactivity of Coolidge had kept national issues in the background. Efforts by the Progressives in 1924 to force consideration of such issues failed. Fundamental differences between the major parties had virtually disappeared. Important problems faced the American people in the 1920's: consolidation and abuse of corporate wealth, Federal control of electric power, the tariff, taxation, and relations with Europe and Asia. Instead of them, most voters were hotly debating the questions of prohibition, the Ku Klux Klan, Romanism, Fundamentalism, and immigration. All but the last of these questions had significance chiefly as symbols in a struggle of rural America against the social, moral, and economic mores of the urban areas, a struggle lost before it began.

The political ideal of the ordinary American was Calvin Coolidge, who had raised "inactivity" to the position of a major policy, and whose banal speeches were actually deemed by some to be gems of economic and political wisdom. The nation had turned from the idealism of the earlier years to worship the goddess of economic success. The business of America, as Coolidge had accurately observed, was business. In brief, the nation had lost its perspective.

Appropriately, the activities of the decade found their climax in the greatest orgy of speculative gambling that the nation had yet seen. It was a perfect counterpart to the election of 1928. Economists have attempted to account for the frenzy of stock-market speculation that swept the land, particularly during 1928 and 1929, and the reasons for its sudden collapse. They note that in August, 1927, during the early days of the boom, the Federal Reserve System lowered its rediscount rate from 4 to $3\frac{1}{2}$ per cent. This was done with the laudable motive of stabilizing European currencies, promoting foreign trade, and at the same time giving a push to American business. Instead of bolstering a weakening Europe, its main effect, as it turned out, was to stimulate the stock market. When a few realists suggested the possibility that stocks were too high, a reassuring word was always forthcoming from high Government sources. Secretary Mellon seemed consistently optimistic, while President Coolidge took an unprecedented step when in January, 1928, he told a press conference that he did not consider brokers' loans too high.

What apparently carried the wave of speculation onward, however, was not so much the brokers' loans of New York banks on their own account, which had but slightly increased during the years 1926–1928; it was mainly the brokers' loans for the account of out-of-town banks, which increased 68.7 per cent during these years, and the loans "for others" which advanced more than 450 per cent. The latter covered the enormous withdrawals of surplus funds by corporations and individuals from customary fields of employment to the call-money market. These loans "for others" increased, it is estimated, from $691,000,000 in September, 1926, to $3,860,000,000 in September, 1929. And why not? Call money by that time was being loaned at 20 per cent.

Actually this was only part of the story. American business was prosperous and the real income of large numbers of people was increasing. The stock market, a rough barometer of business, reflected the growing prosperity. Millions of workers and middle-class people who had never seen a bond or a share of stock until the days of the Liberty Loans and the campaigns for employee stock ownership now became conscious of the stock market. Following the big investors and gamblers, a few began cautiously to purchase stock. As prices went up during succeeding years, more and more people entered the market. The value of American industries actually was mounting, and as this was reflected in the value of stocks, almost any purchase meant a profit. It was an easy way to make money without working, a simple way to get rich quickly. Under the excitement of easy profits the frenzy of speculation grew. Tens of thousands who had never dreamed of entering the market were buying and selling shares. By 1928 the price of stocks became the principal subject of conversation at business and social gatherings, while many an otherwise stable person was neglecting his business or profession to gamble on the stock exchange.

Despite minor economic setbacks, there was a sound basis for the forward movements of most securities. The speculative mania, however, carried prices to fantastic heights. During the final eighteen months of the great boom, from March 3, 1928, to September 3, 1929, the peak of the boom, Montgomery Ward, for example, was pushed up from 132¾ to an adjusted high price of 466½; Union Carbide and Carbon from 145 to 413⅝; Westinghouse from 91⅝ to 313; General Electric from 128¾ to 396¼. Radio skyrocketed from 94½ to 505. According to the Babson index, the value of twenty railroad stocks had advanced from 144.34 in September, 1928, to 189.11 in September, 1929, and of thirty industrial stocks from 241.72 to 381.90. Since 1921 the price of railroad stocks had advanced 138 per cent while the price of industrials had multiplied five times. The traditional and time-honored basis of judging the value of a stock was "ten times earnings." Some of them were now selling at fifty or more times their earnings. The market, as one expert observed, was discounting not only the future but the hereafter. The sight of droves of sheep struggling into the exchanges bleating to be shorn was too much for the leaders of business and finance. They split their stock to make it more easily purchasable; they turned out new issues of stocks and bonds, and perfected methods whereby control might be maintained by the few while the public paid the bill. Any issue which had a respectable name behind it was quickly bought up.

Under these circumstances, it is hardly surprising that the number of shares traded in on the stock exchange increased from 577,000,000 in 1927 to 1,125,000,000 in 1929. In earlier times a million-share day on the stock exchange was almost epoch-making. During October and November of 1929 not a single day dropped below that figure. In 1929 the trading on 122 days exceeded 4,000,000 shares, and on 37 exceeded 5,000,000. October 29, the day of the great crash, saw 16,000,000 shares dumped on the market. Brokers' loans had increased from less than two billion dollars in 1922 to four and one-half billion in 1927, six and one-half billion in 1928, and more than eight and one-half billion in September, 1929. It is probable that at that time the loans on securities made by all the banks in the country were in the neighborhood of eighteen billions. Branch offices of the big Wall Street brokerage houses now appeared in numerous cities where men and women who until recently had never seen a share of stock sat for hours to watch boys mark the changing figures on the board as they came in over the ticker-tape.

There could be but one end to all this, but few

seemed to realize it. Although business had begun to fall off six months before the crash, men high in economics and finance were predicting a "new era" of permanent prosperity and a permanent high level of stock prices. Hoover, more cautious on the market situation than Coolidge or Mellon, was by no means complacent. The Federal Reserve Board raised the rediscount rates to 4 per cent in February, to $4\frac{1}{2}$ per cent in May, and to 5 in June, and on more than one occasion showed its concern. The frenzy of speculation, however, could no longer be influenced by mild Governmental warnings. The break in the stock market came early in September, but no great concern was exhibited until the week of October 21. On October 23 there was a deluge of liquidations; on the 24th the bottom seemed to drop completely out of the market. Faced with a crash, the results of which no one could foretell, J. P. Morgan hastily called to his office the representatives of several great banks who agreed to contribute $40,000,000 apiece to steady the prices of some of the leading securities.

For four days the medicine worked. Then on the 29th came the crash which made earlier breaks seem like the quiet of a rural summer's day:

The big gong had hardly sounded in the great hall of the Exchange at ten o'clock Tuesday morning before the storm broke in full force. Huge blocks of stock were thrown upon the market for what they would bring. . . . Not only were innumerable small traders being sold out, but big ones, too, protagonists of the new economic era who a few weeks before had counted themselves millionaires. Again and again the specialist in a stock would find himself surrounded by brokers fighting to sell—and nobody at all even thinking of buying. . . . The scene on the floor was chaotic. . . . Within a half hour of the opening the volume of trading had passed three million shares, by twelve o'clock it had passed eight million, by half past one it had passed twelve million, and when the closing gong brought the day's madness to an end, the gigantic record of 16,410,030 shares had been set . . . the average prices of fifty leading stocks, as compiled by the *New York Times,* had fallen nearly forty points.*

Like other stock-market crashes, that of 1929 came primarily, as one economist tersely put it, because of "the unwarranted inflation resulting from excessive speculation in borrowed funds." Why it came in October rather than a few months earlier or later is one of those mysteries which seem insoluble. In any event, it was inevitable. Far more important is the fact that the unhealthy stock market was symptomatic of a general economic condition. The collapse was chiefly significant as the signal which marked a widespread economic breakdown and the beginning of a long depression. The illusive bubble had burst.

* Frederick L. Allen, *Only Yesterday* (New York, Harper and Brothers, 1931), pp. 333-334.

As the glittering rush of intense activity ended, economists had no difficulty in discerning some of the fundamental flaws. The decline of important industries and the widespread agricultural depression had weakened the underpinnings of what superficially appeared to be a sound economic prosperity. It now became clear that a fundamental weakness of the decade had been the uneven distribution of the wealth created. There had been, as Professor J. M. Clark pointed out, "an increase in the proportion of the income going to profits (including those left in the business) and a corresponding decrease in the relative proportion going to wages and salaries—this, in spite of a very considerable increase in real wages, reckoned in terms of commodity buying power." This tended, of course, to pile up wealth in the hands of those who would normally use it for further expansion of industrial units rather than of those who would use it to purchase manufactured goods. The American industrial plant, already overexpanded, continued to swell. The fact that even in the boom years the average number of unemployed ran to a million and a half indicated an unhealthy labor condition.

Nor was the international picture free from clouds. Intense nationalism engendered by the war was raising tariff rates to new heights and heightening the barriers to international trade. European gold was being drained to America, producing a situation favorable to inflation and high prices, and further discouraging the purchase of American commodities. Moreover, it should be remembered that no strong or general economic recovery occurred in other parts of the world in the decade after the First World War.

In retrospect the historian sometimes wonders at the prosperity of the twenties rather than at the ultimate collapse. But whichever view we take, the depression quickly demonstrated the weakness of the economic framework. Every phase of economic life suffered the same disaster. Industrial production and retail trade were cut in half during the Hoover Administration. Wholesale prices declined by a third. Foreign trade was hit even harder. Exports declined from approximately $5,241,000,-000 in 1929 to $1,611,000,000 in 1932, and imports from $4,399,000,000 to $1,323,000,000.

One of the weakest pillars of the American economic structure was the banking system. In the decade ending in 1930, 6,987 banks failed, while 2,294 more went down in 1931 and 1,456 in 1932. So bad had the situation become by March, 1933, that Roosevelt on the day after his inauguration declared a nation-wide banking moratorium. The stock market which had so accurately mirrored the hectic speculation and the false hopes of the last years of the decade, revealed as intensely the panic and utter despondency of the owners of industry. From September, 1929, to January, 1933, according to the Dow-Jones index, thirty industrial stocks fell from an average of 364.9 dollars to 62.7 per share, a group of twenty public utilities dropped from 141.9 to 28.0 per share, and twenty railroad stocks declined from an average of 180.0 to 28.1. There were few who escaped the effects of the collapse. It was all-embracing and complete.

For months after the stock-market crash, political and business leaders assured the nation that there was no fundamental weakness in the economic situation and that prosperity would soon return. One conference of businessmen followed another at the White House, where most employers agreed with the President that every effort should be made to maintain wages and employment. Despite exhortations, reassurances, and laudable efforts, the nation sank deeper into the economic morass. Unemployment, according to the American Federation of Labor, had grown by October, 1930, to 4,639,000, and by the early months of 1933 to over 13,000,000. Instead of attaining that end of poverty to which Hoover had optimistically looked forward in his inaugural address, the country found itself in a plight in which one sixth or more of the population was on relief.

Serious as was the loss of wealth and the disappearance of hard-earned savings, they were but minor results of the collapse of 1929. More serious were the disillusionment, the crushed hopes, the breakdown of faith in many social and economic patterns. Upon the morale of millions of hard-working and self-respecting citizens the necessity of seeking public relief fell with disintegrating effect. Quite as disastrous was the position of millions of youth left stranded without jobs and with but little hope for the future. In the despair of a deepening depression many felt that the nation had reached a dead end.

As a whole, the decade had been unsatisfactory. Americans felt that their participation in the World War had played a crucial part in turning the tide of battle toward ultimate victory for the Allies. Enthusiasm had run high; but by the early twenties that victory seemed futile and the people fell into a mood of thorough disillusionment. In this reaction from high idealism and triumphant elation, their one compensation was tremendous activity in the development of the country and in the unabashed search for material prosperity. American enterprise had raised an economic structure which seemed so strong that many believed that the nation had entered a new economic era of permanent prosperity. Then suddenly and with little warning their high-vaulted structure collapsed like a house of cards.

The decade which had begun in frustration and

disillusionment ended in the same mood. What made the situation more difficult was the fact that the nation could find few crumbs of consolation anywhere. Earlier periods of glittering economic activity and hectic speculation had offered lessons which had never been learned or had been quickly forgotten. In the despondency of the economic collapse some of these lessons were recalled, and many were now able to discern the mistakes of the decade. Whether the reaction from the depression would lead to sounder economic policies and a happier future, only time could tell. That the nation had entered a new era was clear enough before the thirties had far advanced; but it was not to be the dazzling "new era" predicted in the inflated twenties.

CHAPTER XI

INTERLUDE

IN one sense the Hoover Administration was merely an epilogue to an essentially unreal and artificial decade. For all practical purposes its history had been written by the time Herbert Hoover took the oath of office in March, 1929. Whatever policies the Government followed in the twenties had been established during the first two years and as a whole they were unfitted to the needs of the time. In a world shaken to its very foundation by a catastrophic war, political leaders eagerly sought to return to an era that could never be revived. Then, blinded by a specious prosperity, they assured themselves that their policies were good. While fundamental issues were ignored or evaded, social, political and economic morality decayed. After the sowing of such a wind, a whirlwind of disaster was almost inevitable.

Hoover reaped the whirlwind. Like the Administration of Van Buren and the second term of

Grover Cleveland, Hoover's Presidency was dominated by a great depression—that which followed the panic of 1929. Except that Hoover had been one of the three key men in the Cabinets of Harding and Coolidge which had formulated the policies of the decade, he could hardly be blamed for the depression. Unfortunately for him, however, his Administration synchronized with the downward sweep of a business cycle. Wiser policies, greater Government control of credit, speculation, and the economic life in general might have delayed the depression and mitigated its severity. Business cycles and periodic depressions had been characteristic of capitalist economy for a century and a half, but those who guided the nation's economy in the 1920's seemed to have ignored the possibility of decline. The country as a whole heaped the blame for the catastrophe upon Hoover and he came to symbolize the depression in the minds of millions.

Hoover himself blamed the depression primarily upon the First World War, and repeatedly emphasized the economic interdependence of the world. The depression, he said as late as 1936,

was the inexorable and inevitable world-wide aftermath of the World War. Its causes lay in the pit of destruction dug by the most titanic struggle in which humanity has yet engaged. Our own credit inflation contributed to our own difficulties. But this depression began in other countries before it touched the United States. No man or no government brought about this depression . . . its sweep was as inexorable as a Caribbean hurricane.

This explanation was quite in line with Hoover's experience. His mining operations on almost every continent of the globe and his long residence abroad made him essentially an international person. He thought in international economic terms. No American President had sojourned in so many parts of the world or experienced more firsthand knowledge of its economic problems. In some ways his prominent position in the nationalist and isolationist governments of Harding and Coolidge was an anachronism. Hoover's first action after his election in 1928 was to go on a good-will tour to Latin America; its object was better understanding, improved relations, and greater economic cooperation.

Few students of the business cycle gave the World War the predominant position described to it by Hoover as the chief cause of the depression. Even fewer followed him in his emphasis upon psychological factors as the fundamental cause for the length and severity of the panic. "Fear and apprehension," declared Hoover in 1931, "whether their origins are domestic or foreign, are very real, tangible, economic forces. . . . All these apprehensions and actions check enterprise and lessen our national activities. We are suffering today more from frozen confidence than we are from frozen securities." While all economists recognize the influence of exaggerated optimism in times of prosperity and a similar pessimism in periods of depression, more fundamental factors were responsible.

One widely held myth regarding Hoover should be examined. He did not, as his political opponents asserted and many of his countrymen believed, sit by and do nothing during the tragic years of his Presidency. His predecessors during earlier depressions—Van Buren, Buchanan, Grant, Theodore Roosevelt, and Wilson, had practically ignored the panics except to make sure that the financial credit of the Government remained impregnable. Cleveland, convinced that the panic of 1893 was caused by the silver legislation, secured its repeal and saved the gold standard. Beyond that he did little. Hoover, on the other hand, made efforts to mobilize the economic resources of the nation, to impress upon private industry and individual initiative their responsibility in the crisis, and he assumed leadership in the field of international finance. That he did not move quickly enough or far enough and that certain of his measures were ill-advised are readily conceded. He did, however, break the earlier precedent, and for the first time attempt to offer Federal leadership.

For this rôle Hoover was not entirely unfitted.

His fundamental opposition to the extension of Government interference in the economic life of the United States did not apply so strongly to international finance. He was so firmly convinced that the center of the economic storm was located in Europe that he was willing to attack the depression at its source. American ills, he believed, could be cured only through world economic stabilization. His debt moratorium of 1931 was the outstanding example of action in this sphere.

Hoover, moreover, was a humanitarian. His important work as chairman of the Commission for Relief in Belgium, 1915–1919, and of similar bodies working in other European countries after the war, was well recalled. His humanitarianism went beyond mere conventional charity. He was earnestly interested in raising the standard of living through improving the public health, greater diffusion of property ownership, and in other ways. The widespread physical and psychological misery caused by the depression distressed him deeply.

It should be added that Hoover resented the charge that he was a believer in *laissez-faire*. He insisted that America had long since abandoned that doctrine.

We have confirmed its abandonment [said he] in terms of legislation, of social and economic justice . . . in part because we have learned that the foremost are not always the best nor the hindmost the worst—and in part because we have learned that social injustice is the destruction of justice itself. . . . We have also learned that fair division can only be obtained by certain restrictions on the strong and the dominant.*

Although it is difficult to think of Hoover as a crusader in the legislative field for equality of opportunity, his philosophy, if his statements mean anything, was not far different from that of Theodore Roosevelt's "New Nationalism" or Wilson's "New Freedom." Said Hoover, "To curb the forces in business which would destroy equality of opportunity and yet to maintain the initiative and creative faculties of our people are the twin objects we must obtain. To preserve the former we must regulate that type of activity that would dominate." †

Despite his background, action, and philosophy Hoover proved unable to meet the depression with any program of rapid and far-reaching action. Fundamental in his thinking was the belief that individual initiative was the structure upon which the economic order rested, and that interference by the Government (except to preserve equality of opportunity) only interfered with the operation and development of an essentially valid system. This theory was strengthened by the conviction

* Herbert Hoover, *American Individualism* (copyright 1922 by Doubleday, Page & Company), p. 10.

† *Ibid.*, p. 54.

that American experience had proved it. He saw here a nation rich in natural resources, adequately supplied with skilled labor and rich in capital. Employment of all these through the medium of an enlightened capitalism would banish poverty and continually raise the standard of living. "We in America today," said he during the campaign of 1928, "are nearer the final triumph over poverty than ever before in the history of any land." Upon enlightened capitalism as the foundation, a greater, richer, and happier nation could be constructed. "Superficial observers," he asserted in his inaugural address, "fail to see that the American people are engrossed in building for themselves a new economic system, a new social system, a new political system."

Although he admitted that "government must, so far as lies within its proper powers, give leadership to the realization of these ideals," he reacted intuitively against anything that tended toward socialism or the transference of initiative from the individual to the Government. Nothing in the political sphere horrified him more than the development of a great bureaucracy. "True American Liberalism," he insisted, "utterly denies the whole creed of Socialism." No one could believe more sincerely than did Hoover in the efficacy of "American individualism" in creating much of what was best in our civilization. "While I can make no claim," said he, "for having introduced the term 'rugged individualism,' I should be proud to have invented it. It has been used by American leaders for over a half-century in eulogy of those God-fearing men and women of honesty whose stamina and character and fearless assertion of rights led them to make their own way in life." *

Another factor in the Hoover psychology which tended to slow action in the depression was his scientific training, which insisted upon obtaining the facts before acting. Among the fact-finding bodies which he created were the well-known Research Committee on Social Trends and the Commission on Law Enforcement. Others included investigations on Child Health and Protection, Conservation of the Public Domain, Bankruptcy Laws, Housing and Home Ownership, Veterans' Hospitalization, and the St. Lawrence Waterway. Altogether he appointed thirty-eight and many of them did valuable work. When criticized for much investigation and little action, he issued a statement pointing out the need of such work, and giving statistics which showed that Hoover's interest in facts was not appreciably greater than that displayed by his predecessors. Congress itself had set up twenty-four such commissions during the Hoover Administration. Slowness of action, more-

* Herbert Hoover, *The Challenge to Liberty* (New York, Charles Scribner's Sons, 1934), p. 54.

over, came also in part from Congress. Hoover erroneously assumed that when facts were established, action would logically follow. This might be the natural procedure in science but it was not in politics. And politics was a business that Hoover never understood.

In his inaugural address, Hoover dwelt on the "disregard and disobedience of law," which he characterized as "the most malign of all the dangers" facing the Government at the moment. He proposed a thorough reform and reorganization of the whole system of justice and its enforcement. He insisted that the election had "again confirmed the determination of the American people that regulation of private enterprise and not government ownership or operation is the course rightly to be pursued in our relations to business." This was to be done in the producing and distributing industries by insisting upon effective competition and in the utilities by regulating services and rates. Reiterating his doctrine that the peace of the world was "interlocked with our progress and prosperity," he urged that the United States should join the Permanent Court of International Justice.

Hoover's Cabinet was of average ability. He retained two of the Coolidge Cabinet (originally appointed by Harding): Andrew W. Mellon in the Treasury and James J. Davis in the Labor Department. Of the new appointees the best known was

Henry L. Stimson, Secretary of State, who had been Secretary of War under Taft and Governor-General of the Philippines under Coolidge. James W. Good, a former Congressman and a Chicago lawyer, became Secretary of War; William D. Mitchell, Solicitor-General under Coolidge, was raised to the Attorney-Generalship, and Walter F. Brown, formerly Assistant Secretary of Commerce, became Postmaster-General. The new Secretary of the Navy was Charles Francis Adams, a Boston financier and amateur yachtsman, and the New Secretary of the Interior was Dr. Ray Lyman Wilbur, a personal friend, who was a physician and President of Stanford University. Arthur M. Hyde, Secretary of Agriculture, was a former Governor of Missouri, and Robert P. Lamont, Secretary of Commerce, was an engineer. After Secretary of Labor Davis was elected to the Senate in 1930 his place was taken by William N. Doak, formerly vice-president of the Brotherhood of Railroad Trainmen, and active in Republican politics.

Like the Cabinets of Harding and Coolidge, that of Hoover was characterized by its essential conservatism. Six of the ten were lawyers; none appeared to have either the resiliency, imagination, or vision to meet the problems of a desperate depression. The Cabinet may have been improved by the promotion of Ogden L. Mills to the Treasury in 1932 after Mellon had been sent as Ambassador

to Great Britain and by the similar promotion of
Patrick J. Hurley to head the War Department
after the death of Secretary Good in November,
1919. Its essential conservatism, however, remained unchanged.

Shortly after his inauguration Hoover called a
special session of the Seventy-first Congress "to
redeem two pledges given in the last election—
farm relief and limited changes in the tariff." The
first was redeemed according to the Hoover formula
in the before-described Agricultural Marketing Act
(Farm Relief Act), signed June 15, 1929. Except
that the act was in many ways a repudiation of
Hoover's famous theory of "rugged individualism,"
it fitted neatly into his idea of how the economic
world should function. It was hoped that through
the encouragement of cooperatives the farmers
would be in a position to do for themselves what
business was doing for itself. Business through
trade associations and other methods had gone far
to control marketing, set prices, and prevent overproduction. Now, it was hoped, the farmers would
do the same. But the farmers were less interested
in voluntary cooperation than in the high prices
which they mistakenly believed the act would insure them. Instead of controlling production, they
expanded it and the surpluses became larger than
ever.

In dealing with the tariff, Hoover failed to make

his position perfectly clear and waited too long
to exert the necessary pressure. Here, also, he ran
into divergent views and into strong partisan politics. His experience was as unfortunate as that
of Cleveland and Taft. If the Hoover Administration ever enjoyed a honeymoon, it ended in the
controversies over the Hawley-Smoot bill.

The Republican platform of 1928 had promised
a revision of the tariff to assist certain industries
which "cannot now successfully compete with foreign producers because of lower foreign wages and
lower cost of living abroad." This certainly
sounded like a call for a higher tariff. Curiously
enough, considering the emphasis which Hoover
put upon tariff revision, there was little interest
or demand for it either before or during the campaign. Hoover, however, firmly believed that both
agricultural and industrial rates should be adjusted
to protect American interests by "equalizing the
difference in costs of production at home and
abroad." His object was to protect the farmer in
the domestic market and stimulate him to diversify
his crops. For industry he would remedy loss of
business or employment which had resulted from
economic shifts since the last tariff. Hoover was
interested in a limited rather than a wholesale
revision and stressed the need of a "flexible"
tariff and a reorganization of the Tariff Commission.

Whatever the original purposes of the bill, they were lost sight of in the log-rolling and politics which ensued. Even the farmer was largely forgotten, but it made little difference because the tariff in any event could offer him little help. If there was anything that the country did not need, it was an extension of the already high rates. Except for a few manufacturers, the bill was virtually friendless. Industrialists interested in foreign trade, bankers concerned with foreign investments, and the ordinary citizen struggling with high prices opposed it. Progressive Senators from the farm states joined with the Democrats to condemn it. As in the weeks preceding the passage of the Payne-Aldrich bill in 1909, various Senators specialized on specific schedules and directed their attack with telling force. In particular, the younger LaFollette fought the increased chemical rates and pointed to the heavy contributions to both parties made by chemical magnates in the previous election. For once even Wall Street opposed a higher tariff.

On the grounds that the bill would raise the cost of living, injure American investments abroad, and further curtail a declining commerce, more than a thousand economists urged the President to veto the bill. It was to no avail. The Hawley-Smoot Tariff was an administrative measure put through by the party machine and no single person was more active than Joseph R. Grundy, president of the Pennsylvania Manufacturers' Association, who became Senator in December, 1929. Insurgent Republicans in the Senate had forced the adoption of a provision for an export debenture to pay bounties to farmers and placed the administration of the flexibility power in the hands of Congress instead of the President. Hoover succeeded in killing both in the House. The bill finally passed the Senate by a narrow margin of 44 to 42 with eleven Republicans, mostly Progressives, voting against it, and five Democrats, won over mainly by the increased duties on sugar, voting for it. It was essentially Hoover's bill and he signed it.

It soon became clear that the Hawley-Smoot Tariff was the highest in our history, with an average *ad valorem* rate of all schedules at 40.08 per cent as against 33.22 in the Fordney-McCumber Act. It provided for a general increase in agricultural duties, including those on raw materials used in American manufacture. The most important increase as it affected the Federal revenue and consumer prices was that on sugar. The duties on numerous manufactured goods, notably on woolens and cottons, were raised and both farmers and manufacturers were pleased with the removal of hides, boots, and shoes from the free list. The powers of the Tariff Commission remained about as before, but the President was empowered to appoint a new body in the hope of improving the quality of the Commission. However beneficial the tariff might appear, experts had no difficulty in discovering the fact that the gainers were a few manufacturers rather than the farmers.

On the day that the first vote was taken in the Senate representatives of foreign nations as well as of domestic interests packed the galleries. During the writing of the tariff many foreign nations had protested; after it was passed they resorted to "defensive" tariffs. As a creditor nation the United States had supported an export trade by large loans and investments in other countries—a policy which allowed foreign nations to maintain unfavorable trade balances and make war-debt payments until the depression of 1929. With the drying up of loans and the erection of higher trade barriers, European nations were forced to raise their tariffs to create export balances for debt payments and thus stabilize their economies. The reaction was so rapid and the deterioration in European finance so sudden that Hoover in 1931 initiated a moratorium on all intergovernmental war debts and reparations. His failure or unwillingness to understand the fundamental importance of the tariff problem was even more evident in 1932 when he vetoed a bill passed by Congress calling for an international conference on tariffs. The retaliatory tariffs, the European economic disintegration, and the reactionary political uprisings which followed in the wake of the Hawley-Smoot Tariff may indeed have made it a turning point in world history.

The healthy, if inconclusive, discussion of prohibition during the Presidential campaign resulted in the passage of the Jones-Stalker Act a few days before Hoover took office. An amendment to the Prohibition Act, the new legislation raised stiffly the fines and prison penalties for violations. This legislation was merely a gesture toward the drys. The main difficulty, as far as the Federal Government was concerned, did not lie in any inadequacy of the existing laws; rather it rested on the unwillingness to appropriate sufficient money or appoint adequate personnel to enforce what laws there were. A more useful act, however, provided for a commission to be named by the President to investigate the problem of law enforcement, including prohibition. This gave Hoover the opportunity to appoint the National Law Enforcement Commission, perhaps the best known of the many advisory and investigation bodies which he created.

Headed by George W. Wickersham and including such distinguished members as Newton D. Baker and Roscoe Pound, the "Wickersham Commission" made an intensive study of the problems of law enforcement and crime. The first part of its report, submitted in 1930, resulted in legislation which transformed the enforcement unit of the Treasury Department into a Bureau of Prohibition under the Department of Justice. Other acts created a Bureau of Narcotics in the Treasury Department, a Bureau of Prisons in the Department of Justice and the creation of two new Federal prisons. As far as the public was concerned the chief interest in the Committee's work was their report on prohibition. Although the majority of the Committee was against outright repeal of the Eighteenth Amendment and the restoration of the saloon, there was division of opinion on the methods of handling the problem. In any event, the Administration chose to ignore this part of the report.

In Hoover's mind the most important Republican commitments in 1928 were farm relief, a new tariff, and more efficient law enforcement. The Agricultural Marketing Act was passed before the stock-market panic of October, 1929, and action had also commenced on the tariff. After the crash in October the policies of the Hoover Administration were dominated fundamentally by the depression rather than by party platforms. Party politics, nevertheless, played an increasingly important rôle after the Congressional elections of 1930. The influence of the depression was evident in the results, which were heavily in favor of the Democrats. When the Seventy-second Congress organized in December, 1931, the Republicans in the Senate had a majority of one. But such control was meaningless, since a half dozen Senators listed as Republicans were Progressives who could not be counted on to support Administration policies. The House was now under Democratic control. From then on the fate of Administration bills rested upon the acquiescence of Democrats and Progressive Republicans.

Unlike many other political and economic leaders, Hoover was skeptical of the runaway stock-market boom and had urged the Federal Reserve Board to exert a restraining influence. Somewhat reluctantly the Board raised the discount rates in June, 1929, but by that time it was too late. As the significance of the crash became evident, the President began in November a series of White House conferences with railroad presidents, industrial and labor leaders, key men in construction and public utilities and leaders in national agricultural organizations. His objective in these and later conferences was to stabilize the business situation by securing declarations favoring the maintenance of normal business activities and prevailing wages and promises from labor that they would withhold demands for higher wages. He urged both business leaders and state and municipal officials to aid the situation by increasing, if possible, their normal programs of construction and expansion. The President was convinced that the economic structure was sound and the stock-market crash was simply

a superficial phenomenon brought on by speculators.

When the Seventy-first Congress met in December, 1929, the President urged a reduction in taxation, increased public works, expansion of the
merchant marine, construction of railroads, departmental reorganization for greater economy, banking reform, and a better regulation of interstate distribution of electric power. Congress responded by
appropriating an extra $230,000,000 for Federal
buildings, making the total appropriation in force
about $500,000,000. It also increased by $50,000,-
000 the annual Federal contribution for state highway construction. Substantial funds were likewise
voted to begin the Colorado River development
and for improving the Gulf-to-the-Lakes Deep
Waterway. Hoover's recommendation for a reorganization of the Federal Power Commission was
complied with and he was authorized to appoint a
new full-time commission. On the other hand
Hoover firmly opposed Government operation of
Muscle Shoals or dealing with the depression
through increased veterans' pensions. However, a
disability pension bill for Spanish War veterans was
passed over his veto. He vetoed another act liberal-
izing the disability clauses for World War veterans,
but signed a second modified to his liking.

Without stressing tax reduction as an emergency
measure to counteract the depression, there can be

no doubt that this was its chief purpose. Thoroughly convinced that the business activity of the 1920's had been stimulated by reduced taxation, the Republicans decided to try again. Reductions in earlier years had brought greater prosperity and larger treasury surpluses, even if it also stimulated speculation. Such a bill was introduced within a few minutes after Congress convened (December 2, 1929) and with virtually no debate went through both houses within twelve days. It cut the normal income-tax rates on personal incomes under $4,000 from $1\frac{1}{2}$ per cent to one-half per cent, on incomes from $4,000 to $8,000 from 3 to 2 per cent, and on those over $8,000 from 5 to 4 per cent. The tax on corporation incomes was reduced from 12 to 11 per cent. These reductions were applicable to income earned in 1929 and payable in 1930. Despite these reductions, the revenues for the fiscal year ending June, 1930, were slightly above those of previous years. After that the magic formula ceased to work. The depression continued and the actual deficit on June 30, 1931, amounted to $903,000,000. It need hardly be added that the "miracle in public finance"—decrease in the public debt along with decrease in taxation—also ended.

Reduction of taxation, the inauguration of an enlarged policy of public works, and the pledge of industry and labor to carry on as usual may have momentarily halted the depression and even slightly stimulated heavy industry in the early months of 1930. Unfortunately the stock market collapsed again in May of that year and the depression deepened. It reached a new crisis with the financial collapse of Central Europe in May, 1931. Hoover believed the situation so serious that he secured consent from the interested governments, and later approval of the American Congress, of a one-year moratorium on intergovernmental debts. This step unfortunately did not prove so effective as he had hoped and did little to improve the immediate situation either in Europe or the United States. In fact, the picture grew darker in September when Great Britain, followed by many others, suspended gold payments, and did so despite aid extended by the Federal Reserve Bank of New York in an effort to bolster her monetary system. Later conferences with Premier Laval of France and Grandi of Italy were largely concerned with bolstering European economy in a critical period. The disastrous effect of all this on the American securities market and in turn upon the solvency of many American banks led Hoover to initiate the organization of a voluntary agency, known as the National Credit Corporation, by means of which the strong banks might help the weak.

Hoover had acted with courage and intelligence in the European situation. At home, however, relief measures bogged down in a conflict between

Hoover's philosophy of private charity and individual initiative and the desire of many members of Congress to extend public relief and Federal leadership. This conflict broke out almost immediately after the opening of the second session of the Seventy-first Congress in December, 1930, over bonus legislation. As finally enacted the bill allowed veterans to borrow up to 50 per cent on the face value of their service certificates. The purpose was primarily to aid veterans caught by the depression. The President vetoed the bill on the ground that it would raise taxes, but Congress immediately passed it over his veto (February 27, 1931). The Bonus Act released almost a billion dollars, but did not halt the depression.

The President also differed with Congress on relief of farmers in certain drought-stricken areas, particularly Arkansas. He signed in January a $45,000,000 appropriation to aid farmers in various ways but opposed a later bill for $25,000,000 to feed the sufferers. Senators insisted that "you cannot rehabilitate farms with dead farmers," and held their ground. In the end the President signed a reworded compromise bill which accomplished the purpose of the Senators. The Hoover philosophy was well illustrated in this session by his veto of a bill sponsored by Senator Wagner which would have created a United States Employment Service as a bureau in the Department of Labor to head a system of employment offices scattered throughout the country. He also vetoed a bill of Senator Norris providing for Government operation of Muscle Shoals.

The depression was more than two years old when the Seventy-second Congress met in December, 1931. It was quite clear by now that Governmental efforts to halt or relieve the catastrophe had failed. It was even more obvious in late January and February of 1932 when the drain of gold became so heavy and bank failures so numerous that business loans and credit were rapidly shrinking. Bank failures and the fear that the United States would follow Great Britain and other European countries in going off the gold standard spread pessimism throughout the business world and started numerous runs on the banks. In many respects February marked the worst crisis of the depression until the final bank debacle a year later.

Although Hoover in his message to Congress warned against excessive expansion in the schedule of Federal public works, he was now in the mood for more strenuous Federal action in the economic crisis. He proposed that the Treasury be empowered to subscribe to further stock in Federal Land Banks to aid agriculture; that a system of home-loan banks be created to aid home owners in saving or improving their homes and that a Reconstruction Finance Corporation with a "reasonable capi-

tal" be established. The last recommendation came
because of the inadequacy of the National Credit
Association in saving banks and providing necessary credit. These were the main proposals as suggested by Hoover after two years' experience and
they comprised the chief program of the Seventy-
second Congress.

The situation had now become so desperate that
Congress acceded to Hoover's proposals with a
minimum of partisan quibbling. A measure amend-
ing the Farm Loan Act was passed in January
increasing the capital stock of the Federal Land
Banks by $125,000,000. This stock, subscribed by
the Treasury, was to increase the resources of the
land banks for lending to farmers. Urged by a special message from the President, Congress also in
January established the Reconstruction Finance
Corporation, the best-known and undoubtedly the
most useful of the agencies set up during the
Hoover Administration to counteract the depression. The RFC was to have a capital stock of
$500,000,000 to be subscribed by the Treasury
with power to issue obligations up to three times
that amount. The act authorized it to loan on
security to banks of various types, trust companies,
building and loan associations, insurance companies, mortgage and loan companies, agricultural
and live-stock credit associations and, with the
approval of the Interstate Commerce Commission,

to railroads. Its life was set at ten years and it was to be governed by a board of seven including the Secretary of the Treasury, the Governor of the Federal Reserve Board and the Farm Loan Commissioner. In the pessimism of the last months of the Hoover Administration many criticized the RFC as simply a means of ladling out credit to the rulers of banks and industries who had already proved themselves incapable of directing the nation's economic life. The fact remains, however, that it saved many a bank, industry, and railroad from destruction and thus played an important part in mitigating some of the disintegrating force of the depression. It proved itself so valuable that the Roosevelt Administration continued it and rested heavily upon it.

Designed particularly to protect the home owner and to stimulate building, the Home Loan Act, passed in July, created not fewer than eight and not more than twelve Home Loan Banks to be supervised by a Home Loan Board. Any building and loan association, savings bank, or the like, might become a member of the Home Loan Bank by subscribing at least one per cent of its own holdings of loans on homes. These amounts might be supplemented by the Secretary of the Treasury up to $125,000,000. With these funds the Home Loan Banks might lend to home-mortgage institutions against the latter's holdings and so supply further home mortgages to an amount not specified. Although the Reconstruction Finance Corporation and the Home Loan Banks were essentially agencies to furnish emergency credit, many hoped that they might contribute to inflation and higher prices. Inflationists, in fact, used the Home Loan Bank Act as a medium for their program. Senator Glass of Virginia introduced a "rider" permitting national banks for three years to issue circulatory notes upon the security of any outstanding bonds of the United States bearing interest at over $3\frac{3}{8}$ per cent. Sponsors of this amendment believed that it would create a potential bank-note inflation of a billion dollars.

So far Hoover's program had enjoyed clear sailing in Congress. Difficulties, however, arose over the demand that the Federal Government do something for state and local governments in the promotion of public and other construction and for the relief of individual distress. Various methods for promoting such a program were introduced into both Houses. Congress finally passed a bill providing for the distribution of over $2,000,000,000, only to have it vetoed by the President, who asserted that it would make the RFC "the most gigantic banking and pawnbroking business in all history" and that it "threatened the credit of the United States." After some reconciliation of views, Hoover signed a new Emergency Relief Act on July 21

which enlarged the loaning power of the RFC to
$3,300,000,000, or by $1,800,000,000 above the
original limit. The RFC was now empowered to
loan to states or to public agencies or corporations
funds to promote self-liquidating projects. It might
do the same to private corporations for the construction of bridges and other such projects of a
self-liquidating nature, to corporations interested in
building low-cost housing, to borrowers seeking to
sell agricultural surpluses in foreign markets and
institutions organized under the law engaged in the
orderly marketing of crops. The act also expanded
the public works program of the Federal Government. Items in the original bill, which Hoover had
vetoed, providing for direct relief were absent in
the final act.

By early 1931 it was clear that the depression
had added an unbalanced Federal budget to the
worries of the Hoover Administration. Few situa-
tions could be more profoundly disturbing to finan-
ciers of the type of Hoover, Mellon, and Mills than
Federal deficits. The depression had brought increased Federal expenditures at a time when receipts from customs revenues and income taxes had
declined rapidly. The deficit of $903,000,000 for
the fiscal year ending on June 30, 1931, grew to
$2,885,000,000 for the year ending in June, 1932.
The national debt during this single year increased
from 16¾ billion to 19½ billion. The Administra-

tion, as a consequence, threw over its early policy of fighting the depression by reduced taxation as tried in the Revenue Act of 1929 and urged substantial advances in 1932.

Congress struggled with the problem for four months during the winter and spring of 1932 with every shade of tax opinion demanding a hearing. Divergent theories of taxation were increased by the political division between a Republican Senate and a Democratic House. The result, nevertheless, was one of the largest increases of taxation ever enacted by the Federal Government in time of peace. The Revenue Act of 1932 raised the rates on corporation and individual incomes; increased the taxes on estates and restored taxes on gifts. It hoped to get about half of the expected additional revenue by manufacturers' excise taxes and numerous sales taxes. Tariff duties were imposed on crude oil, gasoline, coal, lumber, and copper, and other miscellaneous taxes were imposed reminiscent of the First World War. Unfortunately, these new taxes raised but slightly the total Government receipts for the year ending June, 1933; the fiscal deficit for that year rose to over three billion.

The first session of the Seventy-second Congress had spent most of its time struggling with the difficult and discouraging problems of Treasury deficits, increased taxation, and measures to relieve the depression. Nevertheless, two long-overdue reforms

emerged from the session. The first was the passage
by both Houses of Congress of the "Lame Duck"
Amendment, urged for many years by Senator
George Norris. Ratified in 1933, the Twentieth
Amendment abolished the "Lame Duck" session of
Congress after elections and permitted the newly
elected President, Vice-president, and members of
Congress to take office in January instead of
March. Ratification was undoubtedly speeded by
the tragic four months in which the repudiated
Hoover was able to do little to meet a deepening
crisis. Another act sponsored by Senator Norris
and Representative La Guardia did something to
end the abuses of injunctions in labor disputes, particularly their use in upholding the "yellow dog"
contract. The act forbade the use of Federal injunctions in labor cases except on evidence in court
that irreparable damage to persons and property
might ensue in the absence of the injunction. Jury
trials must now be granted to persons accused of
violating such injunctions.

The first session of the Seventy-second Congress
had produced constructive legislation. If it had
come two years earlier, it might have contributed
significantly in mitigating the depression. Like
most of the actions of the Hoover Administration,
it came too late. Nothing could have made this
clearer than the descent upon Washington in May
and June of more than 20,000 veterans demanding

that Congress enact a law for the immediate payment of bonus certificates. The Bonus Expeditionary Force started in Portland, Oregon, under the leadership of Walter W. Waters and was passed on by local authorities from one town to another as the simplest way of dodging the problem. On the whole their discipline was exemplary and the Washington police allotted some vacant Government buildings on Pennsylvania Avenue to the first arrivals. As others came, including several hundred women and children, the main body established themselves in ramshackle huts on Anacostia Flats, a vacant area on the banks of the Potomac. A few tramps, hoodlums, and troublemakers attached themselves to the veterans, but the Bonus Army ejected all not in possession of certificates of honorable discharge.

Under pressure from the veterans, the House passed a bill making immediately available the balance of the adjusted compensation. The Senate turned it down. At this point and with the approval of Hoover, Congress voted funds for transportation and subsistence cost to take the veterans home, the cost to be deducted from ultimate payments on their bonus certificates. Several thousand of the bonus marchers took advantage of this and returned home.

With Congress now adjourned and thousands of veterans still encamped in Washington the situation had reached a stalemate and the authorities were anxious to rid themselves of the Bonus Army. Finally, on July 21 the Chief of the Washington police, Pelham D. Glassford, whose handling of a difficult situation had been unusually commendable, told the Bonus Army that orders had been received for their evacuation of the buildings and property around Pennsylvania Avenue on the following day. At the same time orders were given for complete evacuation of all park areas by August 4. The first order was not enforced until the morning of July 28, when Federal agents and police appeared to execute it. The buildings were evacuated without trouble, but groups from other camps appeared and there was brief rioting in which several veterans and police were injured. Early in the afternoon Glassford with a few police returned to check on the situation. Two policemen, suddenly losing their heads, fired on the crowd of veterans. Two of them died several days later as a result of these shots.

In the meantime the Commissioner of the District of Columbia appealed to Hoover for the assistance of the Federal troops in maintaining law and order. Hoover gave the order and in the late afternoon the army, in full military paraphernalia and directed by General MacArthur, drove the veterans from the area around the capitol. About nightfall the troops descended on Anacostia Flats, ousted the veterans and their families with bayonets and gas bombs and destroyed the camp.

As the weary veterans straggled out of Washington on roads lit by the fires of their burning camp, bitter denunciation was heaped on the President. Hoover defended himself on the ground that the Government could not be coerced by "mob rule" and was obligated to meet "overt lawlessness." It was a sorry ending of an effort misguided by false hopes and badly handled by politicians and the Administration. Four years later Congress passed over Roosevelt's veto a bill similar to that advocated by the Bonus Army.

The last seven months of the Hoover Administration may be divided into two periods, that from the adjournment of Congress on July 18 to the Presidential election in November, and the interregnum from then until the inauguration of Franklin D. Roosevelt. Politically, the first was largely concerned with the campaign; the second, with efforts on the part of the defeated President to win the cooperation and support of Roosevelt to his international and domestic policies. Economically, the first period showed an upturn in the business cycle; the second a deterioration climaxed by the banking panic in February and March of 1933. The Republicans attributed the economic improvement to the growing confidence in the business world inspired by Hoover's policies of improving credit facilities through the RFC and other agencies, of maintaining the gold standard, and of raising taxes to balance the budget. This was their basic argument in the Presidential election of 1932. As against this the Democrats accused the Administration of slowness and timidity in dealing with the depression, of unwillingness to make experiments, and of a program designed largely to bolster the economic structure at the top in the hope that prosperity would then trickle down to the bottom layers. The rebuilding, insisted the Democrats, should begin at the bottom and be all-embracing. In any event, the optimism of the President had little effect on the electorate. Hoover's policies in 1932 satisfied few beyond the business class of the Northeast. Roosevelt won every state south and west of Pennsylvania and the largest electoral majority since 1864. It was essentially a vote against Hoover and the depression.

Not since the election of Lincoln in 1860 had the four months' interval between the election of a new President and his inauguration proved more unfortunate. The nation was clearly finished with Hoover and waiting for a new program, and Hoover himself realized that he could do little with the next Congress, which would naturally take no important action without regard to Roosevelt's views. Republicans attributed the economic decline during these months to business uncertainty as to the program

of the new Administration, particularly with relation to tariff and monetary problems. Whatever
the cause, these were indeed discouraging months.
The production index fell to its lowest point in our
history, unemployment increased, while the banking structure of the nation, beginning in December,
seemed tottering to utter collapse. At the same
time foreign nations were clamoring for a reconsideration of their December debt payments due
this country.

In the face of an obviously serious situation
President Hoover sought the cooperation of Roosevelt in formulating plans for participation in war-
debt negotiations, the Geneva Disarmament Conference, and the World Economic Conference. Such
a move was not only unprecedented, but it raised a
fine Constitutional question regarding the participation of a President-elect in assuming executive
responsibilities before his inauguration. Hoover's
purpose was twofold. He was convinced that the
sources of the American depression were foreign
and that the only threat to America was the international economic instability. If this situation
could be improved, the future was safe. His second
was to involve the newly elected President as
deeply as possible in his own interpretation of the
causes of the depression and in his own program
of meeting it.

To the overtures of Hoover, the President-elect

responded cautiously. He accepted an invitation to
a conference, and with his adviser, Professor Raymond Moley, met the President and Secretary of
the Treasury Mills on November 22. Here the
fundamental divergence between the theories of the
two men became clear. Roosevelt believed that the
primary causes of the depression were not foreign
but domestic, and that the main cause was the
failure of purchasing power to keep pace with production. This must be handled by domestic policies
which might necessitate inflation and price rises
and he was unwilling to commit his Administration
beforehand to any policy of international monetary
stabilization. Roosevelt apparently was already
playing with the idea of a managed currency. On
December 17, President Hoover urged Roosevelt to
join him in selecting a delegation to the impending
World Economic Conference, but the latter declined.

Two months later (February 17, 1933), as the
banking crisis approached a climax, Hoover again
urged the President-elect to action. In a long letter
reviewing the course of the depression and emphasizing the need of restoring confidence, he wrote,

I do not refer to action on all causes of alarm, but it
would steady the country greatly if there could be
prompt assurance that there will be no tampering or
inflation of the currency; that the budget will be unquestionably balanced, even if further taxation is

necessary; that the government credit will be maintained by refusal to exhaust it in the issue of securities.

Roosevelt had no intention of accepting the defeated Administration's interpretation of the causes of the new crisis or to tie his own hands in the future. His answer was delayed for eleven days "through an assumption of my secretary that it was only a draft of a letter." The gravity of the banking situation, replied Roosevelt, was too deep-seated to be helped by "mere statements."

During his final week in office Hoover faced the most serious economic crisis which the nation had ever experienced. Beginning with Louisiana on February 14 every state had declared bank holidays by March 4 when Roosevelt became President. When Governor Lehman closed the banks of New York on March 4 only the Federal Reserve Banks remained open. During this last hectic week Hoover pressed Roosevelt's representatives for cooperation and suggestions in meeting the crisis, but without avail. He himself proposed that he invoke the Trading with the Enemy Act of 1917 to control foreign exchange and hoarding by proclaiming a national bank holiday. His Attorney-General, however, doubted the authority unless Congressional approval was forthcoming.

Hoover then invited Roosevelt to join him in a proclamation of an national bank holiday. Roosevelt believed that the President had the authority to do this, but he himself as a private citizen could not join in such a move. Roosevelt, in fact, seemed opposed on March 3 to any kind of proclamation.

With bankers frantically crying for help and the economic life of the nation virtually at a standstill, Hoover's Administration came to an end. The dismal, rainy skies which greeted his last day in office seemed symbolic of four bitter and unsuccessful years. Despite his best efforts, his policies as a whole had failed to meet the critical problems which he faced. An essentially economic rather than a political person, Hoover struggled with the depression far more actively than had any of his predecessors in a similar situation. But he did so with his mind on the past rather than the future. The foundations of American economic life, he believed, were essentially sound. The causes of the depression as he saw them—speculation, inflation, mismanagement of financial institutions — were superficial and came from human errors. The system itself was fundamentally good. The chief barriers to recovery were the continued dislocations, shocks, and setbacks from abroad. Eager to mitigate domestic evils and to play a part in improving the international economic stability, his efforts were largely checked by a basic dislike to interfere with the existing economic system or to enlarge the activities or powers of the Federal Government.

Hoover's Administration was in reality an interlude between two periods. While this seems clear today, neither Hoover nor his close advisers were able to perceive the fact. It was the future that called, not the past. The old America ended with the crash of 1929; a new America began with the inauguration of Roosevelt. The future was to be one of enlarged Government leadership, wider Federal controls, greater sensitiveness to the welfare of all the people, and eventually a closer identification of America with the other governments of the world.

BIBLIOGRAPHICAL NOTE

PERIODICAL LITERATURE

OF THE hundreds of American newspapers the New York *Times* will probably be found the most satisfactory in following day-by-day developments. Of the current-events periodicals the monthly *Current History* (1914–) is the most valuable for the 1920's. Other weekly or monthly publications which summarized or interpreted events include *Time* (1923–), the *Literary Digest* (1890–1937), *Review of Reviews* (1890–1937), the *Independent* (1848–1928), and *Forum* (1886–1930). The *Survey* (1897–) is particularly valuable for labor and other social history. Interpretations from the liberal point of view will be found in the *Nation* (1865–), and the *New Republic* (1914–).

Yearly summaries of events are given in the *American Yearbook* (1910–1919, 1925–), *New International Yearbook* (1908–), and the *Americana Annual* (1923–). For statistical material see the *World Almanac,* published by the New York *World,* and the *Statistical Abstract* and the *Commerce Yearbook,* both published by the Federal Government.

GENERAL TREATMENTS

GENERAL treatments of the twenties are mostly parts of larger works and are too brief to be of much value. Perhaps the best of these are in Charles and Mary Beard, *The Rise of American Civilization* (rev. ed., 1933) and *America in Midpassage* (1939), largely interpretative; in D. L. Dumond, *America in Our Time* (1947); Harvey Wish, *Contemporary America* (1945); and F. R. Dulles, *Twentieth Century America* (1945). The treatment of James C. Malin, *The United States after the World War* (1930) is essentially political and economic. Although the economic is stressed, Louis M. Hacker, *American Problems of Today* (1938), is a well-rounded summary.

SOCIAL HISTORY

IN *Recent Social Trends* (1934), a Report of the President's Research Committee on Social Trends, the student will find a gold mine of information on almost every phase of social history. R. S. and H. M. Lynd, *Middletown* (1929), is an important survey of American attitudes and ways of living in a typical small city. The most successful effort to summarize and integrate the life of the people is Preston W. Slosson, *The Great Crusade and After* (1931), Vol. XII in the History of American Life Series. Harold E. Stearns, ed., *Civilization in the United States: an Inquiry by Thirty Americans* (1922) is a critical but useful appraisal. Although there is much political history in Mark Sullivan, *Our Times*, Vol. IV: *The Twenties* (1935), there is also a wealth of material on social life. The same is true of Edwin Emerson, *Hoover and His Times*

(1932). The most lively reading of any of the books is Frederick L. Allen, *Only Yesterday* (1931). J. T. Adams, *Our Business Civilization* (1929) is one of the many efforts to interpret America of the twenties. On special phases see Charles Merz, *The Dry Decade* (1931); J. M. Mecklin, *The Ku Klux Klan: a Study of the American Mind* (1924); Felix Frankfurter, *The Case of Sacco and Vanzetti* (1927); and Zechariah Chafee, Jr., *Free Speech in the United States* (1941). The story of the Bonus Army is in W. W. Waters and W. C. White, *B. E. F.* (1933).

ECONOMIC HISTORY

THE economic history of no previous decade has been more thoroughly studied. Innumerable Government studies, surveys, and reports throw light on these years as well as other research projects stimulated by the Government or by private organizations. Of Government-stimulated studies the most valuable is *Recent Economic Changes in the United States* (2 vols., 1929), a Report of the Committee on Recent Economic Changes of the President's Conference on Unemployment, largely done under the auspices of the National Bureau of Economic Research. Among the useful volumes published by the latter organization is Frederick C. Mills, *Economic Tendencies in the United States* (1932). Popular efforts to interpret economic conditions and tendencies during these years include two books by Stuart Chase, *Men and Machines* (1929) and *Prosperity: Fact or Myth* (1929).

For the history of labor the following are essential:

American Labor Yearbook (1916–); Elizabeth Brandeis and Don D. Lescohier, *History of Labor in the United States, 1896–1932* (1935), Vol. III in J. R. Commons and associates, *History of Labor in the United States*, covering labor conditions, labor laws and employee policies; and Selig Perlman and Philip Taft, *History of Labor in the United States, 1896–1932* (1935), Vol. IV in the same series dealing with the history of organized labor. See also Lewis L. Lorwin, *The American Federation of Labor* (1933), and J. S. Gambs, *Decline of the I.W.W.* (1932).

For discussion of the many phases of the labor movement touched on in this book the following will be found useful: C. R. Dougherty, *Labor Problems in American Industry* (rev. ed., 1938); Edward Berman, *Labor and the Sherman Act* (1930); Robert Dunn, *The Americanization of Labor* (1927); P. H. Douglas, *Real Wages in the United States, 1890–1926* (1930); Leo Huberman, *The Labor Spy Racket* (1937); R. F. Foerster and E. H. Dietel, *Employee Stock Ownership in the United States* (1926); Norman Thomas, *Human Exploitation in the United States* (1934); and T. N. Carver, *Present Economic Revolution in the United States* (1925). The steel strike is covered in *Report of the Steel Strike of 1919 by the Commission of Inquiry, the Interchurch World Movement* (1920), and W. Z. Foster, *The Great Steel Strike and Its Lessons* (1920). The report of the Coal Commission set up after the strike of 1922 is in *Report of the United States Coal Commission*, 68th Congress, 2nd Session, Senate Document 195, and is summarized in Edward E. Hunt, F. J. Tryon, and Joseph H. Willets, eds.,

What the Coal Commission Found (1925). In John Lombard's, *Labor's Voice in the Cabinet* (1943), there is a good chapter on "The Red Scare."

H. R. Saeger and Charles A. Gulick, Jr., *Trust and Corporation Problems* (1929), is an excellent introduction to business consolidation. In W. Z. Ripley, *Main Street and Wall Street* (1927), some of the methods used by high finance are described. Probably the most complete picture of consolidation during the decade will be found in Harry W. Laidler, *Concentration of Control in American Industry* (1931). The extent to which it has been carried is developed in A. A. Berle, Jr., and G. C. Means, *The Modern Corporation and Private Property* (1932). Among the numerous excellent books on special phases are J. C. Bonright and G. C. Means, *The Holding Company* (1932); D. M. Keezer and Stacy May, *Public Control of Business* (1930); Arthur R. Burns, *The Decline of Competition* (1936); W. J. A. Donald, *Trade Associations* (1933); and Ferdinand Lundberg, *America's 60 Families* (1937). On concentration in the power industry consult C. O. Hardy, *Recent Growth of the Electric Light and Power Industry* (pamphlet of the Brookings Institution, 1929); H. S. Raushenbush and H. W. Laidler, *Power Control* (1929); and Carl D. Thompson, *Confessions of the Power Trust* (1932), a summary of testimony given before the Federal Trade Commission.

On agricultural legislation of the period the most complete description is in J. D. Black, *Agricultural Reform in the United States* (1929). Also useful are Wilson Gee, *Place of Agriculture in Our Life* (1930);

E. R. A. Seligman, *The Economics of Farm Relief*
(1929); Edwin G. Nourse, *American Agriculture and
the European Market* (1924); National Industrial
Conference Board, *The Agricultural Problem in the
United States* (1926); and the symposium "The Agricultural Situation in the United States" in the *Annals
of the American Academy of Political and Social
Science*, Vol. CXVII (1925). Stuart Chase, *Rich
Land, Poor Land* (1936) gives a popular picture of
what is happening to American soil.

Julius Klein, one-time Director of the United States
Bureau of Foreign and Domestic Commerce (1929) in
Frontiers of Trade (1929) has interpreted the attitude
of the Hoover Administration on developing foreign
commerce. On American foreign investments, Cleona
Lewis, *America's Stake in International Investments*
(1938) is an excellent summary. Literature on the
recent history of the American merchant marine is still
meager, but the following are helpful: W. S. Benson,
The Merchant Marine (1923); National Industrial
Conference Board, *The American Merchant Marine
Problem* (1929); and D. H. Smith and Paul V. Betters,
The United States Shipping Board (Brookings Institution, Service Monographs No. 63, 1931). Most satisfactory summary of internal transportation history
and problems of the 1920's is the report prepared for
the National Transportation Committee by Harold G.
Moulton and associates, *The American Transportation
Problem* (1933). On railroads, consult W. J. Cunning-
ham, *American Railroads; Government Control and
Reconstruction Problems* (1922); D. P. Locklin, *Railroad Regulation since 1920* (1928) and W. N. Leonard,

Railroad Consolidation Under the Transportation Act of 1920 (1946). The following books deal with the automobile industry in the 1920's: R. C. Epstein, *The Automobile Industry* (1928), emphasizing financial and organizational development; E. D. Kennedy, *The Automobile Industry, the Coming of Age of Capitalism's Favorite Child* (1941), a popular history; and C. B. Classcock, *The Gasoline Age, the Story of the Men Who Made It* (1937). On air transportation see F. A. Magoun and Eric Hodgins, *A History of Aircraft* (1931), and John Goldstrom, *Narrative History of Aviation* (1931).

The most suggestive treatment of the business cycle in the years immediately following the First World War is Paul A. Samuelson and Everett E. Hagen, *After the War—1918–1920,* a pamphlet published by the National Resources Planning Board in 1943. A more inclusive treatment of these years is James R. Mock and Evangeline Thurber, *Report on Demobilization* (1944). Taxation in the 1920's is summarized in Sidney Ratner, *American Taxation* (1942). The significance of science and technology is stressed in Roger Burlingame, *Engines of Democracy* (1940), and the development of electric power in Walter N. Polakov, *The Power Age* (1933).

POLITICS AND BIOGRAPHY

Since this book was set in type the first intensive study of the campaign of 1924 has appeared in the excellent volume by Kenneth C. MacKay, *The Progressive Movement of 1924* (1947). R. V. Peel and T. C. Donnelly, *The Campaign of 1928* (1931) and

The 1932 Campaign (1935) are adequate analyses, and Nathan Fine, *Labor and Farmer Parties in the United States, 1828–1928* (1928), is a balanced summary. Selig Adler, "The Congressional Election of 1918," *South Atlantic Quarterly,* XXXVI (October, 1937), No. 4, 447–465, has suggestive interpretations.

A background for an important phase of the politics of these years is in Arthur Capper, *The Agricultural Bloc* (1922). The story of the oil scandals is told in M. E. Ravage, *The Story of Teapot Dome* (1924). Political corruption in New York and Chicago is discussed in W. B. and J. B. Northrop, *The Insolence of Office* (1932); Norman Thomas and Paul Blanshard, *What's the Matter with New York?* (1932); Raymond Moley, *Tribunes of the People* (1932); Lloyd Lewis and H. J. Smith, *Chicago: the History of Its Reputation* (1929), and C. E. Merriam, *Chicago: a More Intimate View of Urban Politics* (1929). Gordon L. Hostetter and Thomas Quinn Beesley, *It's a Racket* (1929), deals with racketeering in Chicago, and F. D. Pasley, *Al Capone* (1930), with the king of the racketeers.

No adequate full-length study of Harding has yet been published. The unpublished thesis of H. F. Alderfer, *The Personality and Politics of Warren G. Harding* (available at the New York Public Library), is probably the most valuable study yet made. The best short sketch is by Allan Nevins in the *Dictionary of American Biography*. Samuel Hopkins Adams, *Incredible Era* (1939), is sprightly reading and reasonably objective. The destruction of the Harding letters after his death by his wife will always handicap his biographers. There is no adequate collection of his speeches and messages.

No really critical or objective full-length biography of Coolidge has yet appeared. All are laudatory or written in a highly appreciative vein. Of the earlier ones perhaps Edward E. Whiting, *President Coolidge: a Contemporary Estimate* (1923) is the most rewarding. Of those which have appeared since his death, William Allen White, *A Puritan in Babylon* (1939) makes on the whole a successful effort at interpreting Coolidge in the light of his times. More informative, but less objective, is Claude M. Fuess, *Calvin Coolidge, the Man from Vermont* (1940). Both are written by experienced biographers, but neither is adequate on many aspects of the Presidential years. Coolidge's speeches are collected in *Have Faith in Massachusetts* (1919) and *Foundations of the Republic* (1926). His *Autobiography* (1929) is brief, meager in information, but nevertheless revealing.

The campaign speeches of Hoover are in *The New Day* (1928) and much of his philosophy in *The Challenge to Liberty* (1934). Excerpts from speeches and various public documents illustrating his philosophy are collected in Ray Lyman Wilber and Arthur M. Hyde, *The Hoover Policies* (1937). See also William Starr Myers, *The State Papers and Other Public Writings of Herbert Hoover* (2 vols., 1934). A strong defense of Hoover is made by William Starr Myers and Walter H. Newton, *The Hoover Administration* (1936), a documentary narrative of the Presidential years. Will Irwin, *Herbert Hoover* (1928) is a well-written campaign biography. An extremely critical estimate is Walter W. Liggett, *The Rise of Herbert Hoover* (1932).

Secretary Mellon is glorified in Philip H. Love, *Andrew W. Mellon* (1929) and caustically appraised in Harvey O'Connor, *Mellon's Millions* (1933). The autobiography of George W. Norris, *Fighting Liberal* (1945), throws light on the decade, while Raymond Moley, *After Seven Years* (1939), contains valuable material on the period between the election of Roosevelt and his inauguration. Good biographies include Alfred Lief, *Democracy's Norris* (1939); Henry F. Pringle, *Alfred E. Smith, a Critical Study* (1937), and Claudius O. Johnson, *Borah of Idaho* (1936). James M. Cox, *Journey through My Years* (1946) includes material on the campaign of 1920.

The Constitutional history of the 1920's is well summarized in Carl B. Swisher, *American Constitutional Development* (1943). Interesting interpretations are in Walter Lippmann, *Men of Destiny* (1927), and *Interpretations, 1931–1932* (1932), the latter edited by Allan Nevins.

After this volume reached the stage of page proof George Soule's invaluable *Prosperity Decade: from War to Depression, 1917–1929* (1947) appeared as Vol. VIII in the "Economic History of the United States Series." It has skillfully integrated much of the scholarly research done on the economic history of this period.

INDEX